Public Sector Communication in the Digital Age

Mandla J. Radebe, Karabo Sitto-Kaunda & Elizabeth Lubinga (Eds)

UJ Press

Public Sector Communication in the Digital Age

Published by UJ Press
University of Johannesburg
Library
Auckland Park Kingsway Campus
PO Box 524
Auckland Park
2006
https://ujpress.uj.ac.za/

Compilation © Mandla J. Radebe, Karabo Sitto-Kaunda & Elizabeth Lubinga 2024
Chapters © Author(s) 2024
Published Edition © Mandla J. Radebe, Karabo Sitto-Kaunda & Elizabeth Lubinga 2024
First published 2024

https://doi.org/10.36615/9781776489909
978-1-7764898-9-3 (Paperback)
978-1-7764899-0-9 (PDF)
978-1-7764899-1-6 (EPUB)
978-1-7764899-2-3 (XML)

This publication had been submitted to a rigorous double-blind peer-review process prior to publication and all recommendations by the reviewers were considered and implemented before publication.

Language Editor: Laurianne Claase
Cover design: Hester Roets, UJ Graphic Design Studio
Typeset in 9.5/13pt Merriweather Light

Contents

Public Sector Communication in the Digital Age:
Insights and Influences from the Global South i
    Mandla J. Radebe

Chapter 1: Ethics and Government Communication 1
    Themba Maseko

Chapter 2: Facebook Communication by
South Africa's Eight Metros 31
    Lakela Kaunda and Ricky Mukonza

Chapter 3: Strategic Communication in Local
Government Collective Bargaining: Proposing
Solutions to Challenges 61
    Pay Shabangu

Chapter 4: Influencing Voter Turnout: Analysing the
IEC's Stakeholder Communication Strategy in the 2021
Local Government Elections 91
    Karabo Sitto-Kaunda

Chapter 5: Public Sector Communications and
Institutionalised Bureaucracy 121
    Margaret L. Dingalo

Chapter 6: The Public Sector Communication of Development Programmes for Small Businesses: An Implementation Challenge in South Africa 147
Maphelo Malgas and Andiswa Mrasi

Chapter 7: Public Health Communication in South Africa: Concepts, Contemporary Issues and Challenges 173
Elizabeth Lubinga

Chapter 8: Analysing Public Policies and Communication Strategies in Zimbabwe's Eye Healthcare Industry 201
Vincent Tshuma and Sibongile Mpofu

Chapter 9: Citizen Engagement and Power Asymmetry in Class Divided Societies: Some Reflections on South Africa 229
Mandla J. Radebe

Chapter 10: Exploring Government Transparency as a Path to Open Government 251
Anna Oksiutycz

Conclusion: Contextualising the Complexities of Public Sector Communication 285
Karabo Sitto-Kaunda

Contributors 295

Public Sector Communication in the Digital Age

Insights and Influences from the Global South

Mandla J. Radebe

Public sector communication in Southern Africa cannot be understood outside the factors shaped by the region's historical context, political transitions and, subsequently, the need for transparent and inclusive governance. This is also the case in the rest of the African continent where effective public sector communication is crucial in promoting transparency and accountability, thus fostering public trust in government institutions. Fundamentally, as Okigbo and Eribo (2004) posit, information and communication play a significant role in development. In recent times, a proliferation of scholarly works has emerged, addressing the detrimental repercussions of ineffective government communication with the public in the African context. These discussions are particularly pertinent as African nations endeavour to construct development-focused and citizen-centric institutions (Adeola, Katuse & Twum, 2022).

Notably, Adeola et al. (2022) have made significant contributions with their comprehensive two-volume edited work, which revolves around marketing communication themes encompassing branding, public relations, trade fairs, exhibitions, and public sector communications. The first volume, *Public Sector Marketing Communications Volume I: Public Relations and Brand Communication Perspectives*, prominently underscores the vital role that public sector marketing communication assumes in bridging the divide between society and the government. "Building a relationship with the public through appropriate communication tools and platforms," they argue, "is sacrosanct to restoring public sector image and trust" (Adeola et al., 2022: vi). This notion closely aligns with the objectives of this current book, *Public Sector Communication in the Digital Age*. Adeola, Katuse and Twum additionally contend that their endeavour revolves around disseminating conceptual and theoretical research regarding the marketisation of Africa's public sector as it aims to engage effectively with the public it serves (Adeola et al., 2022).

In the second volume, *Public Sector Marketing Communications* (Adeola, Twum & Katuse, 2023), the authors delve into both traditional and digital perspectives, offering another convergence with the subject matter at hand. Nonetheless, their foundational premise that the enhancement of public sector image and trust in Africa necessitates the judicious utilisation of suitable marketing communication tools and platforms remains pivotal. There exists scant evidence to counter the argument that strategic communication and its associated tools play a significant role in facilitating interactions between the government and its citizens. This, in turn, fosters inter-governmental and inter-agency cooperation, ultimately fostering a citizen-oriented public sector (Adeola et al., 2023).

While strategic communication tools are posited to play a critical role in citizen and public sector relationships, this current book introduces a more nuanced and ideological perspective, as evidenced by Radebe in Chapter 9. Indeed, in the digital era, there is little doubt, as suggested by Adeola, Twum and Katuse (2023), that the digital revolution presents an opportunity for public sector institutions to align their communication strategies with new technologies, notably by leveraging social media platforms. Several chapters in this volume, such as those authored by Kaunda and Mukonza and Sitto-Kaunda, demonstrate the extent to which digital platforms are shaping the dynamics of how the public sector engages with the citizenry.

Notably, social media has become a cornerstone of public sector communication, as elucidated in volumes like *Social Media and Africa's Public Sector: Perspectives on Contemporary Issues*, which focuses on developing a systematic approach to comprehending the transformations in Africa's public sector social media landscape (Adae, Twum, Hinson, Duh & Odame, 2023). Arguments have been advanced regarding the integration of social media practices into the operational activities of African public sector institutions, aiming to deliver enhanced value to African citizens and consumers of public goods and services (Adae et al., 2023). In the context of this book, these concepts are, *inter alia*, analysed through the praxis of the contributing authors.

South Africa's Evolving Public Sector Communication Landscape

Expectedly, South Africa's public sector communication landscape underwent significant changes in transitioning from the apartheid era to a democratic dispensation (Wasserman & De Beer, 2005; Glenn & Mattes, 2012). For the purposes of this book, by public sector we refer to the part of the country's economic and administrative structure that is owned, operated or controlled by the government. This encompasses various government agencies, departments, ministries and other public institutions responsible for delivering public services, implementing government policies and managing public resources (Mutula & Wamukoya, 2009). However, as it will emerge later, the concept of the public sector is applied within the framework of the state, which, as outlined in the constitutional provisions, is divided among the three branches: the executive (Cabinet), the legislature (Parliament), and the judiciary (Courts of Law). This division aligns with the fundamental principle of the separation of powers (Munzhedzi, 2017).

Before democracy, and particularly during the formal apartheid era (1948–1994), the government exercised strict control over communication channels. This was a clear and deliberate communication strategy to shape public discourse and maintain its oppressive policies. Maseko elucidates this point in this volume. In fact, the media was prohibited from reporting on liberation politics or banned organisations such as the African National Congress (ANC), the South African Communist Party (SACP) and the Pan Africanist Congress (PAC). During apartheid, government communication and state-controlled media served as propaganda tools to promote the apartheid ideology and suppress dissenting voices (Tomaselli, 1997). Often, the concept of 'national interest' was invoked (Wasserman & De Beer, 2005). On the other hand, independent media outlets were subjected to severe restrictions and censorship that limited the flow of information to the public (Radebe, 2006).

The advent of democracy in 1994 ushered in a new era for public sector communication and, notably, represented the inauguration of a democratic government for the very first time. Various aspects of this communication system underwent some serious transformation, with the new democratic government not only recognising, but compelled by its historical principles and mission – and later the new Constitution of the Republic of South Africa (1996) – to respect the significance of transparency, accountability and citizen engagement as critical components of governance. Democracy signalled an end to repressive state regulation of the media (Wasserman & De Beer, 2005). With media freedom and freedom of expression among the rights enshrined in the new Constitution (Radebe, 2021), the foundation for a more open and inclusive communication environment was laid.

Today, South Africa boasts one of the most independent media landscapes in the Global South. Of course, the concept of media independence remains nebulous since the so-called independent media are largely controlled by commercial interests, with advertising and market interests sustaining the funding model. This is also largely the model that has been adopted by digital media platforms. Nevertheless, the commercial print media remains concentrated (Govenden, 2022) and controlled by four oligopolies (Chiumbu & Radebe,

2022). Therefore, public sector communication is a pivotal bridge for the information gap between the government and citizens, fostering a sense of participation and ownership in the democratic process.

Of course, the advent and rapid growth of digital technologies, which have become ubiquitous in South Africa (John, Maama, Ojogiwa & Mubangizi, 2022), has also revolutionised public sector communication. Communication technologies have provided the public sector with much-needed impetus to engage confidently with citizens. In particular, the internet penetration rate, the proliferation of mobile communication, and the ever-growing presence of social media platforms have created new avenues to disseminate information and engage citizens. With South Africa having one of the highest internet and smart phone penetration on the continent (Osei-Appiah, 2021), the burgeoning role of digital technologies is unsurprising. Suddenly, the public sector possesses the ability for real-time interactions with citizens while providing access to government services and information, as discussed by Kaunda and Mukonza in this volume. Of course, it remains to be seen whether these technologies have been effectively utilised beyond being employed to profile government leaders.

Nevertheless, the government is aware of the potential of digital platforms in enhancing citizen engagement and transparency. Hence, many government leaders, from the president to cabinet ministers to the lowest officials, all have some form of social media presence. For example, President Cyril Ramaphosa uses platforms such as X (formerly Twitter) where he has 2.6 million followers, over and above platforms such as Facebook, to drive his engagements. The government has taken advantage of digital technologies through initiatives such as online consultations, e-participation platforms and open data portals (Solomon & Van Klyton, 2020). These efforts are crucial in promoting inclusivity, participation and accountability in the public sector.

These technological developments notwithstanding, challenges with digital communication persist. The digital divide remains a significant hurdle pertaining to access, affordability and, to some extent, digital literacy among different segments of the population (Matli & Ngoepe, 2020; Cariolle, 2021). The challenges of language barriers and cultural considerations are also well documented and affect the potential of public sector communication from reaching diverse communities.

It is precisely these contextual factors with which this books grapples in its endeavour to unravel and theorise the public sector communication landscape, primarily in South Africa, in the context of growing digitisation. Whereas significant progress has been made by the government in its communication efforts across the public sector, thoroughgoing efforts are imperative to overcome some of the challenges and harness the opportunities presented, especially by digital communication platforms.

Factors Influencing Public Sector Communication

The role of infrastructure

For any communication to be effective, robust and reliable infrastructure is essential. Infrastructure, in this context, encompasses various technological and physical components that enable seamless and efficient communication within the public sector. Of course, they have a social dimension (Mamalipurath & Notley, 2022) and are fundamentally value laden since they are closely connected to information and communication flows, and the underlying economic base (Prodnik, 2014).

One crucial aspect of communication infrastructure is information technology (IT). Indeed, technologies have profoundly transformed various facets of contemporary society. They have revolutionised communication methods, information access, work processes, business operations, government interactions and social interactions. Their pervasive influence now extends to the socio-economic landscape, playing an important role in the lives of all citizens (Roztocki, Soja & Weistroffer, 2019). Digital communication platforms have emerged as a vital cog of the communication infrastructure. These platforms encompass email systems, instant messaging applications, video conferencing tools and social networks, among others. Although they have enabled the state's communication with citizens through real-time interactions, allowing the state to disseminate public announcements, policy updates and other essential information to citizens in a timely manner, such platforms are not without challenges. Nevertheless, social media, in particular, is generally recognised for its potential to enhance government communication with the public, improve operational efficiency and increase responsiveness to public concerns (Mwaura, Carter & Kubheka, 2020).

South Africa continues to be ranked among the most unequal societies globally, with a significant prevalence of poverty persisting and opulence co-existing, and hence the importance of physical infrastructure should not be downplayed. Therefore, physical public engagements, such as through *izimbizo* (gatherings), should remain important. Radebe, in this volume, argues that, although useful when properly executed, with benefits for citizens, citizen engagement should not be treated like a silver bullet and thus should be examined for its ability to play the fundamental role of redistribution of power in class-divided societies. Indeed, in supporting effective public sector communication, infrastructure is crucial and forms the foundation for seamless information exchange and stakeholder engagement.

The impact of varying levels of literacy

Literacy, whether media, digital or health literacy, remains one of the contentious issues when dealing with public communication. Any effective communication is dependent on the recipients' ability to decipher and decode transmitted messages. However, varying levels of literacy among citizens and communicators can significantly influence the clarity and efficacy of messages. South Africa has an adult illiteracy rate of about 12%, with about 4.4 million adults still illiterate when compared with the global average of 14%. Literacy is essential in communication since it denotes the ability to "identify, understand, interpret, create, communicate and compute, using printed and written materials associated with varying contexts" (Khuluvhe, 2021: 4).

In an unequal society such as South Africa with diverse educational backgrounds, levels of literacy can vary significantly. Nevertheless, low literacy levels can hinder the comprehension of the communication by the state, leading to inadequate public engagement and basic understanding among certain segments of the population. There is a dialectical relationship between the transmitters and receivers of information since communicators who are inadequately trained may struggle to convey information accurately and understandably, leading to potential miscommunications and inefficiencies.

Effective communication skills

Effective communication is another fundamental aspect that plays a pivotal role in shaping the relationship between the public sector and citizens (McCombs, 2002). Public sector communicators have a critical responsibility in disseminating information to the public and fostering a clear understanding of the policies, initiatives and services of the state. Indeed, the public sector's ability to communicate effectively is fundamental and communication skills to achieve this goal are paramount.

Communication is the backbone of transparency, accountability and trust-building between the public sector and citizens. As Maseko posits in this volume, effective communication must ensure, among other things, that the public is well-informed about the decisions of the state, public policies and administrative processes. The ability to communicate clearly is crucial in democratic societies where transparency in public institutions is required and hence the significance of providing free access to information is acknowledged as a fundamental aspect of democracy (Androniceanu, 2021). One of the central reasons why effective communication skills are vital in the public sector is the complex nature of state information. Given the intricate technical information and legal jargon that government must sometimes deal with (As-Saber, Srivastava & Hossain, 2006), effective communication skills become useful in translating this information into accessible language that the public can comprehend. Communication skills play a pivotal role in reducing information asymmetry between the state and citizens.

In the post COVID-19 era, the era of crisis and emergencies, clear public sector communication is paramount. During disasters or public health crises, the government's ability to communicate vital information promptly and clearly can save lives and maintain public order. As Lubinga argues in this volume, effective communication plays a vital role in informing, persuading and maintaining healthy behaviour among citizens of any society. Again, communications skills help prevent misinformation and panic by providing accurate guidance to the public.

Indeed, effective communication fosters public understanding of the state's actions, leading to increased trust and confidence in public institutions. Transparent communication practices contribute positively to increased inclusivity and citizen empowerment in public engagement. Transparent communication is regarded as "an essential aspect of rationality, progress and good governance" (Florini, 2007; cited in Mohelská & Sokolová, 2017: 236). An informed and engaged public is crucial for democracies, enabling constructive feedback and possessing the agency to hold public officials accountable. It is also argued that such an informed citizenry reduces the levels of distrust in state institutions and their decisions. Certainly, evidence from some studies suggests that the benefits for the public sector from citizen engagement are equally tangible, valuable and, of course, varied (Nambisan & Nambisan, 2013).

Public Sector Communication in the Digital Age

Possessing effective communications skills is also beneficial for public institutions and officials as they contribute to improving their image while enhancing their credibility and perceived competence. Various scholars have found positive associations between perceptions of government and their responsiveness (Liao, Yuan, Dong, Yang, Fielding & Lam, 2020) and thus citizens are likely to participate if they are confident of the government's ability to respond timeously and in their best interest (Sjoberg, Mellon & Peixoto, 2017; Mansoor, 2021).

The significance of effective communication notwithstanding, public sector communicators face numerous challenges in driving messages to the public. Among the challenges are bureaucratic red tape and hierarchical structures that act as barriers to transparent and effective communication. Excessive bureaucracy and red tape in the public sector, just as in the private sector, has a negative influence on the performance of various management systems including communication (Welch & Pandey, 2007). Over and above this, differing communication preferences among diverse populations, such as South Africa's, can complicate the process of disseminating information to the public effectively.

To overcome these challenges, public sector communication must prioritise skills development, among others, as the basis for effective communication. This includes prioritising and incorporating digital platforms, social media and other emerging technologies that can help bridge the gap between the government and the public, reaching a broader audience and engaging citizens more effectively. While the South African government has a relatively high presence in social media, the country still faces many challenges pertaining to the use of digital platforms, such as the digital divide and language barriers (Mwaura et al., 2020). Nevertheless, with high internet and smart phone penetration in the country (Ndulu, Ngwenya & Setlhalogile, 2022), it is logical to invest in communication training programmes for public sector communicators, enhancing their abilities to convey information clearly and concisely.

The significance of accessible communication channels

To reach diverse audiences and enhance engagement with the public, accessible communication channels are essential. Moreover, accessible channels, encompassing both traditional and digital platforms, play a pivotal role in facilitating effective converged communication and engagement with audiences. In a nutshell, communication channels serve as conduits for disseminating information, ideas and messages to a broad spectrum of individuals, transcending geographical, cultural and linguistic barriers.

Traditional communication channels, such as print media, television, and radio, have long been instrumental in reaching diverse audiences since they offer an established and credible means of mass communication, particularly in regions where internet penetration remains limited or uneven. Even in the context of crisis communication, as argued by Coombs (2020), the mix between traditional and digital channels is critical. Hence, thinking "creatively about how to reach the non-digital constituents" under difficult circumstances is important (Coombs, 2020: 995). Although the digital media is on the rise, traditional media still holds sway in rural and marginalised communities and therefore it remains an indispensable tool for engaging with hard-to-reach populations. In many societies such as South Africa's, community media has proven to be the mainstay when engaging the rural and marginalised populations (Shahzalal & Hassan, 2019).

Social media platforms, in particular, are now perceived as acceptable in citizen engagement to drive delivery of services such as healthcare (Stellefson, Paige, Chaney & Chaney, 2020). On the other hand, digital channels empower individuals to participate actively in public discourse and decision-making processes, fostering a sense of inclusivity and empowerment among diverse communities.

Of course, accessibility is a crucial factor in ensuring the effectiveness of communication channels in reaching diverse audiences. However, contextual factors such as language and cultural diversity, as well as socio-economic factors, including the technological divide, are some of the vital factors to consider. Therefore, public sector communication initiatives must be deliberate in being inclusive in the context of South Africa's diverse population. Identifying accessible communication channels is part of the paramount consideration to heighten engagement, increase trust and enhance understanding among the public. We must of course guard against a binary approach in linking engagement and trust. Scholars like Petts (2008) correctly caution against the misplaced optimism that enduring trust is unlikely to spring from engagement itself. Nonetheless, the significance of accessible communication channels, be they traditional or digital, cannot be underestimated in reaching diverse audiences and enhancing engagement.

Media power and public sector communication

The media wields substantial power and influence in shaping public perception and significantly influences the effectiveness of public sector communication. Through its control over information dissemination, agenda setting and framing, the media holds immense power in constructing narratives that influence how the public perceives events and issues (McCombs, Shaw & Weaver, 2018), including government actions. However, it is imperative to acknowledge its limitations since, for example, it has been argued that the South African media tend to portray government negatively (Radebe, 2017). This negative framing is sometimes attributed to the media's lack of transformation, leading to views that its power and hegemony still resides in the hands of the white capitalist class (Jacobs, 2004; M&G Data Desk, 2019).

This situation has led to successive state presidents, from Nelson Mandela to Thabo Mbeki to Jacob Zuma, arguing that this arrangement of media power is used as a tool against the political power of the African majority (Radebe, 2020). The media in South Africa has largely positioned itself as a 'watchdog' against the black elites through state corruption, while on the other hand neglecting corruption in the private sector perpetuated by white capital. Hence it has been accused of racism (Wasserman, 2006; Duncan, 2009) since it largely frames government institutions negatively.

However, there are instances where the media frames public institutions, such as South Africa's supreme audit institution, the Auditor-General of South Africa, positively. Of course, among the drivers of this framing by the media have been, for example, the adverse audit outcomes issued, which are used to frame the government negatively. This has also been the case with other public institutions such as the Public Protector of South Africa under Thuli Madonsela, who was singled out as a corruption buster. It was the findings against the government that catapulted the institution into the limelight. The media power also resides in its agenda-setting function, which is particularly influential in directing public attention to specific issues and topics, while also downplaying or neglecting others (Coleman, McCombs, Shaw & Weaver, 2009). As a result, public sector communication efforts may be overshadowed or distorted by the media's selective focus, thereby affecting the issues that dominate public discourse. Notwithstanding the reduction of the gatekeeping power of traditional media due to the emergence of social media (Gilardi, Gessler, Kubli & Müller, 2022), traditional media remains important in the public sector communication mix for ensuring a wider reach of citizens.

Furthermore, media framing determines how events and policies are presented, influencing the public's interpretation and understanding of government actions (Entman & Rojecki, 1993). By adopting specific frames, the media can either enhance or undermine the effectiveness of public sector communication, shaping the audience's perceptions and attitudes towards governmental initiatives. Moreover, the media's role as a gatekeeper, determining which information is disseminated and how it is presented, can influence public trust in government communication (Shoemaker & Vos, 2014). Biases, sensationalism or partisan reporting can lead to public scepticism, hindering the efficacy of public sector communication efforts. Nevertheless, the media has significance influence and implications for public sector communication.

Political climate impact

The political climate exerts a profound influence on public sector communication. Political factors, in particular, significantly shape the way the public sector communicates with the public. Expectedly, political environments are characterised by power struggles, competing ideologies and varying interests, all of which influence the design, content and delivery of public sector messages. The public environment is a highly politicised and contested space influenced by various factors. One such key aspect is the framing of government initiatives and policies. Governments, for example, often tailor their communication to resonate with their political base or to appease influential interest groups. This is a function of news frames, which are the imprint of power (Entman, 1993). Consequently, messages may be strategically crafted to emphasise certain aspects while downplaying or omitting others, potentially influencing public perceptions and attitudes.

Fundamentally, political dynamics play a role in determining the accessibility and transparency of public sector communication. In periods of heightened political polarisation, for whatever reason, including authoritarianism, some governments may restrict information flow to control the narrative and suppress dissent. In the digital age, censorship and attempts to restrain the internet are common practices. There are many instances across the world where there has been a shutdown of the internet as a whole (Denisova, 2017). Conversely, during times of political openness and accountability, governments may prioritise transparent and inclusive communication to maintain public trust (Hyland-Wood, Gardner, Leask & Ecker, 2021).

The choice of communication channels is also influenced by the political climate. Governments might opt for traditional media to reach broad audiences during

Insights and Influences from the Global South

election campaigns, while using digital platforms to engage with specific demographic groups. Such strategies align with the political objectives of maximising voter support and mobilising constituents. For example, Sitto-Kaunda, in this volume, posits that the South African government employs e-government strategies when it attempts to reach citizens for voting purposes. Essentially, the political environment significantly shapes public sector communication and thus comprehending these dynamics is key, especially when it comes to the assessment of public sector communication.

Some Outcomes of Effective Public Sector Communication

The role of information dissemination is paramount in shaping an *informed citizenry*. Effective public sector communication not only ignites the agency of citizens but equips them with knowledge that empowers them to critically comprehend the socio-political landscape and the underlying power structures. In the context of the evolving communication landscape, characterised by the maturation of social media and the decline of mainstream institutional journalism, there is a trend towards re-evaluating the processes through which information is produced, distributed, assimilated and acted upon, including platforms, analytics, algorithms, ideological media and rogue actors (Entman & Usher, 2018). On the one hand, informed citizens are empowered to advocate for their rights and demand equitable distribution of resources, fostering collective mobilisation for social justice and community development (Wampler, 2000). On the other hand, they are enabled to challenge dominant narratives and question policies that perpetuate inequalities, thereby fostering accountable governance and empowering citizens to engage in responsible decision making (Silver, Scott & Kazepov, 2010).

Another crucial aspect of public sector communication is the establishment of *increased public trust* in government institutions and officials. The challenges previously raised notwithstanding, this is intrinsically linked to transparent and open communication practices. Transparent communication has been argued to foster a sense of accountability and responsiveness, allowing citizens to better comprehend the decision-making processes within the government. Indeed, advocates of greater citizen participation posit that this approach may, among others, "promote democracy, build trust, increase transparency, enhance accountability, build social capital, reduce conflict, ascertain priorities, promote legitimacy, cultivate mutual understanding, and advance fairness and justice" (Callahan, 2007: 1183). Therefore, by providing clear and accessible information, officials can bridge the gap between the governing elites and the governed, promoting a sense of inclusion and reducing feelings of alienation among citizens (Bellamy, 2008).

The encouragement of *meaningful public engagement* in governance processes is important in fostering a sense of ownership and inclusion among citizens. Effective communication that prioritises transparency and accessibility allows citizens to understand and participate in decision-making processes. To this end, e-government is vital in enhancing transparency of decision-making processes (see, for example, Kaunda and Mukonza, in this volume) as it offers opportunities for citizens to directly participate in decision making (Ndou, 2004). Through such engagement, individuals feel empowered to voice their concerns and contribute to policy formulation, challenging the notion of governance as a top-down process controlled by the ruling elite (Althusser, 1971). Meaningful public engagement enables citizens to actively shape their communities and advocate for their rights, thus challenging dominant power structures and promoting a more equitable distribution of resources (Chomsky, 1997).

The Book's Structure

The aforementioned factors define the timeliness of this volume, as each chapter intricately engages and addresses the relevant inquiry concerning the significance of public sector communication in the digital age.

In Chapter 1, **Themba Maseko** reviews the role of the government communication system in South Africa. This is done in the context of the transition from an autocratic apartheid state to our current democratic constitutional dispensation. He explores ways in which government communicators could navigate through ethical dilemmas brought about by the transition. This chapter grapples with ethical dilemmas that confront government communicators, given that the area has not been theorised sufficiently. Maseko helps us identify the gaps and this is what makes this chapter timely and a must-read.

Chapter 2, by **Lakela Kaunda** and **Ricky M Mukonza**, presents a critical assessment of the utilisation of Facebook as a social media platform for public engagement and service delivery purposes. The chapter focuses on South Africa's eight metropolitan municipalities' Facebook pages and their engagement with citizens. Social media, it is argued, with its interactive capability, enables real-time communication with the public. This underlines the urgency of exploring the use of Facebook, and by extension other social media platforms, by South Africa's local government. Indeed, it is becoming apparent that not only can social media be ignored, but local governments must embrace an interactive approach when employing social media platforms. They also highlight the inextricable link between service delivery and communication effectiveness between municipalities and citizens.

The use of strategic communication by local government in collective bargaining has not been adequately theorised in South Africa. With a number of strikes – some illegal – Chapter 3 by **Pay Shabangu** compels us to confront this critical discourse in the context of our highly contentious collective bargaining structures in South Africa as he analyses the challenges in local government collective bargaining and proposes solutions to these. Again, this is another area to which public sector communicators must pay close attention as it frames employee/employer stakeholder relationships in the public sector.

Chapter 4 by **Karabo Sitto-Kaunda** continues with the focus on the public sector communication, but this time using the election as a lens. The chapter explores stakeholder engagement as a key pillar of the Independent Electoral Commission (IEC), in its communication endeavours. Fundamentally, digital and social media is argued to have helped to shift the stakeholder engagement relationship, moving the power of communication into the hands of recipients, such as potential voters. With the increased use of e-government strategies in South Africa for citizen engagement, the evolution of the IEC's communication strategy to digitally led strategic communication activities and its implications are assessed in this chapter.

In Chapter 5, **ML Dingalo** engages with the complexity of public sector communication and the unique environment within which it is practised. The fundamental questions of transparency, accountability and the right to access information from public sector entities are argued as cornerstones of democratic societies. Thus, the chapter explores the citizens' need of information in their quest to understand the entities constituted to serve them and the manner in which policy decisions are made and implemented. Concomitantly, these policies impact on the citizens in their everyday lives. However, how so though, is the critical question with which this chapter grapples.

Chapter 6 further explores the realm of public sector communication, with **Maphelo Malgas** and **Andiswa Mrasi** delving into a critical issue related to the challenges faced in effectively implementing communication strategies for development programmes aimed at small businesses within South Africa. This chapter revolves around the core premise of offering an encompassing and contextually tailored perspective on the prevailing landscape of public sector communication, specifically zeroing in on entities entrusted with fostering the growth of small businesses in

South Africa, notably the Small Enterprise Development Agency (SEDA) and Small Enterprise Finance Agency (SEFA). Ultimately, the primary focus of this chapter rests on presenting a comprehensive proposal for enhancing public sector communication. This proposition entails the introduction of a structured framework designed to facilitate the effective communication of support initiatives tailored to the unique needs of small businesses operating in the South African context.

Elizabeth Lubinga begins the theme of citizen engagement in Chapter 7, albeit from the healthcare perspective. The chapter argues that public health communication is critical to informing, persuading and maintaining healthy behaviour among citizens of any society. However, resource-constrained developing countries such as South Africa are increasingly committing more financial resources to health, which underscores the exigency of using public health communication as a tool to educate and develop a health-literate populace. Most health problems, including both communicable and non-communicable diseases, are preventable and prevention is the most cost-effective strategy to ensure good health among health-literate populaces. The chapter is underpinned by multiple theories relevant to public health communication in order to reflect on the behaviour change required globally and in South Africa.

Vincent Tshuma and **Sibongile Mpofu** continue with the public health communication theme in Chapter 8 where they argue that the strategic dissemination of health information is required to advance the health of the public. Therefore, tailored and targeted messages to individuals, groups and wider communities are key in promoting public health. More so, in the era of digital revolution, the expectations have been that such advancements would aid public health communication efforts to reach an inclusive population and ensure the wellness of society, and ultimately contribute towards the attainment of the Sustainable Development Goals (SDGs). Tshuma and Mpofu focus on the health communication policies of regulatory bodies and the private sector in

Zimbabwe to integrate vital communication in promoting eye and vision health. They identify the communication strategies employed within this sector, together with specific messages regarding eye health and how these contribute to the larger frame of the SDGs.

In Chapter 9, **Mandla J. Radebe** critically analyses the concept of citizen engagement which, he argues, has been valorised as a silver bullet that will drive participation in liberal democracies. It is assumed that citizens will be enabled to make their inputs and benefit in the process. The chapter argues that when properly examined, this seductive concept is unable to play the fundamental role of redistribution of power in class-divided societies such as South Africa's. Instead, in most instances, it is employed to placate the marginalised underclasses and thus is a useful tool to negotiate consent on behalf of the ruling capitalist class. To this effect, the chapter presents some thoughts on approaches to theorising and implementing citizen engagement in the Global South context. It concludes by advocating for a new public sphere that will empower the subaltern to achieve the objectives of redistribution of power through meaningful citizen engagement.

Anna Oksiutycz argues in Chapter 10 that the calls for, and declarations of commitment, to transparency have come from many quarters, putting both government and business organisations under increased scrutiny. Various players, such as the public, media and civil society, are placing emphasis on government and public sector organisations becoming more transparent and consequently accountable to the citizens. The chapter grapples with transparency and accountability as key issues, considering that in South Africa corruption, mismanagement, fraud, misappropriation of funds and other malaises have been identified at all levels of government. Oksiutycz posits that information is not neutral and that providing information is a process loaded with subjectivity, reflecting deliberate choices and the established institutional order and culture. To this end, principles of communication should be applied by governments to foster transparency and its outcomes: accountability, engagement and efficiency.

In providing the concluding remarks to the book, Karabo Sitto-Kaunda provides an overview of the significance of public sector communication to engage citizens. She also draws our attention to the effectiveness of digital technologies to aid in driving more effective strategic communication from public sector organisations, along with the challenges with respect to implementation to date. That COVID-19 and the subsequent period of lockdown forced organisations, including those in the public sector, to rely increasingly on digital communication, is discussed throughout the volume to understand the relational effects among stakeholders of governments. The volume concludes with an understanding of the strategic role citizens play for all government-related public sector communication, which is primarily based on their perceptions of the effectiveness of the service delivery levels received.

References

Adae EK, Twum KK, Hinson RE, Duh HI & Odame DA.
(2023). *Social Media and Africa's Public Sector: Perspectives on Contemporary Issues.* Cham, Switzerland: Palgrave Macmillan. https://doi.org/10.1007/978-3-031-22642-7

Adeola O, Katuse P & Twum KK. (Eds). (2022). Public Sector Marketing Communications Volume I: Public Relations and Brand Communication Perspectives. Cham, Switzerland: Palgrave Macmillan. https://doi.org/10.1007/978-3-031-07293-2

Adeola O, Twum KK & Katuse P. (2023). An Introduction to Public Sector Marketing Communications: Traditional and Digital Perspectives. In: O Adeola, KK Twum & P Katuse (Eds). *Public Sector Marketing Communications, Volume II: Traditional and Digital Perspectives.* Cham, Switzerland: Palgrave Macmillan. 3–18. https://doi.org/10.1007/978-3-031-17863-4_1

Althusser, L. 1971. "Ideology and the State." In Lenin and Philosophy and other Essays. New Left Books.

Androniceanu A. (2021). Transparency in public administration as a challenge for good democratic governance. *Revista Administratie si Management Public (RAMP)*, 36:149–164. https://doi.org/10.24818/amp/2021.36-09

As-Saber SN, Srivastava A & Hossain K. (2006). Information technology law and e-government: A developing country perspective. *Journal of Administration and Governance (JOAAG)*, 1(1):84–101.

Bellamy R. (2008). *Citizenship: A Very Short Introduction*. New York, USA: Oxford University Press. https://doi.org/10.1093/actrade/9780192802538.001.0001

Callahan K. (2007). Citizen participation: Models and methods. *International Journal of Public Administration*, 30(11):1179–1196. https://doi.org/10.1080/01900690701225366

Cariolle J. (2021). International connectivity and the digital divide in Sub-Saharan Africa. *Information Economics and Policy*, 55: 100901. https://doi.org/10.1016/j.infoecopol.2020.100901

Chomsky N. (1997). *Market democracy in a neoliberal order: Doctrines and reality*. Z Magazine. November. https://znetwork.org/zmagazine/market-democracy-in-a-neoliberal-order-doctrines-and-reality-by-noam-chomsky-1/

Coleman R, McCombs M, Shaw D & Weaver D. (2009). Agenda setting. In: K Wahl-Jorgensen & T Hanitzsch (Eds). *The Handbook of Journalism Studies*. 2nd Edition. New York and London: Routledge. 167–180.

Coombs WT. (2020). Public sector crises: Realizations from Covid-19 for crisis communication. *Partecipazione e Conflitto (PaCo)*, 13(2):990–1001.

Denisova A. (2017). Democracy, protest and public sphere in Russia after the 2011–2012 anti-government protests: Digital media at stake. *Media, Culture & Society*, 39(7):976–994. https://doi.org/10.1177/0163443716682075

Duncan, J. (2009). The uses and abuses of political economy: the ANC's media policy. *Transformation*. https://doi.org/10.1353/trn.0.0039

Entman RM. (1993). Framing: Toward clarification of a fractured paradigm. *Journal of Communication*, 43(4):51–58. https://doi.org/10.1111/j.1460-2466.1993.tb01304.x

Entman RM & Rojecki A. (1993). Freezing out the public: Elite and media framing of the US anti-nuclear movement. *Political Communication*, 10(2):155–173. https://doi.org/10.1080/10584609.1993.9962973

Entman RM & Usher N. (2018). Framing in a fractured democracy: Impacts of digital technology on ideology, power and cascading network activation. *Journal of Communication*, 68(2):298–308. https://doi.org/10.1093/joc/jqx019

Florini A. (Ed). (2007). *The Right to Know: Transparency for an Open World*. New York, USA: Columbia University Press. https://doi.org/10.7312/flor14158

Gilardi F, Gessler T, Kubli M & Müller S. (2022). Social media and political agenda setting. *Political Communication*, 39(3):39–60. https://doi.org/10.1080/10584609.2021.1910390

Glenn I & Mattes R. (2012). Political communication in post-apartheid South Africa. In: HA Semetko & M Scammel. (Eds). *The SAGE Handbook of Political Communication*. Los Angeles, London, New Delhi, Singapore, Washington DC: Sage Publications. 494–508. https://doi.org/10.4135/9781446201015.n40

Govenden P. (2022). The power of neoliberalism: Transformation, neo-elitism and class continuities in the post-apartheid media. *tripleC: Communication, Capitalism & Critique*, 20(1):101–120. https://doi.org/10.31269/triplec.v20i1.1301

Hyland-Wood B, Gardner J, Leask J & Ecker UKH. (2021). Toward effective government communication strategies in the era of COVID-19. *Humanities and Social Sciences Communications*, 8(1):1–11. https://doi.org/10.1057/s41599-020-00701-w

Jacobs, S.H., 2004. Public sphere, power and democratic politics: Media and policy debates in post-apartheid South Africa (Doctoral dissertation, Birkbeck (University of London)).

John SF, Maama H, Ojogiwa OT & Mubangizi BC. (2022). Government communication in times of crisis: The priorities and trends in South Africa's response to COVID-19. *Journal for Transdisciplinary Research in Southern Africa*, 18(1):1–10. https://doi.org/10.4102/td.v18i1.1146

Khuluvhe M. (2021). *Adult illiteracy in South Africa*. Pretoria: Department of Higher Education and Training. https://www.dhet.gov.za/Planning%20Monitoring%20and%20Evaluation%20Coordination/Fact%20Sheet%20-%20Adult%20Illiteracy%20in%20South%20Africa%20-%20March%202023.pdf

Liao Q, Yuan J, Dong M, Yang L, Fielding R & Lam WWT. (2020). Public engagement and government responsiveness in the communications about COVID-19 during the early epidemic stage in China: Infodemiology study on social media data. *Journal of Medical Internet Research*, 22(5):e18796. https://doi.org/10.2196/18796

Mail & Guardian (M&G) Data Desk. (2019). *Who runs SA's media is a black-and-white issue*. Mail & Guardian. 4 January. [Retrieved 26 August 2019]. https://mg.co.za/article/2019-01-04-00-who-runs-sas-media-is-a-black-and-white-issue/#:~:text=Who%20owns%20the%20media%20in,run%20mostly%20by%20white%20people.

Mamalipurath JM & Notley T. (2022). Muslim responses to the COVID-19 pandemic in Western Sydney: Understanding the role of community-specific communication infrastructure. *Journal of Intercultural Studies*, 43(6):740–757. https://doi.org/10.1080/07256868.2022.2128088

Mansoor M. (2021). Citizens' trust in government as a function of good governance and government agency's provision of quality information on social media during COVID-19. *Government Information Quarterly*, 38(4):101597. https://doi.org/10.1016/j.giq.2021.101597

Matli W & Ngoepe M. (2020). Capitalizing on digital literacy skills for capacity development of people who are not in education, employment or training in South Africa. *African Journal of Science, Technology, Innovation and Development*, 12(2):129–139. https://doi.org/10.1080/20421338.2019.1624008

McCombs M. (2002). The agenda-setting role of the mass media in the shaping of public opinion. *Mass Media Economics Conference*. Cambridge, UK: London School of Economics: Presentation, June. https://www.academia.edu/download/32748637/The_Agenda-Setting_Role_of_the_Mass_Media_(Maxwell_McCombs).pdf

McCombs ME, Shaw DL & Weaver DH. (2018). New directions in agenda-setting theory and research. In: R Wei (Ed). *Advances in Foundational Mass Communication Theories*. New York and London: Routledge. 131–152. https://doi.org/10.4324/9781315164441-9

Mohelská H & Sokolová M. (2017). Digital transparency in the public sector: Case study Czech Republic. *Economics and Management (E&M)*, 20(4):236–250. https://doi.org/10.15240/tul/001/2017-4-016

Munzhedzi PH. (2017). The role of separation of powers in ensuring public accountability in South Africa: Policy versus practice. *2nd International Conference on Public Administration and Development Alternatives (IPADA)*. Gaberone, Botswana, 26–28 July. http://ulspace.ul.ac.za/bitstream/handle/10386/1882/munzhedzi_role_2017.pdf

Mutula S & Wamukoya JM. (2009). Public sector information management in east and southern Africa: Implications for FOI, democracy and integrity in government. *International Journal of Information Management*, 29(5):333–341. https://doi.org/10.1016/j.ijinfomgt.2009.04.004

Mwaura J, Carter V & Kubheka BZ. (2020). Social media health promotion in South Africa: Opportunities and challenges. *African Journal of Primary Health Care and Family Medicine*, 12(1):1–7. https://doi.org/10.4102/phcfm.v12i1.2389

Nambisan S & Nambisan P. (2013). *Engaging citizens in co-creation in public services: Lesson learned and best practices.* IBM Center for The Business of Government. https://www.businessofgovernment.org/report/engaging-citizens-co-creation-public-services

Ndou V. (2004). E-government for developing countries: Opportunities and challenges. *The Electronic Journal of Information Systems in Developing Countries (EJISDC)*,18(1):1–24. https://doi.org/10.1002/j.1681-4835.2004.tb00117.x

Ndulu B, Ngwenya NX & Setlhalogile M. (2022). The digital divide in South Africa: Insights from the COVID-19 experience and beyond. In: M Qobo, M Soko & NX Ngwenya (Eds). *The Future of the South African Political Economy Post-COVID 19*. Cham, Switzerland: Palgrave Macmillan. 273–295. https://doi.org/10.1007/978-3-031-10576-0_11

Okigbo, C., & Eribo, F. (Eds.). (2004). *Development and communication in Africa*. Rowman & Littlefield.

Osei-Appiah S. (2021). On the question of decolonisation, gender and political communication. In: B Karam & B Mutsvairo (Eds). *Decolonising Political Communication in Africa*. New York and London: Routledge. 109–120. https://doi.org/10.4324/9781003111962-10

Petts J. (2008). Public engagement to build trust: False hopes? *Journal of Risk Research*, 11(6):821–835. https://doi.org/10.1080/13669870701715592

Prodnik, Jernej A. 2014. A seeping commodification: The long revolution in the proliferation of communication commodities. *tripleC: Communication, Capitalism & Critique*, 12(1): 142–168. https://doi.org/10.31269/triplec.v12i1.485

Radebe, M. J. (2006). The coverage of industrial action by the Mail & Guardian, 1999-2004. *Unpublished dissertation*. Johannesburg: University of the Witwatersrand.

Radebe, M. J. (2017). *Corporate media and the nationalisation of the economy in South Africa: A critical Marxist political economy approach* (Doctoral dissertation, University of the Witwatersrand, Faculty of Humanities School of Social Sciences).

Radebe, M. J. (2020). Constructing Hegemony: The South African Commercial Media and the (Mis)Representation of Nationalisation. Pietermaritzburg: University of KwaZulu-Natal Press.

Roztocki N, Soja P & Weistroffer HR. (2019). The role of information and communication technologies in socioeconomic development: Towards a multi-dimensional framework. *Information Technology for Development*, 25(2): 171–183. https://doi.org/10.1080/02681102.2019.1596654

Shahzalal MD & Hassan A. (2019). Communicating sustainability: Using community media to influence rural people's intention to adopt sustainable behaviour. *Sustainability*, 11(3):812. https://doi.org/10.3390/su11030812

Shoemaker PJ & Vos TP. (2014). Media gatekeeping. In: DW Stacks & MB Salwen (Eds). *An Integrated Approach to Communication Theory and Research*. 2nd Edition. New York and London: Routledge. 89–103.

Silver H, Scott A & Kazepov Y. (2010). Participation in urban contention and deliberation. *International Journal of Urban and Regional Research*, 34(3):453–477. https://doi.org/10.1111/j.1468-2427.2010.00963.x

Sjoberg FM, Mellon J & Peixoto T. (2017). The effect of bureaucratic responsiveness on citizen participation. *Public Administration Review*, 77(3):340–351. https://doi.org/10.1111/puar.12697

Solomon EM & Van Klyton A. (2020). The impact of digital technology usage on economic growth in Africa. *Utilities Policy*, 67:101104. https://doi.org/10.1016/j.jup.2020.101104

Stellefson M, Paige,SR, Chaney BJ & Chaney JD. (2020). Evolving role of social media in health promotion: Updated responsibilities for health education specialists. *International Journal of Environmental Research and Public Health*, 17(4):1153. https://doi.org/10.3390/ijerph17041153

Tomaselli, K. (1997). Ownership and control in the South African print media: black empowerment after apartheid, 1990–1997. *Ecquid Novi*, 18(1), pp.67-68. https://doi.org/10.1080/02560054.1997.9653194

Wampler B. (2000). *A guide to participatory budgeting*. International Budget Partnership. 1–32. https://www.changetomorrow.io/docs/a-guide-to-participatory-budgeting-wampler.pdf

Wasserman, H. (2006). Tackles and sidesteps: Normative maintenance and paradigm repair in mainstream reactions to South African tabloid journalism. *Communicare: Journal for Communication Sciences in Southern Africa*, 25(1), 59-80. https://doi.org/10.36615/jcsa.v25i1.1729

Wasserman H & De Beer A. (2005). Which public? Whose interest? The South African media and its role during the first ten years of democracy. *Critical Arts: A Journal of South-North Cultural and Media Studies*, 19(1-2):36–51. https://doi.org/10.1080/02560040585310041

Welch EW & Pandey SK. (2007). E-government and bureaucracy: Toward a better understanding of intranet implementation and its effect on red tape. *Journal of Public Administration Research and Theory*, 17(3):379–404. https://doi.org/10.1093/jopart/mul013

Chapter 1

Ethics and Government Communication

Themba Maseko

This chapter reviews the role of the government communication function in South Africa during the transition from an autocratic apartheid state to a democratic state and explores how ethical theory could enable government communicators to navigate ethical dilemmas brought about by the transition. The government communication function is defined as "the role, practice, aims and achievements of communication as it takes place in and on behalf of a public institution(s) whose primary end is executive in the service of a political rationale, and that is constituted based on the people's indirect or direct consent and charged to enact their will" (Sanders & Canel, 2013: 4).

The chapter argues that government communication during the apartheid era played a pivotal role in defending and promoting apartheid policies in South Africa and abroad, under the leadership of the Ministry of Information and the South African Communication Service (SACS). Following the adoption of a democratic Constitution in 1996, the role of government communication shifted toward promoting transparency and accountability through the GCIS (Glenn & Mattes, 2012). Notably, the Ministry of Information was abolished, and the SACS was replaced by a semi-autonomous GCIS that reported to the Presidency via a Minister without Portfolio. This suggests a deliberate intent to depart from a propagandist Ministry of Information that existed during the apartheid era.

The chapter asserts that a government communication function is contextual and influenced by the nature and character of the state it serves. This chapter uses ethics (moral) theory to evaluate both the system and the conduct of communicators from an ethical standpoint. This is done to inform communicators that all forms of communication have contextual and ethical dimensions that pose dilemmas for those who work in the system. The chapter argues that during the apartheid era, the government communication function was designed to promote apartheid policies, whereas, in the post-apartheid era, the system was designed to promote transparency and accountability in line with the new Constitution and the Bill of Rights.

Although a lot of literature exists about the role, nature, and structure of the government communication function globally, not enough attention has been given to the ethical dilemmas faced by government communicators when countries undergo radical transitions from autocracy to democracy. This discussion seeks to contribute to filling this gap in the South African public sector communication discourse and identifies areas for further study in this regard. Ethical theories are discussed as an analytical tool to identify, analyse, and evaluate the ethical dilemmas encountered by the government communication system and government communicators in post-apartheid South Africa. These government communicators are employees tasked with the responsibility of conveying information, both internally and externally, to diverse audiences regarding agency/departmental office policies, decisions, actions, and/or guiding communication strategy (Ruijer, 2017). I conclude by proposing an ethical theoretical framework that could enable communicators to evaluate their conduct in the exercise of their duties professionally and ethically while remaining loyal to the government of the day. In the end, understanding ethics is important because all forms, contexts, and instances of communication are infused with ethical dimensions (Japp, Meister & Japp, 2005).

Background: Government Communication in South Africa

South Africa held its first democratic elections in 1994 after decades of colonial and apartheid rule. The first democratic parliament embarked on an inclusive process to draft a new Constitution that was finally promulgated as Act 108 of 1996. The preamble of the new Constitution of the Republic of South Africa seeks to "Lay the foundations for a democratic and open society in which government is based on the will of the people and every citizen is equally protected by law".

During the apartheid era, government communication was characterised by a culture of secrecy, disinformation, and restrictions on press freedom (ComTask, 1996). The SACS's mandate was to promote and defend the policies of the apartheid regime and to contribute to the acceptance of apartheid policies in South Africa and abroad. Although no scholarly literature exists regarding the policies and operations of SACS, its primary role was to use various media channels, primarily the South African Broadcasting Corporation (SABC), to promote and defend the ideology of apartheid.

As the government communications function evolved from an undemocratic propaganda machine to an agile system that sought to promote transparency and accountability, the system experienced a new tension that was caused largely by the expectation that the government communication system should serve the narrow purpose of defending a state that was perceived to be corrupt and incapable of addressing the socio-economic needs of the vast majority.

Government communications during the apartheid era

To understand the form and character of government communication, it is important to understand the character of the state that creates the system (Hansson, Belkacem & Ekenberg, 2015). The changing role of the government communication function during the transition requires an understanding of the nature and character of the state in the pre- and post-apartheid era. Goncalves and Santos (2017) define political communication as the communication efforts to disseminate information to the media and the public in order to influence election results. Government communication, on the other hand, is defined as the process of communication and interaction between government and its citizens to convey information about government policies and programmes. The latter is based on the understanding that a healthy democracy requires an informed public and a government transparent and accountable to the electorate (Goncalves & Santos, 2017).

The apartheid state was an autocratic and undemocratic state that did not embrace basic values such equality, law, and socio-economic rights. Hence its reliance on state-sponsored propaganda, stringent security laws, and the use of forces to maintain its survival. It is no accident that its communication system and policies were designed to perpetuate the subjugation of the black majority and to keep the white minority uninformed about the injustices of the system. The apartheid communication system was underpinned by secrecy and suppression of information that exposed the injustices of apartheid and opposition to apartheid in general. Public entities, such as the SABC, were used as a propaganda machine to promote apartheid (Glenn & Mattes, 2012). Legislative frameworks were also used to control the flow of information to the public, control media ownership and ensure that only the government and its supporters had free access to the media platforms.

The communication strategy was designed and implemented by the Ministry of Information with the SACS as its administrative arm. Media ownership was subject to stringent regulation, and numerous laws were in place specifically designed to preserve and propagate the apartheid ideology (Fourie, 2002). Private ownership of both print and electronic media was limited to only a few members of the white – and mainly Afrikaner – elite and a handful of others. However, the concentration of media ownership has persisted into the post-apartheid era (Radebe, 2022). Although bland and progressive journalists took the risk and established alternative media platforms, such as *The New Nation, The*

Sowetan, *Vrye Weekblad*, the *Weekly Mail* and others, these were dealt with harshly by the regime. Several journalists and editors were persecuted, and newspapers were routinely banned by the state (Berger, 2000; Wasserman, 2010). As if controlling the airwaves was not enough, in what became known as the 'Information Scandal' the state went to the extent of using public funds illegally to secretly establish *The Citizen* newspaper at great expense to the taxpayer.

Recruitment to the SACS was purely on a racial and partisan basis at all state levels (Posel, 1999). Just like all aspects of life under apartheid, the SACS was created to serve the narrow interests of the apartheid regime and the ruling elite of the time. Although the government communication system fulfilled its mandate of promoting the unjust policies of an apartheid state and the ruling elite, it cannot be said that the system's character, conduct and work would pass the ethical test.

The post-apartheid state

In the period leading to South Africa's first democratic election, the ANC launched its Reconstruction and Development Programme (RDP) in 1994 stating, among other things, that democratisation requires an efficient, effective, responsive, and accountable government. Following the first democratic elections of 1994, the newly elected government had no choice but to introduce reforms to give effect to the new Constitutional dispensation (Horwitz, 2001). In other words, the ANC planned to establish a state that would be capable of intervening in the economy to deliver improved public services to all South Africans. This language and tone suggest that the ANC embraced the notion of an interventionist state.

A developmental state is defined as a state that, guided by a long-term plan, pursues higher levels of socio-economic development, has the requisite capacity, is run by an elite that is developmental in approach and is appropriately organised to achieve the predetermined goals (Gumede, 2015). Four key elements are identified as pillars of a developmental state, namely:

1. electoral democracy;
2. popular participation in governance;
3. economic growth and state-driven socio-economic development; and
4. state capacity to deliver services (Edigheji, 2005).

The developmental state approach is therefore in direct contrast to the neo-classical economics approach that sees state intervention as tampering with economic growth and disrupting the market (Gumede, 2015). Key ANC documents also emphasise the need for the state to be capacitated to intervene in the market in the interests of higher national development, higher rates of economic growth, and achieving social cohesion (ANC Strategy and Tactics, 2007).

In the 30th anniversary year of South Africa's first democratic elections, although the ideological underpinnings of a developmental and constitutional state exist, several factors have emerged to undermine this trajectory. They include economic decline, high levels of inequality, poverty, unemployment, and corruption, and political infighting among the elite within the governing party, and the tripartite alliance made up of the ANC, Congress of South African Trade Unions (COSATU) and the SACP. The tension within the ANC and its alliance partners points to a contest about two key issues: an ideological fight over economic policies on the one hand, and a fight for control over state resources among the elites within the ruling party (Pillay, 2011). Escalating levels of corruption in the state system suggest that some elements of the governing elite have fallen into the trap of putting personal interests ahead of national interests.

This suggests that while the post-1994 democratic state may have had the characteristics of a developmental state at its inception, it may now be deemed 'anti-developmental' as the state appears to have been derailed from its trajectory. Government appears to be experiencing what Fanon referred to as "... the mishaps of the educated classes who were unprepared, lack practical links with the masses, laziness and cowardice". Further, he writes: "The intellectuals who, on the eve of independence, rallied to the party, now make it clear by their attitude that they gave their support with no other end in view than to secure their slices of the cake of independence. Thus, the party becomes "a means of private advancement" (Fanon,1963).

This context present dilemmas for the government communication system in general and the communicators in particular as the two are caught between an underperforming, untrusted and seemingly unethical state, on the one hand, and an unhappy, distrusting and discontent populace. Edigheji's (2005) characterisation of a development state is useful to evaluate the role, design and character of the South African state; and how the model of a government communication system mirrors his model of a developmental communication system.

The newly elected South African government had to design a state that would be capable of fulfilling the constitutional mandates to address the socio-economic challenges facing the majority. However, the state could not fulfill these objectives without intervening in the market to direct the country's economic trajectory toward the achievement of these goals. In other words, the design of the new state had to confront the relationship between politics and the economy. However, the rising levels of poverty, unemployment, and inequality post-1994 suggest that the state may be failing to fulfill its developmental state role. This failure, real or perceived, is putting strains on the post-1994 government communication system as it struggles to build trust between the state and its citizens.

The post-apartheid government communication system

In 1995, a year after the first democratic elections, the new government established the Communication Task Group in 1995 to conduct a review of the government communication system and recommend a new communication system for

South Africa that would be aligned with the constitutional imperatives of guaranteed political and civil rights, freedom of information, transparency and accountability. The review led to the establishment of the current Government Communication Information System in 1998, which I joined as its Chief Executive Officer in 2009. The GCIS's mission was to "deliver effective strategic government communication, set standards and proactively communicate with the public about government policies, plans, programmes and achievements through media relations, public reporting and responsiveness to citizens' needs" (GCIS, 1998). In addition to being a service to achieve accountability, the new government acknowledged the need for political communication and included a subset of political communicators whose task was to meet the political communication needs of elected representatives.

The establishment of the GCIS resulted in the amalgamation of structures and absorption of personnel from the white administration, the nine ethnically based so-called homeland governments, and four white provincial administrations. Other than the white national administrations and the four provincial administrations, all the government departments had their communication staff, structures, strategies, and systems. Following the recommendations of the Communication Task team, the above-mentioned communication units were integrated into what became known as the GCIS, which included all the racially based communications divisions.

Incidentally, the GCIS adopted the structural model of the SACS with a central Head Office, departmental communications, and provincial communication divisions that reported to their political and administrative heads. Each political head of a ministry or department was allocated the post of a politically appointed media liaison officer whose term of office was linked to the term of office of the political principal.

The recruitment of government communicators was decentralised to each ministry and department and province with no uniform norms and standards. Except for the political communicators, known as Ministerial Liaison Officers (MLO), all communicators were civil servants who were appointed on the basis of communication qualifications, skills, and work experience. The MLOs have no direct reporting line to the heads of administrations in the departments and are not subject to public service rules and regulations. This points to a systemic weakness. The lack of a governance framework to regulate the role and relationship between the political communicators and the heads of communication in the system creates tension within the system. For instance, GCIS's mandate is to develop the national communications framework for national and provincial governments and to manage all communication functions in the organisation, including strategy design and implementation, marketing, and media liaison (GCIS, n.d.). This conundrum could be addressed by creating a dotted reporting line between the departmental head of communication and the MLO to improve coordination and alignment while allowing the MLO to fulfil their political communication responsibilities.

Government and the Media

In a democratic state, the media plays a 'watchdog' role of balancing the executive, legislative and judicial arms of the state by challenging the accuracy of information provided by the government, exposing misinformation and corruption, poor performance and criminality in the public and private sectors in the public interest (Goncalves & Santos, 2017). As previously stated, the relationship between the apartheid state and the media, in general, was frosty at best and non-existent at worst, due to the regime's secrecy laws, intolerance, and an anti-media posture. The alternative press in particular was overtly anti-apartheid (Wasserman, 2010), with many of its journalists and editors imprisoned (Radebe, 2021). The apartheid regime's media function was managed and led by the Department of Information whose mandate was to restrict, monitor and control the flow of information to the public. The SABC was the apartheid regime's mouthpiece and fitted the definition of a state broadcaster rather than a public broadcaster. Essentially, the SABC operated within narrow apartheid logic (Sparks, 2009).

Following the adoption of the new Constitution and the Bill of Rights, the relationship between the state and the media was designed to change as new legislation was promulgated in pursuit of the constitutional imperatives of access to information and a free press (Wasserman & De Beer, 2005). For instance, the post-apartheid Broadcasting Act 4 of 1999 states categorically that the SABC's objectives will include the promotion of democracy, the development of society, and nation-building. The Act also states that the SABC will be owned and controlled by the South African public and not the state. Section 6(2) of the Act provides that the SABC will exercise its powers, and enjoy freedom of expression, and journalistic, creative, and programming independence.

This represented a monumental shift from the apartheid era in which the SABC was a state broadcaster (Fourie, 2003). Further, the Independent Communications Authority of South Africa (ICASA) Act 13 of 2000 was promulgated to establish an independent body to regulate the broadcast media environment. ICASA published a code of conduct that requires all broadcasters to deliver news in a fair manner and without distortion and exaggeration (White, 2006). The jury is still out about whether this policy change was successfully implemented by the previous and current elected representatives and the boards, executives and media practitioners at both the SABC and ICASA.

In the light of the 1996 Constitution, the new laws and policies created a legitimate expectation that the relationship between the state and the media would change for the better. However, cracks emerged between government leaders and the media, suggesting that although the new democratic state was obliged to implement the new Constitution and the Bill of Rights, there were signs that the post-apartheid government was unhappy about the media's role. For instance, South Africa's first democratically elected president Nelson Mandela voiced concerns regarding the ownership and staffing composition of the South African media, predominantly by white males, which he believed contributed to a biased portrayal of the South African experience (Wasserman & De Beer, 2005).

Nevertheless, Valentine (2014), regards former president Nelson Mandela as having laid a firm legacy for media freedom. She cites Mandela's speech at the International Press gathering in 1994: "A critical, independent press is the lifeblood of any democracy. The press must be free from any state interference." Mandela is perceived as having stood firm on media freedom. However, he did have lapses in which he criticised black journalists whom he described as disloyal. This led to a meeting with the South African National Editors Forum (SANEF) in 1996, where Mandela was reported to have reassured the editors that media freedom would never be under threat in South Africa (Valentine, 2014).

Criticism of the media continued under President Mbeki's administration, with government and ANC leaders advocating for stronger regulation of the media (Radebe, 2023). Valentine (2014) submits that in his weekly online article, Mbeki became very critical of black journalists and even went to the extent of branding black journalists as 'Uncle Toms'. President Zuma's relationship with the media was even more acrimonious. For instance, between 2006 and 2010, he is reported to have sued the media and other critics for defamation in 15 cases (Milo, 2023). On 7 June 2023, Zuma lost his legal battle to prosecute a journalist for publishing his medical records ahead of his corruption trial (Hawker, 2023).

Although President Ramaphosa appears not to have taken a negative posture against media freedom, his perceived reluctance to interact directly with the media through media conferences is causing disquiet in the media fraternity. For instance, at the height of the COVID-19 pandemic, Ramaphosa opted for what became known as 'family meetings' at which he communicated with the public through prepared statements on radio and television without allowing journalists to ask difficult questions about the government response to the pandemic and its impact on the economy. Inevitably, these one-sided meetings received criticism (Wasserman & Madrid-Morales, 2022).

Responses to post-1994 government threats against media freedom

Media organisations, civil society bodies and the courts have pushed back on what was perceived as the democratic government's attempt to muzzle the media and limit public access to information. SANEF, together with other civil society organisations, mounted campaigns for media freedom, which included taking the government to court to demand access to information. In response to the call by the ruling ANC to set up a punitive Media Appeals Tribunal, SANEF and media owners set up an independent Press Freedom Commission, chaired by a retired judge, to propose a mechanism to address the concerns raised by the ruling party about media bias (Daniels, 2020). This Commission proposed the establishment of an independent Press Council to strengthen ethical standards for media reporting and to administer a hierarchy of penalties for breaches of ethical standards in the media. This demonstrates the contested nature of South Africa's media (Wasserman, 2020).

The GCIS played a pivotal role in building a bridge between the media and government leaders. This took the form of regular meetings between SANEF and members of the National Cabinet that were convened by the Minister in the Presidency responsible for government communications. Although these meetings served the purpose of managing the tension between the government and the media, the infrequency of these meetings only served to reduce tensions but never dealt with the underlying mistrust, namely: the government's challenge of the media's right to report on all aspects of governance including corruption and governance failures, and government's expectation that the media should under-report on government failures and over-report on government successes. However, there are indications that tensions between the media and the governing party predated the 1994 transition. (Jacobs, 2004).

Ethical Dilemmas

The socio-economic challenges, rising levels of corruption and the state's failure to address service delivery concerns are some of the many factors that are posing ethical dilemmas for government communicators. Ethical theory could play a key role in helping them to evaluate and navigate some of the dilemmas. Some argue that corruption within government departments stems from deficient ethical standards in leadership, consequently resulting in sub-par public service delivery (Mbandlwa, Dorasamy & Fagbadebo, 2020).

The major cause of the trust deficit is the perception that government leaders are driven by self or party interest and are not accountable to the public. For example, since 2008, it is reported that more than 2 million South Africans have taken to the streets in protest at the government's poor service delivery record (Plaut, 2012). Poor state performance and rising levels of corruption often breed discontent as the masses witness the rising living standards of the ruling elites at their expense (Fanon, 1963). The display of arrogance, corruption, and factionalism is evident in the perceived disregard for the poor in numerous municipalities (Ndletyana, 2020). At a macro-level, the primary dilemma facing the communication system relates to balancing personal, government, and societal interests in the performance of the function in an environment characterised by socio-economic and service delivery challenges, and increased corruption.

The GCIS describes its mission as to give the public access to information and create opportunities for the government to hold dialogues with stakeholders to discuss policy implementation and delivery of services. Furthermore, in times of crisis, such as the COVID-19 pandemic, effective government communication plays a crucial role in fostering institutional trust and credibility (Lerouge, Lema & Arnaboldi, 2023) and in convincing stakeholders that government is delivering on its electoral mandate. This opens the government communication service to the risk of being perceived merely as a system that engages in propaganda because of the disconnect between government's messages and citizens' lived experiences.

In such situations, virtue ethics come into play because communicators will have to consider their personal values such as honesty, integrity, consistency, and truthfulness to determine their actions. Essentially, this is about the person's character and the action that caused that character (Alzola, Hennig & Romar, 2020). Therefore, individual communicators may decide not to comply with the demand to engage in propaganda and take the courageous step of exiting the system at great risk to their personal interests, such as career and loss of financial incentives. Similarly, ethical elected leaders also have a choice to either remain or resign as members of an elected executive that is perceived to be corrupt, incapable of delivering services, or that provides misleading information to the public.

Elected leaders and government communicators are often confronted with the conflict between public, party, and personal interests – to be re-elected or retained in a position. For example, when former President Zuma was facing corruption allegations, political leaders from the ruling party and government communicators were torn between defending or criticising him because any decision would attract consequences from either political actors or the public. Many political leaders chose to keep quiet as threats of disciplinary action loomed overhead (Brett, 2020). A similar scenario arose when President Ramaphosa faced serious allegations of corruption and money laundering when large amounts of US dollars were stolen from his private residence (Mahlala, Juta, Chigova & Zweni, 2023). Expectedly, ANC members are often divided about whether to support or criticise their presidents under these circumstances, and government communicators are often caught in the middle of these conflicts.

The central question in both scenarios pertains to the prioritisation of personal and party interests ahead of public interests. Government communicators face similar dilemmas in their day-to-day work. For example, do they prioritise personal, government (employer) or public interest when confronted with instances of governance failure or corruption allegations against their ministries or departments? According to deontology theory, they could rely on codes if such rules exist, to help them make a choice about their communication role in such circumstances. A rule or code could state that 'thou shall not tell lies or mislead the public'. Alternatively, the communicator could rely on their own virtues of honesty and integrity, combine these with their knowledge of the truth, and decide not to be part of the government communication system.

Evaluating government communications from a moral theory perspective

Ethics theories

Understanding ethics is essential to developing an ethical framework to guide and evaluate the government communication system, and for government communicators, as agents of the system, to evaluate themselves. Ethical theories have evolved and have been adopted to inform different disciplines that require certain standards of behaviour and performance from members of their professions.

The word 'ethics' comes from the Greek word *ethos*, which means character and is used in moral philosophy to refer to the evaluation of the character and conduct of a person or persons using the standard of "right or wrong, good or bad, or acceptable or not" (Theroux, 2004). Ethics is described as a system in which ethical behaviour is a good virtue in cultivating responsibility to the self and to the society one exists within, and character may be explained as the qualities which an individual, organisation or society finds acceptable (Dieffenbach, 2020). Therefore, each stakeholder or agent of government communication who faces ethical dilemmas in the performance of their duties could use one or more of these theories to evaluate their conduct and the conduct of others. These theories could be used by stakeholders to evaluate the conduct of individuals in the system and or the performance and role of the system.

Elected representatives are often faced with a tension between their personal interests, such as career and material benefits on the one hand, and public interests on the other. During the COVID-19 pandemic, politicians across the world were caught out for undermining the very stringent regulations they were enforcing in their respective countries (Guttman & Lev, 2021). These violations included issues in their private lives, allegations of corruption, nepotism, and favouritism. Civil servants in government communication face the dilemma of choosing between giving priority to the interests of the government as their employer, the public interests and their values.

Ethical shortcomings become more pronounced when a government communicator is managing a communication crisis because they must make a choice between telling the truth and protecting the image of the government or telling half-truths (spin) to protect the elected leader, thereby putting the government's reputation at risk (Goncalves & Santos, 2017). This challenge primarily arises from the inherently political nature of government communication, which frequently confronts communicators with the dilemma of navigating between conveying factual information and potentially propagandistic messaging, as well as balancing the needs of the public with those of political parties (Brown, 2012).

For the purposes of this discussion, the view is taken that government communication under apartheid fell within the framework of political communication as the system was designed to defend and promote the state's apartheid ideology. Ethical theory contributes to society's evaluation of the conduct of both the government communication system and the agents. However, these theoretical tools are also available for use by the agents to evaluate themselves.

Different philosophies have emerged over time and the question that often arises is which theory applies to the field of study in question. In most cases, different theoretical approaches exist in the same field, which requires theorists and practitioners to choose the best theoretical tool to apply. According to Goncalves and Santos (2017), three ethical theories are applicable to the study of government communications:

1. utilitarianism;
2. deontology; and
3. virtue ethics.

The first theory, utilitarianism, provides that an action or conduct of an agent is deemed ethical if the overall consequence of the action provides the greatest possible good to most people. This is calculated by adding together the partial 'good' that makes up the whole society and minimises the negative consequences that may arise for the minority (Goncalves & Santos, 2017). In this instance, government communication's task is to justify the action or conduct based on benefits that accrue to the majority. This theory is criticised for its majoritarianism.

The second theory, deontology, places emphasis on ethical principles and morality to evaluate human action. In other words, no ethical shortcoming of an act can be justified or rationalised by a cost-benefit analysis, however great the aggregate good that arises from the action or inaction. This theory advocates for the institutionalisation of ethics through codes and rules that regulate and evaluate whether rules have been broken. Its downside is that there cannot be rules for every situation or circumstance and that agents always find ways around rules. Agents ask, "What is my duty, and which rule is applicable?" (Goncalves & Santos, 2017).

The third theory, virtue ethics, states that an agent's action is guided largely by character traits that drive them to act in a particular way, such as having the courage to take risks to perform a particular good, and acting rationally without following rules. The use of codes is not simply banned but should be more aspirational than prescriptive. This theory favours internalisation and application of ethical values by agents themselves, who apply them in every situation (Goncalves & Santos, 2017). For instance, an agent internalises truthfulness, honesty, and integrity in the exercise of their duties and does not need rules or codes to apply these values in their personal, organisational and societal capacities.

Goncalves and Santos (2017) adopt the view that although virtue ethics theory is more useful as a tool to evaluate the performance of the government communication system, deontological theory's adoption of ethical codes to guide government communications also has a place because professionalisation of the function may not be achievable without adopting codes to guide good practice. This is the context that presents ethical dilemmas for those who have the task of communicating on behalf of a state that seems incapable of executing its ideological and constitutional obligations to build a capable developmental state. The dilemmas are essentially about how a government communication system positions an incapable state. Government communication is a product of, and is shaped by, the character of the state of which it forms part.

Government communicators are also appointed in terms of the Public Service Act of 1994, Batho Pele Principles (Public Service and Administration, 1994), the Public Service Regulations of 2016, and the Code of Conduct for Public Servants (Public Service Regulations, 2016).

The premier legislation that directs the communicators' conduct is the Constitution of 1996, which requires that a high standard of professional ethics must be promoted and maintained in public service (Semono, 2020). Further, Chapter 2 of the Public Service Regulations (2016) provide an ethical framework that regulates the conduct of all public servants, including government communicators. These regulations include the promotion of unity and wellbeing of all citizens, not receiving bribes, serving with impartiality, and politeness, being accessible, providing a high standard of service, the right of access to information, and refraining from participating in political activities in the workplace. These principles and values are designed to achieve efficiency and effectiveness and can be used to evaluate the conduct and performance of public servants.

Other than the GCIS broad frameworks, there is no code of conduct that guides communicators when faced with ethical challenges. In the examples previously stated, communicators could either follow the party line and defend the presidents or choose to be guided by their virtues. However, one of the Batho Pele Principles that states: "Citizens should be given full and accurate information about the services they are entitled to receive" comes close to providing a tool that communicators could use to evaluate their conduct. When confronted with a specific or broader ethical challenge such as providing misleading information, defending wrongful and unethical behaviour of elected and appointed government officials, or using communication tools and platforms to justify poor performance by the government, a communicator could use this Batho Pele principle to refuse to comply and face the consequences, which could include dismissal. Similarly, the communicator could choose to exit the system on account of being unwilling to defend a government whose values and performance record are contrary to his or her own.

Discussion

Indeed, government communication is a tool at the disposal of government and the character of the state it serves defines its character (Sanders & Canel, 2013). In other words, the public communication system is designed to serve the government of the day. This could lead to a dilemma for communicators who experience a conflict between their values and the values of the government they serve. Examples of this conflict include instances where a government communicator embraces liberal and democratic values while working for an autocratic apartheid state and an ethical communicator who is employed by a corrupt and incompetent state. In these instances, a communicator who is confronted by this dilemma has a choice whether to align their conduct with the interests of the state as their employer or put their ethical interests first and exit the system. For example, should a progressive-minded communicator continue to work for a racist company at which they are expected to promote and defend the racist or homophobic policy of their employer?

In a government context, ethical shortcomings often become more pronounced when government communication is managing a communication crisis because the agents in the system may have to choose between telling the truth and protecting the image of the government or telling half-truths (spin) to protect the leader, thereby putting the government's reputation at risk (Goncalves & Santos, 2017). In these circumstances, the South African government communication system and its agents have tended to either err on the side of caution or align their conduct with the policies of the government of the day. Although understandable from a career and personal interest point of view, this approach carries reputational risks for the individual concerned. In most cases, government communicators opt out and become unavailable for comment for fear of being seen to be defending what they consider indefensible policies of the employer or the conduct of political principals. This is largely due to a lack of theoretical tools that could enable them to navigate difficult situations. The opting-out option creates another problem for elected leaders as communicators are then evaluated as inefficient, incompetent, or not communicating sufficiently because they expect communicators to defend the government at all costs.

The fundamental question is what these 'agents' should do under these circumstances. In terms of virtue ethical theory, communicators must internalise virtue ethics and if they conclude that simply complying and defending the indefensible would be contrary to the ethical beliefs they have internalised, the option might be to choose to exit the system (Goncalves & Santos, 2017; Alzola, Hennig & Romar, 2020). This requires courage on the part of the professional communicator. Similarly, those government communicators who worked in SACS, the apartheid government communication agency, would have had to make a judgment call on whether to stay or exit the government system if they considered the apartheid system as racist and unjust.

Sometimes it is not good enough to say, "I'm just doing my job". The suggested route for communicators is to follow their personal character traits and beliefs, such as honesty, without needing a rulebook. In other words, take what they believe is the right course of action with a full understanding that this carries risks and could be career-limiting when dealing with unlawful and unethical directives from an elected leader or superior. Government communication is a pivotal part of governance as it promotes transparency and accountability, and strengthens democracy by providing avenues for citizens to become actively involved in the policy implementation processes and to hold the government accountable (Canel & Luoma-aho, 2018).

In these instances, two possible scenarios exist for consideration by professional and ethical communicators who face these dilemmas. Firstly, a communicator could remain in their post and continue to tell half-truths, provide misleading information to the public, defend corrupt practices, and could justify their conduct by arguing that they were just doing their job, and didn't break any code or rule. In other words, they would have chosen to suppress their virtues in the hope that they would be rewarded and evaluated sympathetically because of loyalty to the government of the day. Secondly, they could choose to exit the system on account of irreconcilable conflict between their personal ethical standards and rules, on the one hand, and the values and practices of the government they serve, on the other. Although this may be the most ethical or 'right thing to do', this may have negative consequences for the individual, which may include loss of income.

Conclusion

Government communicators will need to empower themselves with theoretical tools that enable them to evaluate their role as they navigate the complex and sometimes toxic political context. Virtue ethics theory is the most viable framework for navigating through the ethical dilemmas that communicators and elected leaders face in the performance of their duties. This theory suggests that, as they confront ethical dilemmas in the performance of their duties, these agents of the communication system need to internalise character traits such as: honesty, courage, coherence, trust, skills, and rational action. Furthermore, deontological codes may be useful as an attempt to professionalise the service and to provide a guide, so long as they are seen as aspirational and not judicial because codes cannot anticipate every ethical challenge that communicators may face.

In conclusion, ethical codes and prescriptions holding to account communication agents who break the 'codes' will not lead to the disappearance of ethical dilemmas from government communication systems primarily because the system itself is political, located as it is at the interface between government and the citizens. Like most public service departments that are at the coal face of service delivery, elected representatives will always struggle to resist the temptation to use the government communication function to advance their narrow party-political interests. Therefore, those who choose to join the government communication service will always be exposed to these ethical dilemmas as they will be subject to – and expected to organise and manage – the government communication system so as to support the political class's electoral mandate and political objectives. Most importantly, they could be required or be expected to defend conduct, practices or policies that may conflict with their personal virtues and traits.

Government communicators must be alert and understand that all communication conduct is infused with ethical dimensions and that deliberately lying is more potently unethical and could cause serious reputational damage. Equally, telling half-truths in an attempt to win acceptance from an elected leader or a section of the public is itself unethical. Deliberately lying may attract immediate consequences such as dismissal or snubbing by journalists or communities, whereas merely glossing over aspects of truth to protect an elected principal or to hide government failures may not necessarily attract immediate consequences as this approach may be less easy to detect. Both are decidedly unethical and should be always avoided (Japp, Meister & Japp, 2005).

References

African National Congress (ANC). (2007). *Adopted strategy and tactics of the ANC. Polokwane: 52nd National Conference.* Africa National Congress. 20 December. [Retrieved 12 August 2023] https://www.anc1912.org.za/adopted-strategy-and-tactics-of-the-anc/

Alzola M, Hennig A & Romar E. (2020). Thematic symposium editorial: Virtue ethics between east and west. *Journal of Business Ethics,* 165:177–189. https://doi.org/10.1007/s10551-019-04317-2

Berger G. (2000). Publishing for the people: The alternative press 1980–1999. In: N Evans & M Seeber (Eds). *The Politics of Publishing in South Africa.* London: Holger Ehling Publishing; Scottsville: University of Natal Press. 73–106.

Brett P. (2020). Politics by other means in South Africa today. *Journal of Law and Society,* 47(S1):S126–S144. https://doi.org/10.1111/jols.12248

Brown DCG. (2012). The administrative dilemmas of government communications. *Canadian Political Science Association Annual Conference.* Edmonton, Canada: University of Alberta. Presentation, 13 June.

Canel MJ & Luoma-aho V. (2018). Public Sector Communication: Closing Gaps Between Citizens and Public Organizations. USA: John Wiley & Sons. https://doi.org/10.1002/9781119135630

ComTask. (1996). Communications 2000: a vision for government communication in South Africa: final report of the Task Group on Communications to Deputy President Thabo Mbeki. Retrieved April 20, 2024 https://www.gcis.gov.za/content/resource-centre/reports/comtask

Daniels G. (2020). Power and Loss in South African Journalism: News in the Age of Social Media. Johannesburg, South Africa: Wits University Press. https://doi.org/10.18772/12020075997

Dieffenbach DM. (2020). Professional Codes of Ethics and How They Apply to Mediated Communication. Com 530: Law & Ethics: A Line in the Sand. New Hampshire, USA: Southern New Hampshire University.

Edigheji O. (2005). *A democratic developmental state in Africa: A concept paper*. Centre for Policy Studies Research Report 105. Johannesburg.

Fanon, F. (1963). *The Wretched of the Earth*. New York: Grove Press.

Fourie PJ. (2002). Rethinking the role of the media in South Africa. *Communicare: Journal for Communication Sciences in Southern Africa*, 21(1):17–40. https://doi.org/10.36615/jcsa.v21i1.1826

Fourie PJ. (2003). The future of public service broadcasting in South Africa: The need to return to basic principles – Policy. *Communicatio: South African Journal of Communication Theory and Research*, 29(1-2):148–181. https://doi.org/10.1080/02500160308538025

Glenn I & Mattes R. (2012). Political communication in post-apartheid South Africa. In: HA Semetko & M Scammel (Eds). *The SAGE Handbook of Political Communication*. Los Angeles, London, New Delhi, Singapore, Washington DC: Sage Publications. 494–508. https://doi.org/10.4135/9781446201015.n40

Goncalves G & Santos JM. (2017). What ethics for governmental communication? Ethics issues on government public relations. *Revista International De Relaciones Públicas*, 4(7):165–182. https://doi.org/10.5783/revrrpp.v7i14.493

Gumede V. (2015). *Political Economy of Post-Apartheid South Africa*. Dakar, Senegal: Council for the Development of Social Science Research in Africa (CODESRIA). https://doi.org/10.2307/j.ctvh8r1rm

Guttman N & Lev E. (2021). Ethical issues in COVID-19 communication to mitigate the pandemic: Dilemmas and practical implications. *Health Communication*, 36(1):116–123. https://doi.org/10.1080/10410236.2020.1847439

Hansson K, Belkacem K & Ekenberg L. (2015). Open government and democracy: A research review. *Social Science Computer Review*, 33(5):540–555. https://doi.org/10.1177/0894439314560847

Hawker D. (2023). *SLAPP down — Jacob Zuma fails in attempted private prosecution of Billy Downer and Karyn Maughan*. Daily Maverick. 7 June. https://www.dailymaverick.co.za/article/2023-06-07-slapp-down-jacob-zuma-fails-in-attempted-private-prosecution-of-billy-downer-and-karyn-maughan/

Horwitz RB. (2001). *Communication and Democratic Reform in South Africa*. Cambridge, UK: Cambridge University Press. https://doi.org/10.1017/CBO9780511510151

Jacobs SH. (2004). Public Sphere, Power and Democratic Politics: Media and Policy Debates in Post-Apartheid South Africa. PhD dissertation. Birkbeck: University of London.

Japp PM, Meister M & Japp DK. (Eds). (2005). *Communication Ethics, Media & Popular Culture*. New York: Peter Lang Publishing.

Lerouge R, Lema MD & Arnaboldi M. (2023). The role played by government communication on the level of public fear in social media: An investigation into the Covid-19 crisis in Italy. *Government Information Quarterly*, 40(2):101798. https://doi.org/10.1016/j.giq.2022.101798

Mahlala S, Juta L, Chigova L & Zweni A. (2023). Conduits of political corruption and patronage in South African government. *International Journal of Social Science Research and Review*, 6(11):16–25.

Mbandlwa Z, Dorasamy N & Fagbadebo, O. (2020). Ethical leadership and the challenge of service delivery in South Africa: A discourse. *TEST Engineering & Management*, 83:24986–24998.

Milo D. (2023). *The role of the judiciary, the media and parliament in slapping back*. Inaugural lecture hosted by Freedom Under Law and University of Stellenbosch Department of Journalism. [Retrieved 14 February 2024]. https://www.freedomunderlaw.org/wp-content/uploads/2023/08/SLAPP-Speech-2023-Stellenbosch-27-July-004.pdf

Ndletyana M. (2020). Anatomy of the ANC in Power: Insights from Port Elizabeth, 1990–2019. Cape Town: HSRC Press. https://doi.org/10.1515/9780796926111

Pillay D. (2011). The tripartite alliance and its discontents: Contesting the 'National Democratic Revolution' in the Zuma era. In: J Daniel, P Naidoo, D Pillay & R Southall (Eds). *New South African Review 2: New Paths old Compromises?* Johannesburg: Wits University Press. 31–49. https://doi.org/10.18772/22011105416.6

Plaut, M. (2012). Behind the Marikana massacre. *The New Statesmen*, 20 August 2012.

Posel D. (1999). Whiteness and power in the South African civil service: Paradoxes of the apartheid state. *Journal of Southern African Studies*, 25(1):99–119. https://doi.org/10.1080/030570799108777

Radebe MJ. (2021). South Africa's post-apartheid media and democracy. In: M Williams & V Satgar (Eds). *Destroying Democracy: Neoliberal Capitalism and the Rise of Authoritarian Politics*. Johannesburg: Wits University Press. 163–178.

Radebe M. (2022). New features of media imperialism: The South African online media and the coverage of the Ukrainian war. *Communicare: Journal for Communication Sciences in Southern Africa*, 41(2):75–89. https://doi.org/10.36615/jcsa.v41i2.1407

Radebe, MJ. (2023). Constructing Hegemony: The South African Commercial Media and the (Mis) Representation of Nationalisation. Taylor & Francis. https://doi.org/10.4324/9781032632186

Republic of South Africa. Department of Public Service and Administration (DPSA). (1994). Batho Pele Principles.

Republic of South Africa. Government Communication and Information System (GCIS). (1998.) Annual report [Retrieved 20 April 2024] https://www.gcis.gov.za/content/resourcecentre/reports/annual-reports/1998.

Republic of South Africa. Government Communication and Information System (GCIS). (n.d.). *Government communicators' handbook 2014–2017.* https://www.gcis.gov.za/government-communicators-handbook-2014-2017

Republic of South Africa (2016). Public Service Regulations. Pretoria: Government Printer

Ruijer HJM. (2017). Proactive transparency in the United States and the Netherlands: The role of government communication officials. *The American Review of Public Administration*, 47(3):354–375. https://doi.org/10.1177/0275074016628176

Sanders K & Canel MJ (Eds). (2013). *Government Communication: Cases and Challenges*. New York and London: Bloomsbury Publishing.

Semono CA. (2020). The Impact of Organisational Culture on Integrated Communication: The Case of the Government Communication and Information System (GCIS) in Polokwane. PhD dissertation. Polokwane: University of Limpopo.

Sparks C. (2009). South African media in transition. *Journal of African Media Studies*, 1(2):195–220. https://doi.org/10.1386/jams.1.2.195_1

Theroux JP. (2004). *Ethics: Theory and Practice*. 8th Edition. New Jersey, USA: Pearson/Prentice Hall.

Valentine S. (2014). *Mandela's legacy of media freedom stands its ground*. https://cjp.org/2014/02/attacks-on-the-press-south-africa/

Wasserman H. (2010). *Tabloid Journalism in South Africa: True story!* Bloomington, Indiana: Indiana University Press.

Wasserman H. (2020). The state of South African media: A space to contest democracy. *Publizistik*, 65(3):451–465. https://doi.org/10.1007/s11616-020-00594-4

Wasserman H & De Beer AS. (2005). A fragile affair: The relationship between the mainstream media and government in post-apartheid South Africa. *Journal of Mass Media Ethics*, 20(2-3): 192–208. https://doi.org/10.1080/08900523.2005.9679708

Wasserman H & Madrid-Morales D. (2022). The messenger, the message, and the receiver: South African government communication during the COVID-19 pandemic. In: PJ Maarek (Ed). *Manufacturing Government Communication on Covid-19: A Comparative Perspective.* Cham, Switzerland: Springer Nature. 319–333. https://doi.org/10.1007/978-3-031-09230-5_16

White J. (2006). Independent Communications Authority of South Africa (ICASA). In: S Woolman, R Roux, J Klaaren, P Stein, A Chaskalson & M Bishop (Eds). *Constitutional Law of South Africa.* 2nd Edition. Cape Town: Juta Law. 24E1–24E16.

Chapter 2

Facebook Communication by South Africa's Eight Metros

Lakela Kaunda  *and Ricky Mukonza*

The dawn of social media has changed the way people work, live and play, given the proliferation of digital communication tools at their fingertips. It has also added new platforms to the instruments that government and the public can use to communicate. Using the development communication approach as a theoretical framework, this chapter explores how the eight South African metropolitan municipalities use social media – particularly the Facebook platform – to engage in two-way communication with the public. Local government was selected for study as it is regarded as the sphere that is closest to the people (Mkhize, 2018). The delivery of basic services such as as electricity, access to potable water, proper sanitation and waste removal, street lighting, cutting the grass on the verges of the roads, repairing potholes and ensuring correct billing systems for both households and businesses, are delivered by municipalities (Madumo, 2015; Mkhize, 2018).

The post-1994 democratic policy and legislative framework of the country created a developmental local government system which emphasises the involvement and participation of the people in the work of municipalities, as articulated in the White Paper on Local Government (DPACD, 1998) and in Chapter 7 of the Constitution. In section 152(1), local government is given the task of amongst others, encouraging the involvement of communities and community organisations in the matters of local government. Legislation, such as the Local Government Municipal Systems Act 7 of 2000 (SA, 2000), also directs municipalities to encourage the involvement of communities and community organisations in local governance. The legislative framework has thus institutionalised public participation in local government and the need for government to communicate with communities it services. Municipalities are required to publish the annual budget and the Integrated Development Plan (IDP) and invite members of the public to comment on them (Brand, 2016; Breakfast, Mekoa & Maphazi, 2015). The IDP of a municipality should outline what the council will do to promote socio-economic development and build a safe and healthy environment, and the information should be provided to citizens as a basic step in promoting accountability (Brand, 2016).

This study found that besides the statutory consultation mechanisms, members of the public seek to engage with municipalities on an ongoing basis on issues relating to electricity, water, refuse removal and other basic services. Such engagement is catered for in the Government Communication Policy – adopted by the South African Cabinet in November 2018 – which is anchored on the development communication framework (GCIS, 2018) (see Maseko in this volume).

Government defines development communication as the use of communication to facilitate social and economic change, with the principle of involving the people in activities that affect their lives, through ongoing engagement with government (GCIS, 2018). The policy enjoins government to disseminate information that will assist people to improve their livelihoods. It also underscores the need for government to listen to the people and respond to their inquiries (GCIS, 2018). The common denominator between developmental local government and government's development communication paradigm is the participation of members of the public in governance and the need for ongoing communication with the citizens.

The 'development communication' paradigm is attributed to Filipino Professor Nora C. Quebral, who is known as the mother of development communication, having first used the concept in 1971 according to Concepcion (2020). The scholar linked communication with development and the improvement of the quality of life, and defined the field as, "the art and science of human communication applied to the speedy transformation of a country and the mass of its people from poverty to a dynamic state of economic growth that makes possible greater social equality and the larger fulfilment of the human potential" (Quebral, 2011: 4).

Quebral (2011) also describes, as a major shift, the marriage of the technology of information and of communication which, in her view, revolutionised how information is exchanged, even in developing societies. In South Africa, government has introduced electronic government or e-government, which is the use of information and communication technologies (ICT) to provide services to the public, according to the Department of Telecommunications and Postal Services (DTPS, 2017). ICT-enabled communication platforms such as social media, portals and websites have been developed to share information with the public (Palvia & Sharma, 2019; DTPS, 2017).

Using the qualitative research method, data was collected from the official Facebook pages of the eight South African metropolitan municipalities – commonly known as metros – and the content was thematically analysed. It has been established that all the metros have official Facebook accounts and post information daily on their official Facebook pages. Information disseminated on the pages relates to the provision of basic services such as water, electricity and refuse removal, including interruptions in the provision of services. The municipalities also distribute information about forthcoming events such as official openings and infrastructure projects, activities of the mayors and members of mayoral committees or other leaders, economic activities such as business exhibitions, health issues such as COVID-19 and notices on bylaws.

The study has found that the information route is unidirectional. Municipalities provided the information but did not engage or discuss the content with users in the majority of cases during the period of the study, November

2021. Members of the public responded to the information with questions and comments, especially in relation to the delivery of basic services or lack thereof, but these were ignored. The interactive capability of the Facebook platform was not taken advantage of to engage the users and respond to their inquiries, in line with the spirit of the development communication paradigm and the public participation ethos of developmental local government.

Background: Social media changing the way people communicate

The term social media generally refers to the computer-based and internet-based technology that is used to share ideas, thoughts and information using virtual networks (Dollarhide, 2021). A common feature of social media is its interactive capability. People communicate and share information 24 hours a day in an interactive manner, and anyone can create content for social media and share it as and when they want to do so (Jordaan, 2019). Social media platforms include social networking sites such as Facebook, Twitter, WhatsApp, Telegram, Signal and Instagram or content production sites such as video platforms TikTok and YouTube (Jordaan, 2019; Apuke, 2017).

Facebook allows users to create their own profiles on which they can upload pictures and videos, as well as share messages. Twitter enables users to tweet short messages on their walls, which attracts comments from other users, while WhatsApp is a mobile social network that allows the sharing of information, pictures, videos, voice notes and other vital messages (Apuke, 2017). Facebook was established by global entrepreneur Mark Zuckerberg in 2004 as a platform for Harvard University students to connect with other students (McFadden, 2020). The site became immediately popular and within 24 hours of the launch, around 1 200 students had signed up. Facebook had more than 4.7 billion monthly active users globally in 2021, according to McFadden (2020).

The Facebook social media platform was selected for the study due to the large numbers of users in the country, its interactive capability, as well as the wide reach within the metropolitan municipalities that formed the sample of the study. Two studies have indicated high figures for the usage of the platform in South Africa. The DataReportal annual digital report for 2022 put Facebook users at 24 million, quoting advertising data obtained from the Facebook owners, Meta (Kemp, 2022).

The 2022 Social Media Landscape report for South Africa described Facebook as the most popular platform with an estimated 22 million local users (Goldstuck & Turner, 2022). Major metropolitan municipalities such as Johannesburg, Tshwane, eThekwini and Cape Town were found to have the highest level of numbers of people using Facebook according to the report. The breakdown of usage among provinces with metropolitan municipalities indicated the highest usage in Gauteng at 37.6%, followed by: KwaZulu-Natal (11.9%), Eastern Cape (9.58%), Free State (6.38%) and the Western Cape (8.18%) (Goldstuck & Turner, 2022). The Facebook reach therefore makes it an appropriate platform to gauge the way municipalities utilise social media platforms for interactive communication with the public.

Jakoet-Salie (2020) moots that the use of internet technology may greatly enhance citizen participation and improve government to citizen relations, given the access to public information and interaction that it provides. The public sector, as stated in the Government Communication Policy (GCIS, 2018), embraces social media and states that it provides an opportunity for interactive communication between government and citizens, partners and stakeholders. The Government Communication Policy (GCIS, 2018) also states that social media has increased the frequency and speed of engagement. Social media has also provided an important platform for municipalities to communicate with, or keep track of the views of, the public on service delivery issues and governance, in addition to institutional mechanisms such as ward committees (Kaunda, 2021)

Communicating for change and development using ICT-enabled platforms

The essence of the development communication paradigm is that change must occur in the lives of those who are recipients or beneficiaries of government's communication efforts. Quebral (2011) described development communication as centred on change, and on the poor and the marginalised in a developing society who were to be supported in a move towards a better life. The theme is taken further by Odoom (2020), who introduces a link between communication, empowerment and participation. Odoom (2020) contends that development communication is used to promote participation in development activities and to provide people with the information and knowledge they need to improve their lives. Meanwhile, Ihsaniyati, Sarwoprasodjo, Muljono & Gandasari (2023) indicate that development communication and social development are not only limited to providing access to, or dissemination of, information, but also as a process that enables dialogue and public participation.

Pypers and Bassuday (2016) posit that municipalities invite citizens to actively participate in governance as voters, citizens, consumers and organised partners. The purpose is to ensure accountability on the part of the elected political leadership for the policies they wish to introduce Pypers and Bassuday (2016). The authors also differentiate between 'invited' spaces and 'invented' spaces of public participation (Pypers & Bassuday, 2016). Community protests are regarded as invented spaces, a form of public participation used by aggrieved citizens, while the 'invited' spaces are the formal mechanisms that are used to provide inputs into the work of municipalities such as the ward committees and public meetings or sending written submissions to council.

The growth of ICT platforms has enabled the development of e-participation or electronic participation of citizens in governance. E-participation is regarded as a subset of both public participation and e-government (Palvia & Sharma, 2007). E-participation is defined as encompassing all forms of political participation which is carried out using digital media according to Lindner and Aichholzer (2020). E-participation in this study is used to mean the participation of citizens via the Facebook platform to provide their views about the information the municipalities post, as well as other issues that are of concern to them.

The South African Government produced an E-Government Strategy and Roadmap in 2017, which defines e-government as referring broadly to the innovative use of ICTs to link citizens and the public sector with the interest of improving governance and promoting collaboration and efficiency according to the erstwhile Department of Telecommunication and Postal Services (DTPS, 2017). Jakoet-Salie (2020) posits that e-government enables participatory democracy in the sense that it makes it possible for citizens to directly communicate with and debate with government about issues that affect them. The citizens can provide feedback to government about the services that are provided, posits the author (Jakoet-Salie (2020). According to the E-Government Strategy and Roadmap, e-government operations may take three forms: Government-to-Government (G2G), Government-to-Business (G2B) and Government-to-Citizens (G2C). The G2C services are described as including applications that enable citizens to interact with government departments and institutions and pose questions. It also refers to services such as filing income tax returns or renewing driver's licences which are enhanced by the use of ICT applications (Pavlia & Sharma, 2019; DTPS, 2017). Government has also established a web portal called the *Batho Pele Gateway* from which the public can source government legislation and policy documents (Jakoet-Salie, 2020). The official government social media platforms form part of the G2C services.

Social media has become popular as an easily available tool during crises in the country (Allen, 2021). The South African government, especially the Department of Health (DoH), used social media extensively to communicate about the COVID-19 pandemic in its early stages, in addition to using traditional media forms. Government research indicated that 90% of South Africans know what protocols to follow to avoid being infected by the virus, which was taken to mean the communication strategy had been a success, according to then GCIS director-general Phumla Williams (Williams, 2020). The social media platforms were also used widely during protests in South Africa, for example, the civil unrest that accompanied the arrest of former President Jacob Zuma in July 2021 (Allen, 2021), as well as the #FeesMustFall protests by higher education students in 2016 (Ntuli & Teferra, 2018). Ntuli and Teferra observe that the 2016 student protest wave was characterised by the successful use of social media to mobilise participation in the protests across the country.

Parkyn (2017) also cites the characteristic of social media as an organising tool, and refers to the Arab Spring, where social media was used to mobilise against governments in North Africa. However, the author (Parkyn, 2017) also argues that social media may be less effective in representing the interests of ordinary people on a sustained basis. Other scholars have noted that while social media is useful for quick communication during a crisis and as a participation tool, there are risks of misinformation and disinformation and spreading harmful messages (McNeill & Briggs, 2014). The fake news or false information that was distributed via social media in South Africa during the COVID-19 pandemic included a conspiracy theory that fifth generation (5G) ICT played a role in the conception of, or the spread of, the pandemic (Malinga, 2020).

The value of ICT and e-government services is also hampered by the digital divide, given that there are still many citizens who lack access to digital technologies. Mlaba (2021) breaks down South Africa's digital divide into three factors: access to hardware, understanding the digital tools and affordability. The author (Mlaba, 2021) contends that these factors have had a negative impact on access to education and employment opportunities.

Ihsaniyati et al. (2023) define the digital divide as the rural-urban gap, as well as a divide caused by demographics such as age, education, gender and income. However, statistics indicate a growth in access to the internet, despite the concerning digital divide. DataReportal's Digital 2021: South Africa report pointed out that there were 38 million internet users in South Africa in 2021, with the internet penetration rate standing at 64% in January 2021 (Kemp, 2021). Meanwhile, The SA Social Media Landscape Report 2022 indicated the growth of social media users from 25 million in 2020 to almost 30 million in 2021 (Malinga, 2022). The platforms LinkedIn, Twitter and TikTok showed the fastest growth, while Facebook continued to be South Africa's most popular social network (Malinga, 2022). The report also indicated that most people with internet access use smartphones to connect.

Digital 2021 reported that there were more than 100 million cellular phone connections in the country in 2020 (Kemp, 2021). The information about the extensive use of cellular phones in South Africa is corroborated by the 2020 General Household Survey released by Statistics South Africa (StatsSA) (StatsSA, 2020), which reported that 89.4% of South African households exclusively use cellular phones. Using mobile phones to access the internet made it more accessible to residents in rural areas, according to Stats SA (2020). The General Household Survey also stated that 74.1% of South African households had at least one member who had access to or used the internet. They accessed the internet at locations such as their homes, work, place of study, internet cafés or public hotspots according to Stats SA (2020). The use of mobile internet access devices in rural areas was at 52.9% while the same use in urban areas was 71.6% and 66.8% in metropolitan areas (Stats SA, 2020).

The Minister of Communications and Digital Technologies Khumbudzo Ntshaveni outlined government's plans to ensure that 80% of South Africans have access to the internet through smart devices as part of bridging the digital gap (Ntshavheni, 2022). This would be achieved through Phase 2 of the South Africa/SA Connect programme, which sought to connect 44 000 government institutions and over 33 000 community Wi-Fi hotspots through a partnership of government and the private sector. Ntshavheni (2022) also stated that government sought to automate government frontline services and take at least 50% of government services online. The Minister conceded that the plan would require that the poor and those in rural areas obtain basic digital skills to access government.

Research has however indicated that ensuring the availability of ICTs and communication applications does not necessarily lead to uptake by citizens. Muridzi (2019) examined the usage of ICTs by citizens in municipalities and found that while metropolitan municipalities had provided access to e-government services, the response from citizens had been slow. In the same vein, Okeke-Uzodike and Dlamini (2019) examined e-participation in municipalities in KwaZulu-Natal, Western Cape and Gauteng. The study found that Gauteng and KwaZulu-Natal had low levels of public participation using e-participation platforms and that municipalities were still using traditional forms of citizen participation. On the other hand, findings in the Western Cape province showed several e-participation projects being implemented. The authors recommended that effective implementation of an e-participatory platform would reduce protests and contribute to easing the divide in society.

Two studies revealed a muted response by government to inquiries by the public on official platforms. Mawela (2016) assessed how provincial government departments and municipalities use social media applications for electronic participation. The study established that citizens demonstrated increasing access and interest in social media and were ready to use the electronic platforms to interact with government departments. However, the departments responded sporadically to the responses of the public. Fashoro and Barnard (2021) undertook a qualitative study exploring social media platforms that are used by South African provincial departments and municipalities and how these platforms are used for public participation activities. The study found that all provinces and municipalities have social media accounts. However, the platforms are used mainly to disseminate information or as an extension of the government websites where information is posted. The two studies bear resemblance to the focus of this chapter, the difference being that they focus on social media in general in various provincial government departments and in local government, while this paper specifically targets metros and the Facebook platform.

The state of local government

Local government has been selected for the study given its importance in the government system as the sphere that is closest to residents (Mkhize, 2018; Kaunda, 2023). It has also been chosen due to the serious challenges facing many municipalities. In the 2022 Municipal Audit Report, the Auditor-General of South Africa (AGSA, 2022) highlighted shortcomings facing municipalities as being accountability and service delivery failures, poor governance, weak institutional capacity and instability.

The Auditor-General reported that by June 2021, 23 municipalities were under administration or provincial intervention, which further increased to 33 municipalities by February 2022 (AGSA, 2022). In the 2018 Cooperative Governance and Traditional Affairs (COGTA) Budget Vote speech, the then COGTA Minister Dr Zwelini Mkhize announced that only 7% of the country's municipalities were classified as well-functioning, while others ranged from reasonably functional to dysfunctional or distressed (Mkhize, 2018). In the 2022 report, the Auditor-General also reported a slight improvement as 27 municipalities were able to maintain their clean audit status throughout the term of the previous administration, while 14 achieved their first clean audit (AGSA, 2022).

The weaknesses in governance and financial administration coupled with poor communication with the public has been cited in official reports and studies by scholars as being responsible for service delivery protests. The 15 Years Review of Local Government report, produced by the South African Local Government Association (SALGA, 2015) cited poor public participation and poor communication with the public as one of the main causes of community protests around the country. Other research studies have found a link between the dysfunctionality of municipalities and community protests. Reddy (2016) investigated service delivery protests in South African townships and highlighted service delivery failures that anger the public such as non-functioning traffic lights, uncut grass on the verges of the roads, broken or leaking water pipes, potholes on the roads and unanswered telephones. Reddy (2016) also cited the politicisation of local government and interference by politicians in administrative matters as a serious problem that led to dysfunctionality and distress.

The view on the causes of protests is shared by Morudu (2017), who explored the link between the increase in service delivery protests and the level of services delivered by local municipalities in 234 municipalities. The study recommended that to minimise the number of protests, local municipalities should increase the provision of basic services. Botes (2018), who concurs with Morudu (2017), investigated why service delivery protests continued despite an increase in the delivery of services by government. The study found that people needed to see a tangible improvement where they live for the protests to end. The author also emphasised the need for participatory democracy to be widened and consolidated in order to stop the protests.

Methodology

Research techniques and operationalisation of the study

Facebook was selected for the study given its standing as the most popular and most widely used social media platform (Malinga, 2020). The metros were selected through purposive sampling. Bertram and Christiansen (2020) point out that a purposive sample is chosen for a particular purpose which could be either because it is representative of the population or encapsulates a number of issues which exist in the population.

The metros were specifically chosen given reports that social media penetration is higher in urban areas (Malinga, 2020).

The Auditor-General of South Africa (AGSA, 2022) describes described as large urban complexes with populations of more than one million people. The metros account for the largest portion of municipal expenditure, serve the highest number of households and were responsible for a budget of R247.48 billion in 2020/21 according to the AGSA (2022). Data was collected in November 2021. This was the period of the South Africa local government elections, which took place on 1 November 2021. This period also overlapped with the period of the COVID-19 pandemic which incidentally made social media and other digital tools more important for communication as in-person public meetings were restricted (NICD, 2020).

Information sought from the metropolitan municipalities' Facebook pages included the number of followers of the official page, the information distributed by the municipality on the page, the responses and comments of members of the public or followers, and the nature of engagement on the page, for example, whether the information flow is two-way or unidirectional. The Facebook pages of the municipalities were scrutinised daily, monitoring the posts and engagement between the municipalities and the users and, where there was none, observing the lack thereof. A thematic analysis of the data was undertaken. Willis (2013: 323) describes thematic analysis, which explores the presence of themes, both pre-determined and themes observed within the data, as the most used form of analysis in qualitative research. The themes and findings are discussed in the next section.

Discussion

Dominance of service delivery issues

It was established that all metros selected for the study have an official presence on the Facebook platform, with information being posted daily during the period under review – November

2021 – except for Mangaung Metropolitan Municipality, which had sporadic posts (Facebook, 2021; Kaunda 2021). The common topics gleaned from the data collected are service delivery interruptions and maintenance, infrastructure development, announcements of public events, consultations on policy or bylaws or surveys, and the introduction of new municipal political leadership following the 2021 local government elections. The overriding theme in the responses by the social media users is service delivery and access to basic services such as water, electricity and refuse removal.

Users wrote about water problems, electricity outages or refuse removal interruptions even in municipal posts that had nothing to do with service delivery. For example, municipal posts on COVID-19 attracted questions about an electricity outage in an area. The metros featured a considerable amount of information on COVID-19 on their Facebook pages, including alerts about rising case numbers, vaccination sites, COVID-19 prevention methods and information on trends. The responses from users tended to be negative or cynical about COVID-19 and also diverted to service delivery issues instead. For example, on 29 November 2021, eThekwini Municipality posted information on the new COVID-19 adjusted levels following an address by President Cyril Ramaphosa (Facebook, 2021). The responses from users were primarily about water and electricity outages. "We do not have water in the Sawpit area, it's been a whole week now. *Aniscabangeli nina* (You don't care about us)." The municipality responded with contact details of where the fault could be reported.

The Ekurhuleni metro posted COVID-19 prevention methods and the president's speech on the COVID-19 lockdown (Facebook, 2021). The responses from users also focused primarily on water and electricity. For example, "We have power outage here at Clayville ext 71 since yesterday around 13:00, are you aware of it?" and: "Food is getting rotten". Responses to notices about forthcoming public events also veered towards complaints about service delivery issues. On 22 November 2021, the City of Tshwane posted about the Birding Big Day, which would take place on 27 November ((Facebook,

2021). The users responded with service delivery issues: "We don't have electricity in extension 11 and 8 since the early hours of the morning in Soshanguve South Ext 8 and 11" and "We don't have power as well in some parts of Atteridgeville". On 25 November 2021, the City of Johannesburg announced that the Johannesburg Open golf tournament would be hosted by the city at the Randpark Golf Club featuring international golfers (Facebook, 2021). The comments by users included: "Is playing golf part of service delivery?"

Infrastructure delivery announcements also attracted cynical comments, in the main. Mangaung Metropolitan Municipality published an announcement on 25 November 2021 informing the public about the Hauweng bus infrastructure that had been designed to accommodate people with disabilities (Facebook, 2021). One of the users wrote in response: "It is not like there is a shortage of public transport in MMM. Just create job opportunities and forget this nonsense". The municipality did not respond to the comments. The City of Cape Town metro attracted more favourable comments (Facebook, 2021). On 26 November 2021, the metro thanked customers for their patience during routine maintenance of electrical infrastructure and indicated that routine regular planned maintenance was taking place daily in various parts of the city. The City's Facebook page received positive responses as follows: "At least you do maintenance"; "Just grateful you do maintenance"; "Maintenance done in Glencairn on Wednesday. Very efficient with only a couple of interruptions". One resident indicated that she needed help with sewage spillages in her area too and other users advised her to email the member of the mayoral committee and also to speak to the local councillor. There was no response from the municipality to the inquiry. Buffalo City Municipality announced a water outage in East London areas on the 30th of November 2021 with a promise that the water would be restored in the afternoon (Facebook, 2021). Comments indicate that the promise was not kept. "*BCM is there any news on the water issue? Please be honest and frank and allow us to make additional plans with correct information at hand.*

Not everyone has a swimming pool or tank connected that can be used to shower. Most of us need to work." Another Facebook user responded: *"Afternoon has come and gone and still no water in Nahoon Valley Park as promised by yourself earlier of water to be restored by afternoon, besides water being necessary for hydration and hygiene we are also in the middle of a pandemic, please advise".* There was no response from the municipality to the several comments on the same issue.

The focus on basic services confirms that the effective delivery of basic services remains a pivotal issue for local government as indicated in the studies done on this subject (Botes, 2018; Morudu, 2017; Reddy, 2016), as well as the report of the Auditor-General (2022).

One-way communication

The study has found that all eight metros use the Facebook pages to share information in a unidirectional way. Users continue engaging following the posting of information but there is no response from the administrators of the page. The state of affairs confirms the finding by Fashoro and Barnard (2021) and Mawela (2016), who examined the social media accounts of provincial government departments and municipalities and found that the social media accounts were used for one-way communication from government to the people. In failing to entertain the inquiries and responses from the public, the municipalities were unable to benefit from the interactive capability of social media.

Among the advantages of social media is that users benefit from socially interacting with other users while organisations providing the social media platform – in this case, municipalities – gain a captive audience (O'Brien, 2018). The author also posits that for business, the two-way process is beneficial as users engage and provide their views on products. The residents or citizens of the eight metros provide their views on the products or services provided, which is beneficial to the municipality.

The need to respond to the comments and queries from the public is summed up by a user on the Mangaung Metropolitan Municipality Facebook page (Facebook, 2021), responding to the announcement of the new bus service for Mangaung on 25 November 2021:

> The most offensive thing about this page of Mangaung Municipality is that they would throw things here for the information of the citizenry, which is a move I applaud. However, when we give feedback on what they have provided, they keep quiet and not interact, which defeats the whole objective of having this page in the first place (Facebook, 2021).

The lack of two-way communication confirms the outcome of other studies. For example, Mawela (2016) found that while citizens were willing to use platforms provided to engage with government departments, the departments responded sporadically. In addition, Fashoro and Barnard (2021) found that social media platforms in provincial and local government departments are used mainly for information dissemination and as an extension of the government websites. The metros were not engaged to ascertain the reasons for the lack of systematic ongoing responses to issues raised by the users on their official accounts as that exercise is beyond the scope of this study. Further work in this regard would be valuable.

Public notices requiring responses from the public

The study demonstrated that Facebook pages are not ideal for the sharing of information on policy issues that require feedback from residents or ratepayers to enable or contribute to decision-making. Residents either responded flippantly or raised service delivery issues that were not related to the matter. A public notice was posted on the Facebook page of the City of Tshwane inviting comments on the City of Tshwane Events Compliance Bylaw (Facebook, 2021). The notice attracted three comments. Two of the comments requested Eskom electricity loadshedding schedules and the third was a spam post on love potions. The reference to loadshedding schedules demonstrated yet again that the public view the work of municipalities as being to provide basic services. There was no comment on the policy document.

The City of Ekurhuleni issued an invitation to members of the public to comment on its draft Integrated Waste Management Plan on its Facebook page (Facebook, 2021). The responses from users focused on immediate service delivery issues such as refuse not being removed for six weeks, failure to cut grass and electricity outages in specific areas. A user chastised the municipality for using Facebook to seek comments and recommended the undertaking of a roadshow instead to ensure the inclusion of residents who do not have access to social media. Such notices may fall within the ambit of matters on which the public should be formally consulted. For example, municipalities are required by law to publish the IDPS, the annual budgets, and to invite members of the public to comment on them (Breakfast, Mekoa & Maphazi, 2015).

Job opportunities posted by municipalities

Information on job opportunities falls within the ambit of communication that empowers citizens and provides opportunities. The exchanges on the City of Johannesburg Facebook page relating to jobs demonstrated the value of two-way communication with citizens, and it was one of the few instances where municipalities responded to users (Facebook, 2021). On 24 November 2021, the City of Johannesburg metro posted information looking for seasonal lifeguards, cashiers and cloakroom assistants for swimming pools. A user wrote: "I do love seeing these posts, they do give me a purpose, I hope one day I get to score a vacancy from Joburg", to which the municipality responded: "Best wishes".

The City of Johannesburg also announced a partnership with National Treasury inviting unemployed youth to participate in the Infrastructure Skills Development Grant (Facebook, 2021). A user asked for a clearer application form and the municipality responded with assistance to obtain the form via an online link. Another user complained that the opportunity did not apply to people who were over the age of 35 and the municipality directed the user to the general vacancies page.

However, unlike the City of Johannesburg, a Nelson Mandela Bay metro announcement on possible job opportunities did not attract an enthusiastic response from users. The municipality announced on 26 November 2021 that the new municipal leadership would assist in resolving a potential bottleneck in the implementation of work opportunities and that R400 million had been set aside (Facebook, 2021). There was only one response to the post and it was related to service delivery: "Electricity has been off since yesterday in Motherwell NU3, the call centre cannot assist as the matter is with the electricity department."

Recommendations and proposals

The Government Communication Policy promotes two-way communication between the government and citizens (GCIS, 2018). One-way communication with the public is not in line with the policy or the development communication paradigm, nor with the developmental local government framework, which call for an interactive engagement with the public. It is recommended that the GCIS should promote the implementation of the policy and highlight the benefits of social media as a tool for enabling more effective participation and two-way engagement of citizens who have access to the internet.

The GCIS manages and coordinates inter-governmental communication forums across the three spheres of government. The forums include the National Government Communicators' Forum, the Provincial Government Communicators' Forum, District Communicators' Forum, the Local Communicators' Forum and the Intergovernmental Communicators' Forum (GCIS, 2018). The South African Local Government Association manages the SALGA National Communications Forum (NCF), which brings together municipal communication officials, marketers and municipal spokespersons, as well as COGTA and GCIS (SALGA, 2023). SALGA held its sixth forum meeting on 11 April 2023 and said the meeting was convened to deliberate on the impact of technology and how it can be better managed to complement the rollout of service delivery and improve governance systems in local government (SALGA, 2023). The forums provide viable platforms for engagement and mobilisation of communicators to use technology more efficiently for the benefit of citizens in a developmental manner, in line with the development communication paradigm and the Government Communication Policy (GCIS, 2018).

Quebral (2011: 5) posits that development communication was seen as a "confluence of the development process and the communication process". Meanwhile, the Government Communication Policy directs government communicators, referred to as "development communicators", to engage in work that will "uplift the quality of life of the South African public, not only socially, but also economically and culturally, using a range of communication tools" (GCIS, 2018).

Municipalities should thus assign communication staff to monitor the official Facebook pages and respond to the public inquiries on a regular basis, especially those from users seeking information about the delivery of basic services in their areas, as well as updates on outages and interruptions.

The methodology followed in the study did not include engagement with municipal staff to establish the reasons for not systematically responding to the public. A further study looking into the social media strategies and human and financial resources allocated to manage the social media platforms in the metros, would contribute further to knowledge on the use of social media for communication with the public in metropolitan municipalities.

This study has found that service delivery is a high priority for users of the metro Facebook pages. The various areas where service delivery backlogs or interruptions are being experienced are also mentioned. The content of the Facebook pages therefore provides valuable information and indicates the mood and views of the users of municipal services. It is recommended that municipalities should use the Facebook pages for research purposes to assist in planning for future interventions and to respond to the immediate needs raised by users or citizens.

Conclusion

The study has contributed to knowledge on the utilisation of e-government services, – in particular, social media platforms – to communicate with the public in an interactive manner. It has found that the capability of the social media technologies is not utilised to the fullest by metropolitan municipalities as they engage in unidirectional communication with the public. In addition, the municipalities are not in line with the development communication and developmental local government frameworks of government, which underscore public participation in governance and service delivery. Municipalities are encouraged to utilise the social media platforms more effectively. GCIS, as the lead department in communication coordination, is encouraged to spearhead municipal implementation of the Government Communication Policy, with its attendant principles of public participation and usage of social media to enhance service delivery.

References

Allen K. (2021). *Social media, riots and consequences*. Daily Maverick. 16 July. [Retrieved 8 November 2022]. https://www.dailymaverick.co.za/article/2021-07-16-social-media-riots-and-consequences/

Apuke OD. (2017). Social and traditional mainstream media of communication: Synergy and variance perspective. *New Media and Mass Communication*, 54:83–86. https://doi.org/10.29333/ojcmt/2614

Bertram C & Christiansen I. (2020). *Understanding Research: An Introduction to Reading Research*. 2nd Edition. Pretoria: Van Schaik Publishers.

Brand D. (2016). South Africans have made their voices heard. Now what for local councils? The Conversation. 15 August. [Retrieved 2 August 2023]. https://theconversation.com/south-africans-have-made-their-voices-heard-now-what-for-local-councils-63854

Breakfast N, Mekoa I & Maphazi N. (2015). Participatory democracy in theory and practice: A case study of local government in South Africa. *Africa's Public Service Delivery & Performance Review*, 3(3):31–51. https://doi.org/10.4102/apsdpr.v3i3.88

Botes L. (2018). South Africa's landscape of social protests: A way forward for developmental local government? *African Journal of Public Affairs*, 10(4):241–256.

Concepcion DL (2020). *UP President Danilo L. Concepcion pays tribute to the "Mother of DevCom", Dr Nora C Quebral*. University of the Philippines. 28 October. [Retrieved 24 April 2023]. https://up.edu.ph/up-president-danilo-l-concepcion-pays-tribute-to-the-mother-of-devcom-dr-nora-c-quebral/

Dollarhide M. (2021). Social media definition. Investopedia. 23 February. [Retrieved 3 August 2021]. https://www.investopedia.com/terms/s/social-media.asp

Facebook (2021). *Buffalo City Metropolitan Municipality Facebook page*. [Retrieved 8–11 November 2021]. https://www.facebook.com/BuffaloCityMetro/

Facebook (2021). *City of Cape Town Metropolitan Municipality Facebook page*. [Retrieved 8–11 November 2021]. https://www.facebook.com/CityofCT/

Facebook (2021). *City of Johannesburg Metropolitan Municipality Facebook page*. [Retrieved 8–11 November 2021]. https://www.facebook.com/CityofJoburg/

Facebook (2021). *City of Ekurhuleni Metropolitan Municipality Facebook page.* [Retrieved 8–11 November 2021]. https://www.facebook.com/CityOfEkurhuleni/

Facebook (2021). *City of Tshwane Metropolitan Municipality Facebook page.* [Retrieved 8–11 November 2021]. https://www.facebook.com/CityOfTshwane/

Facebook (2021). *EThekwini Metropolitan Municipality Facebook page*: [Retrieved 8–11 November 2021]. https://www.facebook.com/eThekwiniM/

Facebook (2021). *Mangaung Metropolitan Municipality Facebook page*: [Retrieved 8–11 November 2021]. https://www.facebook.com/MangaungMetropolitanMunicipalityOfficial/

Facebook (2021). *Nelson Mandela Bay Metropolitan Municipality Facebook page.* [Retrieved 8–11 November 2021]. https://www.facebook.com/NMBayM/

Fashoro I & Barnard L. (2021). Assessing South African government's use of social media for citizen participation. *The African Journal of African Information Systems*, 13(1):1936–0282.

Goldstuck A & Turner B. (2022). *Facebook analysis.* In: *Social Media Landscape Report: The Metaverse. Is it a David vs Goliath Play?* Ornico/World Wide Worx. [Retrieved 31 October 2023]. https://website.ornico.co.za/wp-content/uploads/2022/06/The-SA-Social-Media-Landscape-Report-2022.pdf

Ihsaniyati H, Sarwoprasodjo S, Muljono P and Gandasari D. (2023). The Use of social media for development communication and social change: a review. *Sustainability* 2023, 15(3): 2283. https://doi.org/10.3390/su15032283

Jakoet-Salie A (2020). E-government Strategies in South Africa: A Plausible Attempt at Effective Delivery of Services. *Administratio Publica*, 28(3). https://journals.co.za/doi/pdf/10.10520/ejc-adminpub-v28-n3-a2Jordaan L. (2019). Broken beats: The state of South Africa's newsrooms. The Media Online. 5 November. [Retrieved 10 October 2021]. https://themediaonline.co.za/2019/11/broken-beats-the-state-of-south-africas-newsrooms/

Kaunda L. (2023). Beat reporters needed for local govt. *Politicsweb*, 30 November. [Retrieved: 12 February 2024]https://www.politicsweb.co.za/opinion/local-govt-important-sphere-of-government

Kaunda L. (2021). Public participation platform: Municipalities must actively engaged with citizens. *Daily Maverick*, September 12. [Retrieved: 23 March 2022]. https://www.dailymaverick.co.za/opinionista/2021-09-12-public-participation-platform-municipalities-must-actively-engage-with-citizens-on-social-media/

Kemp S. (2021). Digital 2021: Global Overview Report. DataReportal. 27 January. [Retrieved 21 July 2021]. https://datareportal.com/reports/digital-2021-global-overview-report

Kemp S. (2022). Digital 2022: South Africa. DataReportal. 15 February. [Retrieved: 31 October 2023]. https://datareportal.com/reports/digital-2022-south-africa

Lada A, Wang M & Yan T. (2021). How does news feed predict what you want to see? Facebook. 26 January. [Retrieved: 4 November 2022]. https://about.fb.com/news/2021/01/how-does-news-feed-predict-what-you-want-to-see/

Lindner R & Aichholzer G. (2020). E-Democracy: Conceptual foundations and recent trends. In: L Hennen, I van Keulen, I Korthagen, G Aichholzer, R Lindner & RØ Nielsen (Eds). *European E-Democracy in Practice*. Cham, Switzerland: Springer Open. 11–45. https://doi.org/10.1007/978-3-030-27184-8_2

Madumo OS. (2015). Developmental local government challenges and progress in South Africa *Administratio Publica*, 23(2): 153–166.

Malinga S. (2020). *Dr Zweli Mkhize debunks 5G-coronavirus link theories*. ITWeb. 1 April. [Retrieved: 20 February 2021]. https://www.itweb.co.za/content/LPp6V7rDW3xqDKQz

Malinga S. (2022). *Half of SA's population now active on social media*. ITWeb. 1 July. [Retrieved: 20 April 2023]. https://www.itweb.co.za/content/rW1xLv5nGyP7Rk6m

Mawela T. (2016). Exploring the role of social media in the G2C relationship: A South African perspective. *Information Development*, 33(2): 117–132. https://doi.org/10.1177/0266666916639743

McFadden C. (2020). *A brief history of Facebook and its major milestones*. Interesting Engineering. 7 July. [Retrieved: 25 April 2023]. https://interestingengineering.com/culture/history-of-facebook

McNeill A & Briggs P. (2014). *Theoretical perspectives on the usage of social media in the propagation of health messages*. [Retrieved: 12 February 2021]. https://hcihealthcarefieldwork.files.wordpress.com/2013/11/theoryhealthchi2014_submission_2.pdf

Mkhize ZL. (2018). Local government is everybody's business. *Tabling of the COGTA budget vote*. Cape Town: National Assembly. Speech, 15 May. https://www.cogta.gov.za/index.php/2018/05/14/speech-by-minister-zweli-mkhize-during-the-local-government-week-event/

Mlaba K. (2021). *How is South Africa's digital divide making inequality worse in the country?* Global Citizen. 3 August. [Retrieved 21 March 2023]. https://www.globalcitizen.org/en/content/south-africa-digital-divide-makes-inequality-worse/

Morudu HD. (2017). Service delivery protests in South African municipalities: An exploration using principal component regression and 2013 data. *Cogent Social Sciences*, 3(1). https://doi.org/10.1080/23311886.2017.1329106

Muridzi G. (2019). Framework for E-governance to Improve Service Delivery for Local Authorities in South Africa. PhD thesis. North-West University. https://dspace.nwu.ac.za/handle/10394/35328

Ntshavheni K. (2022). Unlocking the potential of South Africa's digital economy. *NASPERS/DCDT Stakeholder Forum*. Sandton, Johannesburg. Speech, 23 March. https://www.polity.org.za/article/sa-khumbudzo-ntshavheni-address-by-communications-minister-at-the-naspersdcdt-stakeholder-summit-under-the-theme-unlocking-the-potential-of-south-africas-digital-economy-230322-2022-03-23

Ntuli ME & Teferra D. (2018). Implications of social media on student activism: The South African experience in a digital age. *Journal of Higher Education in Africa*, 15 (2):63–80. https://doi.org/10.57054/jhea.v15i2.1481

O'Brien T. (2018). *Why social media is important for your business.* Engageware. 16 August. [Retrieved 23 October 2022]. https://engageware.com/blog/why-social-media-engagement-is-important-for-your-business/

Odoom MD. (2020). Understanding development communication: A review of selected literature. *E-Journal of Humanities Arts and Social Sciences (EHASS)*, 1(5): 37–48. https://doi.org/10.38159/ehass.2020055

Okeke-Uzodike OE & Dlamini B. (2019). Citizens' e-participation at local municipal government in South Africa. *Journal of Reviews on Global Economics*, 8:458–468. https://doi.org/10.6000/1929-7092.2019.08.39

Palvia SCJ & Sharma SS. (2007). E-Government and e-governance: Definitions/domain framework and status around the world. In: *Proceedings of the 5th International Conference on E-governance*. Hyderabad: Hyderabad Central University. 5(1):1–12.

Parkyn R. (2017). *The role of social media in development*. BBC. 31 March. [Retrieved 20 April 2023]. https://www.bbc.co.uk/blogs/mediaactioninsight/entries/63e297a8-83b6-456d-aff5-67dc55f45d27

Pypers E & Bassuday J. (2016). Public participation in local government. *Southern African Catholics Bishops' Conference Parliamentary Liason Office*. Briefing Paper 421. December. https://www.cplo.org.za/wp-content/uploads/2016/02/BP-421-Public-Participation-In-Local-Government-December-2016.pdf

Quebral NC. (2011). Devcom Los Baños Style. *Honorary Doctorate Celebration Seminar*. London, UK: University of London. Lecture, 7 December. https://www.lse.ac.uk/media-and-communications/assets/documents/events/past-events/Professor-Nora-Cruz-Quebral-Dec-2011-lecture.pdf

Reddy PS. (2016). The politics of service delivery in South Africa: The local government sphere in context. *The Journal for Transdisciplinary Research in Southern Africa*, 12(1):a337. https://doi.org/10.4102/td.v12i1.337

Republic of South Africa. Auditor-General. (AGSA). (2022). Consolidated General Report on Local Government Audit Outcomes: MFMA 2020/21. [Retrieved 23 April 2022]. https://mfma-2022.agsareports.co.za/

Republic of South Africa. Constitution of the Republic of South Africa. (1996). Government Gazette No. 25799. Pretoria: Government Printer.

Republic of South Africa. Department of Cooperative Governance and Traditional Affairs. (COGTA). (2020). Municipal Profiles. District Development Model. [Retrieved: 23 October 2021]. https://www.cogta.gov.za/ddm/index.php/documents/

Republic of South Africa. Department of Provincial Affairs and Constitutional Development (DPACD). (1998). The White Paper on Local Government. Pretoria: Government Printer.

Republic of South Africa. Department of Telecommunications and Postal Services (DTPS). (2017). National E-Government Strategy and Roadmap. Government Gazette No. 41241. 10 November. Pretoria: Government Printer. [Retrieved 24 April 2023]. https://www.gov.za/sites/default/files/gcis_document/201711/41241gen886.pdf

Republic of South Africa. (2018). Government Communication and Information System (GCIS). Government Communication Policy. [Retrieved 10 April 2022]. https://www.gcis.gov.za/sites/default/files/Government%20Communication%20Policy%20Cabinet%20Approved%20Oct%202018.pdf

Republic of South Africa. Independent Electoral Commission (IEC). (n.d.). More about municipalities. [Retrieved 25 October 2021]. https://www.elections.org.za/content/Elections/2016-Municipal-Elections/More-about-municipalities/

Republic of South Africa. National Institute for Communicable Diseases (NICD). (2020). *First case of COVID-19 announced – An update.* NICD. 5 March. [Retrieved 15 October 2021]. https://www.nicd.ac.za/first-case-of-covid-19-announced-an-update/

Republic of South Africa. Statistics SA (StatsSA). (2020). General Household Survey. [Retrieved 20 April 2023]. https://www.statssa.gov.za/publications/P0318/P03182020.pdf

South African Local Government Association (SALGA). (2015). *15 Years of developmental and democratic local government: 2000–2015.* [Retrieved 21 July 2021]. https://www.salga.org.za/Documents/Knowledge-products-per-theme/Plans-N-Strategies/15%20Years%20of%20Developmental%20and%20Democratic%20Local%20Government.pdf

South African Local Government Association (SALGA). (2023). SALGA to convene the 6th Annual SALGA National Communicators' Forum in Cape Town. [Retrieved 18 April 2023]. https://www.salga.org.za/event/ncf-23/ncf/documents/Media%20Release%20SALGA%20to%20convene%20the%206th%20Annual%20SALGA%20National%20Communicators%20Forum%20in%20Cape%20Town.pdf

Williams P. (2020). *The importance of leading communication during epidemics.* SANews. 3 September. [Retrieved 10 February 2021]. https://www.sanews.gov.za/south-africa/importance-leading-communication-during-epidemics

Willis K. (2013). *Analysing qualitative data.* In: Walter, M. (ed.). *Social research methods.* 3rd ed. Victoria, Australia: Oxford University Press.

Willis (2013: 323)

Chapter 3

Strategic Communication in Local Government Collective Bargaining: Proposing Solutions to Challenges

Pay Shabangu

The South African Constitution identifies local government/ municipalities as one of the three spheres of government. However, on collective bargaining matters, the local government sector bargains within a distinct bargaining council separate from those of the national and provincial government spheres. The Public Service Co-ordinating Bargaining Council (PSCBC), for instance, oversees collective bargaining for the national and provincial government. On the other hand, collective bargaining for local government take place through the South African Local Government Bargaining Council (SALGBC).

This chapter is mainly concerned with analysing collective bargaining challenges in the local government sector and proposing solutions to these.

In August 2022, what looked like a peaceful local government employee strike at the small town of Middelburg in Steve Tshwete Local Municipality, Mpumalanga Province, ended in a deadly shooting. In a confrontation between striking municipal employees and a private security company, one employee was shot and killed while five others were admitted to hospital with gunshot wounds. The employees were demanding better wages and working conditions, among other demands (SAMWU, 2022b). That killing of a Steve Tshwete Local Municipality employee is not unprecedented in South Africa's labour relations. In 2011, a clash between the City of Tshwane's striking bus and refuse workers led to the

61

death of a municipal employee who was a trade union member (M&G, 2011).

In 2020, in another local government labour-relations-related confrontation, the City of Ekurhuleni Metropolitan Municipality dismissed 52 employees for what the trade unions called an act of silencing union leadership and members for voicing their frustrations. The SALGBC ruled against the municipality's decision and instructed that the employees be reinstated as of May 2022 (SAMWU, 2022a). In a separate case, also in 2020, the City of Tshwane Metropolitan Municipality claimed that the fixed-term contract of 627 employees had expired and dismissed them. Again, the municipality's decision was overruled by the SALGBC. The trade unions criticised the municipality, claiming that employees are led by people who have no sympathy or empathy (Moatshe, 2022).

These are a few instances of labor relations cases that showcase the difficulties in collective bargaining within the South African local government sector. All these cases came after the World Economic Forum (WEF) had ranked South Africa the worst in the world for competitiveness in labour-employer relations cooperation. Of the 137 countries included in the WEF quantitative study, South Africa was ranked last (WEF, 2017).

The local government collective bargaining data presented in this chapter is based on qualitative research conducted in 2020 and 2021 in South Africa's Gauteng Province. Research participants interviewed for this study comprised representatives from two local government collective bargaining trade unions, the Independent Municipal and Allied Trade Union (IMATU) and the South African Municipal Workers Union (SAMWU), as well as the local government employer organisation, SALGA, and the SALGBC. Semi-structured interviews were carried out simultaneously with an analysis of official, publicly accessible documents produced by the three collective bargaining stakeholders, namely: the employer organisation, trade unions, and the bargaining council.

The stakeholder theory was utilised to understand the complexities surrounding conflicts and the dynamics of relationships among stakeholders in local government negotiations. Based on this study and its findings, this chapter identifies and discusses the dynamics of collective bargaining challenges in local government sector; proposes strategic communication principles as to address these challenges; and defines and contextualises the concept of strategic communication in relation to local government collective bargaining. It also explains the bargaining process, identifies and briefly outlines the roles of leach ocal government collective bargaining stakeholders, and describes and explains the 'new stakeholder' concept.

Background: Strategic Communication in Collective Bargaining

As one of the objectives of this chapter is to propose a strategic communication approach as an answer to collective bargaining challenges, it is appropriate to commence with an explanation of the concept of strategic communication. Since 2007, when the first journal in this field was published, the *International Journal of Strategic Communication*, a myriad of definitions of the concept have come forth. I take a critical view of some of these definitions to create an understanding of the field.

The seminal work of Hallahan, Holtzhausen, Van Ruler, Verčič and Sriramesh (2007:3) defines strategic communication as a "purposeful use of communication by an organisation to fulfil its mission". In the realm of the collective bargaining function, as highlighted in the Labour Relations Act 66 of 1995, the mission of local government is to encourage employee involvement in workplace decision making and effective problem solving of collective bargaining disputes. In the local government cases discussed in the introduction to this chapter, engagement among collective bargaining stakeholders appears to have failed to achieve the expected mission.

Strategic communication has the potential to strengthen engagement among local government stakeholders and, in turn, improve employee involvement in decision making and dispute resolution. As a field of study, strategic communication has always been interdisciplinary in nature and, as such, can make an impact in the industrial relations field (Verwey & Benecke, 2021). Most importantly, strategic communication research has consistently sought to outline commonalities across the several disciplines that engage in this interdisciplinarity (Holtzhausen & Zerfass, 2013).

Strategic communication goals, as applied in this chapter, are to encourage collaboration, co-creation, meaningful dialogue and creation of trust among collective bargaining stakeholders. These goals are proposed to mitigate the identified collective bargaining challenges. This sets strategic communication apart from integrated communication by emphasizing how organizations can effectively communicate across various organizational initiatives while considering future strategic actions (Mahoney, 2011).

Zerfass and Huck (2007) highlight the role of strategic communication in building trust among an organisation's stakeholders, and argue that, strategic communication, as a practice, makes a multifaceted contribution. Besides from establishing trust among stakeholders, it develops organisational reputation and manages symbolic connections with stakeholders. Unlike the kind of communication that supports daily activities in an organisation, Strategic communication readies an organization for an unpredictable future. It stands apart from other fields of communication by prioritizing the fundamental elements crucial for achieving organizational success (Zerfass & Huck, 2007).

According to Farwell (2012), strategic communication, from a modernist perspective, is a type of engagement that involves psychological operations, propaganda, public affairs and public diplomacy. Psychological operations and propaganda refer to the type of communication aimed at distributing selected content to recipients with the intention to influence their thinking and ultimately the behaviour of their governments and other stakeholders. Psychological operations and propaganda are not characteristic of the field of strategic communication as understood for the purpose of identifying and addressing collective bargaining challenges. The act of concealing information for the purpose of influencing stakeholders is not a suitable mechanism for reducing conflict in an organisation.

On the contrary, in organised labour settings characterised by stakeholder activism, openness and transparency between trade unions and employer organisations becomes a significant component of engagement.

An effective strategic communication analysis can identify the challenges confronting an organisation through research and suggest possible opportunities for how these can be resolved (Hallahan, 2015). In such instances, 'strategic communication is understood as a multidimensional and post-modernistic stakeholder engagement approach that promotes transparency, openness, collaboration and knowledge-sharing for organisational success and conflict mitigation' (Shabangu, 2021). Contrary to the modernistic perspective characterised by control and manipulation, a post-modernistic perspective encourages a dialogic matrix (Overton-de Klerk & Verwey, 2013). In a collective bargaining environment, strategic communication encourages labour unions' and employers' cooperation to conduct a smooth engagement. Strategic communication examination reveals that such communication is post-modernistic and interdisciplinary in nature and encourages 'new stakeholder' behaviour.

Local Government Collective Bargaining

Collective bargaining is the backbone of public sector labour relations, most processes of which can either be bolstered or weakened through collective bargaining. It establishes a forum where labour unions and employer representatives discuss terms of employment and associated matters in a broader societal context (Nel, Kirsten, Swanepoel, Erasmus & Jordaan, 2016). In the local government sector, the SALGBC brings together representatives involved in collective bargaining and guarantees their compliance with the collective bargaining regulations outlined in the Labour Relations Act, the SALGBC Constitution and the Main Collective Agreement.

Local government collective bargaining happens at two separate levels – national and divisional – depending on the nature of contractual agreement or labour issue under discussion. Collective bargaining issues that are managed at a divisional level are: acting allowance, standby allowance, night work allowance, shift allowance, special leave, emergency work, long service bonus, additional paid sick leave, measures to manage the taking and accrual of sick leave, administrative measures for the taking of leave and legal indemnification (SALGBC, 2015).

The SALGBC comprises the following thirteen divisions in totality: Gauteng; Johannesburg Metropolitan; Cape Town Metropolitan; eThekwini Metropolitan; Western Cape; Eastern Cape; Free State; KwaZulu-Natal; Limpopo; Mpumalanga; Northern Cape; North-West, and Tshwane Metropolitan Division (SALGBC, 2017/ 2007?). Each division has divisional committees that are made up of an equal number of trade union and employer representatives.

In researching local government collective bargaining, this chapter's data was collected at the three divisional levels in Gauteng Province, namely Johannesburg, Tshwane, Gauteng – which includes the Ekurhuleni Metropolitan Municipality, the Sedibeng and West Rand District Municipalities. These three divisions comprise bargaining committees that are given powers to settle collective agreements relating to terms and conditions of service or any other matter referred to them. It is mostly the efficiency of these bargaining committees that contributes to the success of collective bargaining within a specific division. The collective bargaining process's success is determined by a peacefully reached and formally written agreement called a Collective Agreement, which binds collective bargaining stakeholders for a number of years or until a particular matter necessitates changes (Shabangu, 2021).

The main objectives of the Collective Agreement are to promote employee participation in decision making; promote fair treatment of employees; promote and maintain industrial peace; create uniform procedures for all stakeholders covered by the agreement; and to ensure effective labour relations (Finnemore & Koekemoer, 2018; SALGBC, 2015). The collective bargaining challenge is that there is little or no adherence at all to these objectives within the collective bargaining network. The perceptions about the concept 'collective bargaining' varies from one labour relations stakeholder to another. Employees, for instance, look at collective bargaining as a monetary value-creating platform for members of a labour union and good working conditions. Employers, on the other hand, regard collective bargaining as a process embarked upon when a need arises for engagement on employment conditions and salaries (Heald, 2016). Numerous scholars in labour relations offer varying viewpoints on the predominant interpretation of collective bargaining.

According to De Wet (1987) and Du Doit (2007), the idea of collective bargaining was initially brought forward by Beatrix Potter Web, the British labour movement pioneer, in 1891. According to the Webbs (1896), barter between groups of workers or stakeholders and between individuals must be heralded by some form of negotiations, through authorised representatives. Fox (2006) and Bendix (2019) concur. Similarly, in the local government sector of South African, collective bargaining occurs between representatives of the employer organisation (SALGA), recognised labour unions (SAMWU and IMATU) and the bargaining council (SALGBC).

Local Government Collective Bargaining Challenges

Collective bargaining in the local government sector starts from a structure called a Local Labour Forum (LLF) (Shabangu, 2021). One stipulation in the Collective Agreement mandates that each municipality must create an LLF structure, which fosters dialogue between representatives of employers and employees. Issues that an LLF can engage or consult on, according to the Main Collective Agreement (SALGBC, 2015), are Issues relevant to a specific municipality but beyond the jurisdiction of the bargaining council or its divisions; issues referred to the LLF by the bargaining council; and the concluding of Minimum Service Level Agreements (operational issues within a respective local government). Agreements taken at the LLFs would then be escalated to the division's bargaining committee for ratification (SALGBC, 2015).

Collective bargaining fundamentally revolves around communication process hence it presents challenges that are commonly associated with communication (Nel, Kirsten, Swanepoel, Erasmus & Jordaan, 2016). The collective bargaining challenges outlined are based on qualitative research data sourced from the local government sector collective bargaining stakeholders in Gauteng between 2020 and 2021. The collective bargaining challenges discussed in this chapter are not exhaustive, and further research work might discover additional challenges.

Politicisation of collective bargaining

Following substantial engagement with the three stakeholder groups involved in local government collective bargaining in Gauteng, it was revealed that internal politics within political parties somewhat contribute to the confrontational nature of collective bargaining. The extended exercise of political power in the collective bargaining processes by councillors representing the employer organisation politicises collective bargaining. They might be representing particular political parties in the council of a particular municipality, but in the SALGBC they only represent the employer organisation (Shabangu, 2021). One Gauteng Division research participant, for instance, commented on how political interference has become a challenge to the collective bargaining issues:

"Remember the South African Municipal Workers Union (SAMWU) is a member of the Congress of South African Trade Unions (COSATU). COSATU is affiliated to the ANC, so when we are seated at the Local Labour Forum (LLF), and we talk to councillors, we talk to ANC councillors; so, if ANC councillors have their own divisions at branch level they bring them here, and then they divide labour. Those are the things we have identified, and we have not come up with an answer on how we are going to deal with it."

The indirect involvement of political parties creates unease and has a detrimental impact on collective bargaining. A participant from the Tshwane Division expressed concern about the challenges of collective bargaining when certain stakeholders introduce political party dynamics into the process. The participant explained that:

"You might find that a lot of us as shop stewards are ANC members. Even when you are in meetings and you're planning something, some of your shop stewards will tell them [the ANC] that, hey, we are planning something, and we are coming for you."

Likewise, a research participant from the Johannesburg Division also indicated the interference that party politics has on collective bargaining within local government:

"For your understanding, all these collective bargaining problems are caused by political parties."

Coercive collective bargaining

Coercive collective bargaining refers to a bargaining environment where one stakeholder consciously intimidates other stakeholders and adopts a 'leader stakeholder' posture. A "leader stakeholder" is a term used to describe a stakeholder who asserts dominance over other stakeholders in situations like collective bargaining, believing that decisions made should primarily serve their own interests rather than those of other stakeholders. Typically, this is followed by putting pressure on other stakeholders to agree with their negotiation stance through intimidation (Shabangu, 2021). As elucidated by a participant from the Tshwane Division:

> "We have been followed; we have been threatened; but we don't care anymore. But you see, there's one thing that you must realise as a union is that you must be sure of your strength."

The leader stakeholder hypothesis was further emphasised by one participant from the Gauteng Division:

> "The employer would actually be a problem here because if both trade unions agree that things should be done this way, the employer is the one that complicates issues, this [is] because they [the employer] have authority over the implementation of collective bargaining resolutions."

The leader stakeholder hypothesis is operationalised using intimidation and coercion, giving rise to the idea of coercive collective bargaining. The reality of the coercive collective bargaining concept is, moreover, explained in the following SAMWU Gauteng Division press statement:

> "[The] Municipal Manager with his deputy have been using their positions of authority to intimidate, threaten and cause division among our members and employees of the Midvaal Local Municipality in general. The threats started during the demonstration that they will deal with all SAMWU members after elections and, indeed, after elections they started to suspend our members following ambiguous and witch-hunt allegations, instilled fear among employees, caused division and suspended our members, including all shop stewards within Midvaal in an attempt to ban the union so they can push their devious agendas." (SAMWU, 2016a)

In that same year, the trade union released another statement expressing comparable views on collective bargaining within the province:

> "We have heard of the offensive that has been launched against the working class by municipalities [as] a direct attack on trade unions by the employer. We will be defending ourselves against the employer who has shown no regard to collective bargaining and wants to run municipalities as though they are someone's private property." (SAMWU, 2016b)

Such a positional approach towards engagement damages trust and the possibility of value creation among stakeholders. Solving challenges becomes a difficult exercise and trust is diminished under such circumstances (Lewicki, Elgoibar & Euwema, 2016). Confrontations that, at times, have led to killings in the labour relations environment remain a worrying factor, demonstrating a need for a co-creation approach in collective bargaining.

Trade unions and political parties' alliances

Historically, trade unions have been working side by side with political parties such as the ANC and the Inkatha Freedom Party (IFP). Some of these trade unions shared ideological beliefs with these political parties. The United Workers Union of South Africa (UWUSA), for instance, had an alliance with the IFP, while COSATU has an alliance with the ANC (Bennett, 1988; Bennett & Howe, 1986). The collaboration between trade unions and political parties proved effective during the fight against apartheid. Bhorat, Naidoo and Yu (2014) argue that COSATU played a vital role in shaping the course of economic restructuring and the path of transformation within the nation. This research has confirmed, however, that some stakeholders involved in the collective bargaining hold differing views on such collaborations nowadays.

One Gauteng Division's research participant, for example, pointed out the alliance between trade unions and political parties as one of the challenges facing the process of collective bargaining. The research participant explained:

> "If you look at other countries abroad, you'll find that very few labour federations have this historical alliance with political parties that govern a country. In South Africa, we blur the lines (between trade unions and political parties). When shop stewards are aggrieved with management and the structures of collective bargaining in the municipality, the unions will approach the political leadership and try to strike a deal, and then want to come with that gentleman's agreement outside the structures of collective bargaining and want to implement it in this collective bargaining arena, and that is what causes these tensions and problems."

The challenge posed by alliances between political parties and trade unions was also shared by a research participant from the Gauteng Division. The participant stressed:

> "There is a confusion of roles. Remember, I am a member of the ANC at branch level. Then I would attend a branch meeting of the ANC where I am just an ordinary member and come to the union where I am now secretary. Then I stand in front of members and articulate issues. Now, when I am in the union position, I want to address the issue from the ANC branch meeting on the wrong platform, which is the main problem that we need to address. Yes, it is the national alliance, but the trade union needs to have their own rules otherwise these things [misunderstanding of roles] are not going to fall off."

A Tshwane Division study participant clarified that the factional dynamics within the ANC extend to shop stewards in the union who also hold membership in the ANC. Then trust among shop stewards of one trade union in the collective bargaining process is disrupted. The participant expressed that:

"Some shop stewards will say, this one is pushing a particular agenda because he belongs to a different faction [a grouping in the ANC]."

Poor consultation

Consultation stands out as a fundamental level of stakeholder engagement. It is during consultation that an organisation presents information to stakeholders and receives feedback. Consultation is essential among stakeholders for an effective functioning of an organisation (Larson & Williams, 2009). Local government collective bargaining is characterised by poor consultation, which negatively affects efficiency and progress in stakeholders' engagement processes.

In a consultation process, stakeholders' feedback is valued and considered at a leadership level. Most collective bargaining challenges would be detected early if the local government's consultation machinery were functioning well. Meaningful dialogue and inclusive consultation could solve labour relations problems before erupting into conflicts, as explained by a Tshwane Division participant:

> "So, if you engage us properly, we are prepared to make a deal out of the situation – to say, 'Maybe let's take this route". We [trade unions] are not difficult people; it's just about proper consultation and engagements."

Consultation is not a stakeholder engagement process that is done for the sake of it. Failing to value consultation can also create problems among the stakeholders involved. The main problem associated with poor consultation in collective bargaining is that the employer tends to have the upper hand. This manifests through the taking of decisions without involving other collective bargaining stakeholders (Shabangu, 2021). This happens with matters impacting all stakeholders, as stated in the following SAMWU Gauteng Division statement:

> "We have noted decisions which have been taken without following due processes and consulting with organised

labour, such as the decision to convert day shifts into night shifts. We are, however, glad that the South African Local Government Bargaining Committee declared that move invalid as there has been no agreement between trade unions and the city in the LLF." (SAMWU, 2017:1).

Meanwhile, the terms of reference of the LLF in the City of Johannesburg (2018: 6) make it clear that the basis of sound and sustained labour relations is effective communication and cooperation among collective bargaining stakeholders. This means the opposite of that would be unsound labour relations and would therefore pose a challenge to the stakeholders and the process.

A Tshwane Division participant stressed:

"They [the employer] fail, on a regular basis, to communicate with employees. They would just apply certain resolutions without consulting with employees, and I think if they do that [consulting], it would bring much more stability in the organisation."

Consultation is not only helpful for sourcing feedback from stakeholders, but it also contributes to building a working relationship. The following SAMWU Johannesburg Division statement stresses consultation's relevance in this regard:

"If the Mayor is serious about having a cordial relationship with the trade unions, he should begin by consulting with trade unions before making decisions that would impact employees." (SAMWU, 2017:1).

Now that challenges associated with the collective bargaining process have been identified, the following section proposes some solutions to the challenges.

Solutions to the Collective Bargaining Challenges Identified

In an organisational environment where there is a multiplicity of voices, such as local government collective bargaining, strategic communication practice accentuates stakeholder collaboration, co-creation and dialogue as ideal approaches for minimising engagement challenges (Shabangu, 2021). Therefore, stakeholder recognition and co-creation, resolving collective bargaining issues collaboratively, meaningful dialogue, and building and strengthening trust among stakeholders are some strategic communication principles that can be integrated in an organisation facing engagement challenges similar to those previously discussed.

Stakeholder recognition and co-creation

Figure 1: Stakeholders ought to recognise each other and encourage co-creation. Source: Author

To achieve co-creation, stakeholders need to value, involve and recognise each other, hence the importance of stakeholder recognition. Such recognition is one of the levels of stakeholder engagement and is central to facilitating stakeholder co-operation leading to the minimisation of engagement challenges. Stakeholder recognition in local government collective bargaining should not be confused with identification of stakeholders (Shabangu, 2021). Stakeholders in the local government collective bargaining environment are clearly identified in the Main Collective Agreement (2015-2020). The agreement does not include political parties as stakeholders; it only mentions trade unions and the employer organisation. Recognition of these stakeholders is key to ensuring co-creation in solving challenges.

The main principle of stakeholder recognition involves recognizing and embracing the perspective that all stakeholders should be included in collective bargaining processes and decision-making. Moreover, they ought to treat each other with respect and value each one's contribution. Such an approach obviates any unwelcome interference by those not recognised by the agreement in the collective bargaining (Shabangu, 2021).

The stakeholder recognition principle is anchored in the 'stakeholder involvement' factor. By engaging stakeholders in decision-making and governance processes, it becomes simpler to achieve organizational accountability and responsibility (Greenwood, 2007; Fisher & Hopp, 2020). Acknowledging stakeholders is crucial because when employees feel acknowledged and connected to an organisation, they tend to align their decisions with the organisation's strategic objectives and exhibit behaviours beneficial to the organization, such as cooperation and demonstrating good organizational citizenship (Shabangu, 2021).

There are many ways in which organisations can put into action the principle of stakeholder recognition. Firstly, this can be achieved by providing additional avenues for listening. By actively listening, an organization can gain deeper insights into stakeholders' thoughts and feelings.

Secondly, an organisation can organise platforms such as seminars where stakeholders engage each other openly on issues impacting collective bargaining. Most importantly, these seminars must be convened in a neutral setting where all parties feel unrestricted and not compelled to adhere to the directives of any leader stakeholder. Skilled labour relations consultants can be hired to help facilitate such occasions. Such seminars must result in summarized reports featuring actionable steps and clear timelines, as these will be beneficial to stakeholders, enabling them to monitor the seminar's progress and feel personally involved as contributors to the report's development (Shabangu, 2021).

Resolving collective bargaining issues collaboratively

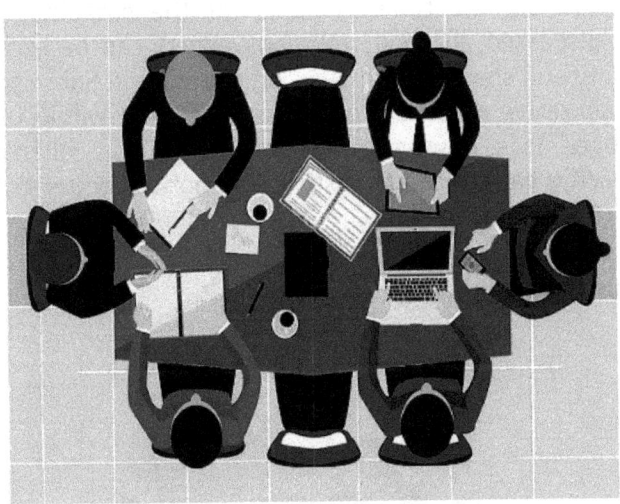

Figure 2: Collaboration is grounded on continuous stakeholder interaction and tolerance. Source: Author

Stakeholder collaboration can help resolve problems such as coercive collective bargaining in many different ways. Firstly, through stakeholder collaboration an environment where an organisation can achieve a task that could not be easily accomplished in any other way is created. Collaboration helps to create a favourable environment for constructively building a future-focused stakeholder relationship. Secondly, the local government's ability to solve collective bargaining problems that an individual stakeholder cannot solve, could be strengthened through stakeholder collaboration (Shabangu, 2021).

The main aim of a collaborative approach is to facilitate a group creative brainstorming exercise with wider stakeholder inputs, through the creation of a collaboration space. This is a space where local government collective bargaining stakeholders can express their opinions and have these taken into account. A suggested approach to this is that a local government can publicise a contested bargaining issue in an internal communication platform such as intranet, newsletter or WhatsApp groups and invite stakeholders to respond. Depending on the time available for the bargaining issue being discussed, a labour relations expert can be invited to facilitate and share perspectives on the subject. Subsequently, a collaborative response to the issue at hand would then be developed. It is, however, important to say that collaborative approaches cannot be exhaustive, and none is better than the other (Shabangu, 2021).

Meaningful dialogue

Figure 3: Meaningful dialogue creates a sense of belonging and adds value to all stakeholders. Source: Author

Meaningful dialogue refers to an engagement that creates a sense of belonging and adds value to all stakeholders in a conversation. Dialogue becomes meaningful when all stakeholders appreciate the engagement's purpose. This is done by showing respect to each other and valuing each one's contribution in an engagement session (Shabangu, 2021).

Meaningful dialogue is essential in an era where a post-modernistic stakeholder emerges in organisations. The emerging stakeholder – the new stakeholder – wishes to be part of the decision-making process in an organisation. The local government collective bargaining challenges outlined above show that the emerging new stakeholder can indeed be identified in the sector. Turning to the challenge of poor consultation in local government collective bargaining, it is again apparent that the new stakeholder is eager to be recognised and empowered through involvement in the organisation's processes (Shabangu, 2021).

The emergence of the new stakeholder is precipitated, among other things, by the proliferation of technology. Technology moves information easily from one point to the other. This empowers the new stakeholder, who now has unlimited access to information. Therefore, using platforms such as social media, the new stakeholder can question leadership on issues that previously were deemed 'for management' only.

Meaningful dialogue is therefore proposed as an alternative resolution to the local government collective bargaining process. Through meaningful dialogue, different perspectives from stakeholders are considered and integrated into organisational planning. This is done to emphasise that stakeholders should not be viewed as resources or units of production but as equals in the organisation (Shabangu, 2021).

Build and strengthen trust among stakeholders

Figure 4: Trust is one significant factor in organisational relationships. Source: Author

In collective bargaining, trust refers to reciprocal expectations of respect, honesty, support and transparency in the relationship between the trade unions and the organisation. Research in the local government collective bargaining environment has established that failure to respect and abide by agreed performance measures causes a breakdown of trust among collective bargaining stakeholders. In addition to that, the blaming of trade unions and political parties' alliances as one of the reasons for disruptive collective bargaining could be reason enough to demonstrate how necessary it is for collective bargaining stakeholders to work on trust-building among themselves (Shabangu, 2021). In a confrontational collective bargaining scenario where there are high levels of trust among stakeholders, they tend to display cooperative behaviour, while relationships characterised by low trust produce the opposite (Elgoibar, Munduate & Euwema, 2016).

Building trust attributes is neither a simple nor a short-term exercise. There is no one approach that can respond to all trust related problems. However, constant interactions between stakeholders is one of the strategies identified as a trust-builder in a collective bargaining environment. This strategy, which is explained by the fact that stakeholders get to know about each other's interests, needs and commonalities, can be achieved by allocating time and resources in informal and personal interaction between the senior management team and trade unions representatives (Lewicki et al, 2016). Moreover, these scholars add that constant communication between stakeholders and open communication channels, even during periods of conflict, are effective in building trust.

Conclusion

Most significantly is that the interdisciplinarity of strategic communication is not only restricted to organisational communication, public relations and marketing communication but can be extended to other fields such as labour relations in the local government sector. Local Labour Forums and Bargaining Committees are two critical structures of the local government collective bargaining in the Tshwane, Johannesburg and Gauteng divisions of the Local Government Bargaining Council in the Province. The discussion further shows that the local government sector collective bargaining resembles the 'all channel' and 'chain communication' network.

The collective bargaining challenges identified and discussed have demonstrated engagement challenges in labour relations in the local government sector. In a collective bargaining space, where one stakeholder believes their voice is not heard, and where the blaming of the other is common, promoting trust-building has been discussed as an ideal solution. The chapter has shown that trust promotes collaborative engagement, which allows protagonists to collectively develop solutions.

The importance of meaningful dialogue as a solution to collective bargaining, characterised by the proliferation of technology and the emergence of the phenomenon known as the new stakeholder. Stakeholder recognition and co-creation are some of the strategic communication objectives that have been discussed as ideal solutions to public sector collective bargaining challenges.

References

Baker R & Angelopulo G. (2006). *Integrated Organisational Communication*. Cape Town: Juta.

Bendix S. (2019). *Labour Relations: A Southern African Perspective*. 7th Edition. Cape Town: Juta.

Benecke DR & Phumo T. (2021). A road less travelled: Re-charting future strategic communication in Southern Africa. In: DR Benecke, S Verwey & T Phumo (Eds). *Strategic Communication: South African Perspectives*. Cape Town: Oxford University Press Southern Africa.

Bennett M. (1988). UWUSA: Tied to the last outpost. *Indicator SA*, 5(3):75–79.

Bennett M & Howe G. (1986). Contenders for labour in 'KwaNatal': The UWUSA initiative. *Indicator SA*, 4(1):108–111.

Bhorat, H; Naidoo, K & Yu, D. (2014). Trade unions in an emerging economy: The case of South Africa, World Institute for Development Economics Research Working Paper, No. 2014/055. https://doi.org/10.35188/UNU-WIDER/2014/776-9

Botan CH (2018). *Strategic Communication Theory and Practice: The Cocreational Model*. USA: Wiley Blackwell.

Broch C, Lurati F, Zampirini A & Mariconda S. (2018). The role of social capital for organizational identification: Implications for strategic communication. *International Journal of Strategic Communication*, 12 (1):46–66. https://doi.org/10.1080/1553118X.2017.1392310

Cacciattolo K. (2015). Defining organisational communication. *European Scientific Journal*, 11(20):79–87.

City of Johannesburg (2018: 6)

Clarke AR (2007) Public Service Labour Relations: Centralised Collective Bargaining and Social Dialogue in the Public Service of South Africa (1997 to 2007). Master's thesis. Cape Town: University of the Western Cape.

Cornelissen J. (2011). Corporate Communication: A Guide to Theory and Practice. London: Sage Publications.

Republic of South Africa. Department of Employment and Labour (DEL). (2020.) Annual Industrial Action Report

De wet, L. (1987). Collective bargaining at local government level with particular reference to Natal, Dissertation submitted in part fulfilment of the requirements for the degree Master of Public Administration (MPA) in the Department of Public Administration in the Faculty of Commerce and Administration at the University of Durban-Westville.

Du Toit, D. (2007). What is the Future of Collective Bargaining (And Labour Law) in South Africa? 28 *ILJ* 1405-1435.

Elgoibar P, Munduate L & Euwema M. (2016). Building trust and constructive conflict management in organizations. In: P Elgoibar, M Euwema & L Munduate (Eds). *Building Trust and Constructive Conflict Management in Organisations*. Cham, Switzerland: Springer International Publishing. https://doi.org/10.1007/978-3-319-31475-4

Falkheimer J & Heide M. (2015). Strategic communication in participatory culture: From one- and two-way communication to participatory communication through social media. In: DR Holtzhausen & A Zerfass (Eds). *The Routledge Handbook of Strategic Communication*. New York and London: Routledge. 337–350. https://doi.org/10.4324/9781315621555

Falkheimer J & Heide M. (2018). *Strategic Communication: An Introduction*. London: Routledge.

Farwell JP. (2012). *Persuasion and Power: The Art of Strategic Communication*. Washington DC: Georgetown University Press.

Finnemore M & Koekemoer GM. (2018). *Introduction to Labour Relations in South Africa*. 12th Edition. Durban: LexisNexis.

Fisher J & Hopp T. (2020). Does the framing of transparency impact trust? Differences between self-benefit and other-benefit message frames. *International Journal of Strategic Communication*, 14(3):203–222. https://doi.org/10.1080/1553118X.2020.1770767

Fox M. (2006). *Managing Organisational Behaviour*. Cape Town: Juta.

Gobind J. (2015). *South African Employment Relations in Context*. Randburg: KR Publishing.

Greenwood M. (2007). Stakeholder engagement: Beyond the myth of corporate responsibility. *Journal of Business Ethics*, 74(4):315–327. https://doi.org/10.1007/s10551-007-9509-y

Hallahan K. (2015). Organizational goals and communication objectives in strategic communication. In: DR Holtzhausen & A Zerfass (Eds). *The Routledge Handbook of Strategic Communication*. New York and London: Routledge. 244–265.

Hallahan K, Holtzhausen D, Van Ruler B, Verčič D & Sriramesh K. (2007). Defining strategic communication. *International Journal of Strategic Communication*, 1(1):3–35. https://doi.org/10.1080/15531180701285244

Heald G. (2016). *Why is Collective Bargaining Failing in South Africa: A Reflection on How to Restore Social Dialogue in South Africa*. Randburg: KR Publishing.

Heide M, Simonsson C, Nothhaft H, Andersson R & Von Platen S. (2018). *The Communicative Organization: Final Report*. Stockholm, Sweden: Swedish Association of Communication Professionals.

Holtzhausen DR & Zerfass A. (2013). Strategic communication: Pillars and perspectives on an alternate paradigm. In: K Sriramesh, A Zerfass & JN Kim (Eds). *Current Trends and Emerging Topics in Public Relations and Communication Management*. New York: Routledge. https://doi.org/10.1007/978-3-531-18961-1_4

Jainarain S. (2020). A Critical Analysis of Violent Strikes in South Africa. Master's thesis. University of KwaZulu-Natal.

Kent ML & Lane AB. (2017). A rhizomatous metaphor for dialogic theory. *Public Relations Review*, 43:568–578. https://doi.org/10.1016/j.pubrev.2017.02.017

Larson S & Williams LJ. (2009). Monitoring the success of stakeholder engagement: Literature review. *Desert Knowledge Cooperative Research Centre*, 45(7): 251–298.

Labour Relations Act 66 of 1995 and CCMA Related Material. (2019). Cape Town: Juta.

Lewicki R, Elgoibar P & Euwema M. (2016). The tree of trust: Building and repairing trust in organizations. In: P Elgoibar, L Munduate & M Euwema (Eds). *Industrial Relations and Conflict Management: Building Trust and Constructive Conflict Management in Organisations*. Cham, Switzerland: Springer International Publishing. https://doi.org/10.1007/978-3-319-31475-4

Macnamara J & Gregory A. (2018). Expanding evaluation to progress strategic communication: Beyond message tracking to open listening. In: KP Werder, H Nothhaft, D Verčič & A Zerfass (Eds). *Future Directions of Strategic Communication*. New York: Routledge. https://doi.org/10.1080/1553118X.2018.1450255

Mahoney J. (2011). Horizons in strategic communication: Theorising a paradigm shift. *International Journal of Strategic Communication*, 5:143–153. https://doi.org/10.1080/1553118X.2011.537603

Mail & Guardian (M&G). (2011). *COSATU condemns death of SAMWU worker.* [Retrieved 3 April 2023]. https://mg.co.za/article/2011-03-07-cosatu-condemns-death-of-samwu-worker/

Moatshe R. (2022). *Union weighs in on more than 500 workers fired by Tshwane.* Pretoria News. [Retrieved 1 July 2022]. https://www.iol.co.za/pretoria-news/news/union-weighs-in-on-more-than-500-workers-fired-by-tshwane-d7ccb56a-159a-4a09-8a65-2fbe242c2aa2

Modebadze V. (2010). The term politics reconsidered in the light of recent theoretical developments. *International Black Sea University Scientific Journal,* 4 (1):39–44.

Muff K. (2014). *The Collaboratory: A Co-Creative Stakeholder Engagement Process for Solving Complex Problems.* United Kingdom: Greenleaf Publishing.

Neher WW (1997). *Organisational Communication.* Butler University: Allayn and Bacon.

Nel PS, Kirsten M, Swanepoel BJ, Erasmus BJ and Jordaan B. (2016). *South African Employment Relations: Theory and Practice.* 8th edition. Pretoria: Van Schaik.

Neville BA & Menguc B. (2006). Stakeholder multiplicity: Toward an understanding of the interactions between stakeholders. *Journal of Business Ethics,* 66:377–391. https://doi.org/10.1007/s10551-006-0015-4

O'Connor A & Shumate M. (2018). A multidimensional network approach to strategic communication. *International Journal of Strategic Communication,* 12 (4):399–416. https://doi.org/10.1080/1553118X.2018.1452242

Overton-de Klerk N & Verwey S. (2013). Towards an emerging paradigm of strategic communication: Core driving forces. *South African Journal for Communication Theory and Research,* 39(3):362–382. https://doi.org/10.1080/02500167.2013.837626

South African Local Government Bargaining Council (SALGBC). (2015). Main Collective Agreement, 2015–2020. Pretoria: Government Printers. https://salgbc.org.za/wpfd_file/maincollectiveagreement2015/

South African Local Government Bargaining Council (SALGBC). (2017/2007?). Constitution of the South African Local Government Bargaining Council.

Sandhu S. (2009). Strategic communication: An institutional perspective. *International Journal of Strategic Communication*, 3(2):72–92. https://doi.org/10.1080/15531180902805429

Shabangu PE. (2021). Towards a Framework Using Stakeholder Engagement as a Strategic Communication Approach in Mitigating Conflict in the Local Government Collective Bargaining Process. PhD thesis. Johannesburg: University of Johannesburg. https://hdl.handle.net/102000/0002

Sloan P. (2009). Redefining stakeholder engagement: From control to collaboration. *Journal of Citizenship*, 34 (1):25–40. https://doi.org/10.9774/GLEAF.4700.2009.wi.00005

Sommerfeldt EJ & Yang A. (2018). Notes in a dialogue: Twenty years of digital dialogic communication research in public relations, *Journal of Public Relations Research*, 30 (3):59–64. https://doi.org/10.1080/1062726X.2018.1498248

South African Municipal Workers Union (SAMWU). (2016a). *DA-Led Midvaal uses apartheid strategy to suspend workers.* Press statement. [Retrieved 31 July 2018].

South African Municipal Workers Union (SAMWU). (2016b). *SAMWU to continue with listening campaign.* Press statement.

South African Municipal Workers Union (SAMWU). (2017:1). *SAMWU condemns Ekurhuleni's compromise of service delivery.*

South African Municipal Workers Union (SAMWU). (2017:1). *Statement on the proposed reintegration of CoJ Municipal-owned entities.*

South African Municipal Workers Union (SAMWU). (2022a/b?) Mpumalanga Province. Press statement.

South African Municipal Workers Union (SAMWU). (2022 a/b?) *SAMWU secures reinstatement of 52 unfairly dismissed workers*. Press statement. SAMWU Ekurhuleni region.

Terms of Refence: Local Labour Forum, City of Johannesburg (2018).

Van Ruler B. (2018). Communication theory: An underrated pillar on which strategic communication rests. In: KP Werder, H Nothhaft, D Verčič & A Zerfass (Eds). *Future Directions of Strategic Communication*, New York: Routledge. https://doi.org/10.1080/1553118X.2018.1452240

Venter R & Levy A. (2014). *Labour Relations in South Africa*. 5th Edition. Cape Town: Oxford University Press.

Verwey S & Benecke DR. (2021). Strategic communication paradigm and symbolic intermediation. In: DR Benecke, S Verwey & T Phumo (Eds). (2021). *Strategic Communication: South African Perspectives*. Cape Town: Oxford University Press Southern Africa.

World Economic Forum (WEF). (2017). The Global Competitiveness Report 2017–2018. Geneva: World Economic Forum. https://www.weforum.org/publications/the-global-competitiveness-report-2017-2018/

Webb, S & Webb, B. (1896). *The history of trade unionism*, 2nd edition. London: Longmans, Green and Co.

Zerfass A & Huck S. (2007). Innovation, communication, and leadership: New developments in strategic communication. *International Journal of Strategic Communication* 1(2):107–122. https://doi.org/10.1080/15531180701298908

Zerfass A, Verčič D, Nothhaft H & Werder KP. (2018). Strategic communication: Defining the field and its contribution to research and practice. *International Journal of Strategic Communication*, 12(4):487–505. https://doi.org/10.1080/1553118X.2018.1493485

Chapter 4

Influencing Voter Turnout: Analysing the IEC's Stakeholder Communication Strategy in the 2021 Local Government Elections

Karabo Sitto-Kaunda

The Independent Electoral Commission is a Chapter 9 institution tasked with all responsibilities related to voter education and communication in South Africa and is thus a key public institution. The right to vote is protected by the institution, given South Africa's political past, which politically excluded a significant majority of the population. The decreasing voter turnout is therefore of great public concern, with record lows in the numbers of voters casting their ballots for the local government elections of 2021. These local government elections were contentious for numerous reasons, including the limitations on electioneering due to COVID-19 regulations (Mokoena, 2021).

As the custodian of free and fair elections in South Africa, the role of the IEC is pivotal to the evaluation of the low voter turnout for the 2021 local government elections. Citizens who are eligible to vote – meaning those 18 years of age or older – have been showing up in steadily declining numbers at the polls, raising questions about some of the possible reasons for their absence, as well as the democratic implications thereof. Eligible voters, who are key stakeholders of the IEC, need to see the value for them personally of exercising their right to vote, and this should be conveyed through a clear and consistent communication strategy. Stakeholder engagement is a key pillar of the IEC, requiring good faith in its communication to balance the power inequalities among various stakeholders,

91

especially the citizens as voters. Digital and social media have helped to shift the stakeholder engagement relationship, moving the power of communication into the hands of recipients (Overton-de Klerk & Verwey, 2013), such as potential voters.

The fourth industrial revolution (4IR) has been hailed as a great enabler of inclusion and participation for stakeholder communication and engagement. The South African public sector has pursued an e-government strategy to increase its reach and optimally use the limited resources to communicate the government's service delivery efforts. The evolution of the IEC's communication strategy to digitally led strategic communication activities has had some implications because of the increased integration of digital communication. Developing countries such as South Africa struggle to deliver basic community services such as running water, electricity and healthcare, which tend to be considered a higher priority than the technological integration of 4IR (Kayembe & Nel, 2019). Internet access is critical for meaningful participation in the 4IR and yet Africa's low internet penetration persists even as the United Nations in 2011 declared internet access as a catalyst for the enjoyment of human rights (Salway, 2020).

South Africa's national estimated rate of internet access has increased dramatically from 28% to 78% through various means, including access at places of work and study, public access points or internet cafes (Lewis, 2023). However, the internet penetration rate in South Africa is evidence of the geographical and technological urban/rural divide and the digital connectivity divide, defined along the lines of economic affordability. In rural South African households, an estimated 1% of households have internet access, compared to 17% of urban households, a gap that has been linked to affordability (Lewis, 2023). As one of the most unequal societies in the world, South Africa has some of the highest data costs – in some instances double those of neighbouring countries (Mwareya & Simango, 2023). The introduction of digital channels for public sector engagement has seemingly also not considered the full implications of the digital generational divide and media consumption preferences of diverse stakeholders, such as those of the IEC.

The COVID-19 pandemic increased the public sector's reliance on digital technologies to maintain social distance, and the government aimed to quickly increase its public communication reach. South Africa's 2021 local government elections took place amid the COVID-19 pandemic, with preparations delayed because of the third wave of the virus (Mokoena, 2021). The declaration of the voting date – ultimately, 1 November – was delayed because of the COVID-19 behavioural imperatives hampering ordinary campaigning by political parties to their supporters. In April 2021, the parliament's Portfolio Committee on Cooperative Governance and Traditional Affairs raised concerns with the IEC in respect to readiness and committee members advocated for the postponement of the 2021 local government elections (Gerber, 2021). The IEC stated to the committee at the time that a postponement of the 2021 local government elections would be unconstitutional and raise legitimacy issues for elected councillors due to the end of their terms (Gerber, 2021). Yet, in July 2021, the IEC petitioned the Constitutional Court for a postponement over concerns of low voter turnout (Njilo, 2021).

Consistent, sustained public communication is critical for the IEC to reach some of the most marginalised South Africans, who are often reliant on free public media resources, particularly in relation to their meaningful participation in voting. Past public communication campaigns by the IEC included voter education via television programmes (e.g. *Khululeka* on SABC), roadshows and other communication strategies that were designed to reach as many South Africans as possible (Malada, 2015). The question of meaningful participation in the voting process in South Africa, where the cost of data is prohibitive (Harrisberg & Mensah, 2022), particularly in the face of the IEC's increased reliance on digital communication technologies, merits evaluation in terms of the public communication landscape. This chapter analyses articles from mainstream media and research sources on the issue of low voter turnout, thematising the key reasons and linking them to the responsibility of the IEC towards citizens as key stakeholders. The chapter argues that limiting IEC communication to periods leading up to the elections – such as for the 2021 local government elections – through a digital-first approach that gives preference to digital channels over traditional media (PMG, 2022) – has had an influence on how citizens understand their role in upholding a healthy democracy through voter participation. The right of all eligible South African citizens to vote may be diluted through limited access to critical information from the IEC because of its limited engagement and digital-first communication strategy.

The Right to Vote

The right to vote is paramount in South Africa, given the past dispensation of segregation where the majority were excluded from participating in the selection of political leaders in the country. The advent of democracy and the first elections held in 1994 stand out in South African history, as does the establishment of the IEC as an independent Chapter 9 institution tasked with the management of free and fair elections in South Africa (IEC, n.d.). The South African political system is a representative democracy where citizens elect political party representatives to represent them in government (Parliament of the Republic of South Africa, n.d.); thus, voters select a political party registered with the IEC that will then select its candidates to represent the party at various levels of government, whether national, provincial or local (municipal).

In South Africa, as with other African states, there is a marked age difference between political leaders and their constituencies, with Africa having the youngest median population age in the world (Lubinga & Sitto, 2021). This age gap influences the norms of communicating with voters. A significant part of the IEC's role is to manage elections by ensuring the participation of all stakeholders, including citizens, the media, political parties and civil society (IEC, n.d.). The IEC must demonstrate impartiality in all its dealings with this diverse set of stakeholders, including being responsive and transparent (see Oksiutycz in this volume on transparency). The various aspects of the IEC's management require clear, concise and intentional communication efforts by the organisation to ensure free and fair elections through knowledgeable citizens voting.

The elections in South Africa include two main events:

- The national and provincial elections, which take place every five years,
- The local government elections, which also take place every five years, two years after the national elections.

In between, there may be by-elections for various reasons including run-offs, the loss of a councillor or reports of election mismanagement (IEC, n.d.).

Local government elections are critical elections as municipalities are the first port of call and closest means of interaction that citizens have with government. Local government elections strengthen democracy and work towards basic service delivery (Mudau, 2021), following the principle of proportional representation and direct election of ward councillors. To ensure good local government elections, engagement needs to take place between the IEC and multiple stakeholders, including legislative bodies and institutions, citizens, political parties and civil society.

Citizens as the IEC's Stakeholders

Communication professionals are tasked with creating value for stakeholders and must consider the socio-economic and generational uses of communication tools to do so effectively. South Africa is a diverse country, made up of citizens from varying backgrounds and socio-economic statuses. In a population of approximately 60 million people in South Africa (Worldometers, 2022), there are 26 039 335 registered voters as at 2023 (IEC, 2022). In 2021 the number of registered voters was approximately 63.9% of the voting age population

(Human Sciences Research Council, 2021). The number of registered voters in 2021 had decreased from 74.6% in 2019 of the voting age population registered to vote (Human Sciences Research Council, 2021). Of those registered voters in 2021, the demographic spread of voters indicates that those in the age groups 18–29 and 60–80 are the least number of registered voters proportionally. The voter registration proportions signify some challenges concerning stakeholder engagement across generational divides, especially with the South African population median age being 27.6 years (Worldometers, 2022).

The focus of stakeholder theory is on the purpose of the organisation and the responsibility it has to stakeholders to develop or create shared value (Freeman, Wicks & Parmar, 2004). Citizen stakeholders are entitled to have input into matters that affect them, beyond the election ballot, and thus have a vested interest in all communication efforts of the IEC, primarily centred on the protection of a free and fair democracy. The challenge for organisations such as the IEC is how to become more creative in developing shared value through their communication strategies to build and maintain citizen-stakeholder relationships – even beyond voting season – to preserve the connection to participatory democracy. Often stakeholders that are treated well tend to respond with positive attitudes and behaviours towards an organisation and its communication. Thus, to balance interests among stakeholders and the organisation, stakeholder engagement needs to be conducted in good faith by organisations such as the IEC. Good faith in stakeholder communication encourages engagement while preserving individual autonomy to pursue self-interest, and while helping to balance power inequalities among stakeholders (Dawkins, 2014). According to Dawkins (2014), good faith is important for meaningful stakeholder engagement and the success of communication, fostering a culture of collectivity, especially where a complexity of interests exists. The IEC is tasked with balancing multiple interests that may not always enjoy mutuality and thus stakeholder engagement needs to be practised in good faith through strategic communication, requiring the IEC to be reflexive in its communication approach.

The Power Shift in Organisational Communication

Organisations no longer have control in a world where internet-driven communication technologies have empowered stakeholders – more so than ever before – to act as key players in organisational communication. The 4IR, which is expected to be the new normal, has been hailed as a transformative period for organisations, with disruptions that will revolutionise almost all industries (Xing & Marwala, 2017). 4IR-powered technology has been earmarked as a way for organisations to build capacity with minimal need for additional or costly resources. The IEC, as part of the overall public sector e-government strategy, invested in an upgraded website in October 2022. The organisation has also invested time in developing social media accounts on YouTube, Instagram, Twitter (now X) and Facebook (the largest social media network in South Africa) (BusinessTech, 2021). However, across these social media platforms, the number of followers collectively for the IEC as at 2023, did not exceed 700 000, which is a small number compared to the size of the voter registration base, especially when considering the possible reach of these platforms.

The IEC as an organisation is increasingly interacting with their stakeholders online through various channels and platforms, although the digitally connected still represent a small proportion of stakeholders. The official IEC social media hashtag for the local government elections, #LGE2021 brought up numerous results online, with a mixture of commentary from citizens on the performance of the various political parties but limited direct mention of the IEC by social media users. The most notable aspect of the social media accounts for the IEC is the low engagement and interaction with content shared, with comments closed on some videos loaded. The social media strategy of the IEC seems, from the content evaluated, to focus on sharing the various activities of the organisation primarily through broadcasting, media releases, outcomes of court actions, election outcomes and event live streaming, with limited engagement with online users or responses to direct questions or comments posted by them.

The pattern of use reflects some of the findings with respect to government use of digital media discussed by Sitto et al. (2022), demonstrating that government digital communication strategies during the COVID-19 pandemic did not make full use of the advantages of engagement through digital media. The IEC seems to experience the strategic communication challenges with their social media activities which Navarro, Moreno and Al-Sumait (2017) discuss with the incorporation of social media into organisational communication strategies, namely:

- limiting engagement – for example, by disabling comments – because of organisational fear of loss of control;
- inappropriate use of channels selected for message dissemination – for example, full media releases shared;
- underinvestment in online time for meaningful engagement;
- not using stakeholder feedback from social media to help improve relations; and
- a lack of proactive engagement for dialogue measurement.

While the power of political parties in the South African voter communication landscape has grown as they use the media to drive their messages to attract voters, the visibility of IEC's public communication strategy has simultaneously diminished across converged media platforms – i.e. a mix of traditional and digital media. A large contributor to the shrinking voice of the IEC on the converged media landscape has been a diminishing budget (Parliament of the Republic of South Africa, 2022).

The COVID-19 pandemic exposed the deep socio-economic inequalities in the country and further extended the digital divide. Even as global internet penetration rates continue to rise, the digital divide in South Africa continues to widen along socio-economic and urban/rural lines. The internet penetration rate in South Africa remains lower than the global average (Internet World Stats, 2022), with internet access primarily through mobile, using expensive data and concentrated in urban centres (StatsSA, 2019). South Africa's internet connectivity costs are among the highest on the African continent and globally (Kahla, 2019). The digital divide has implications for how different citizen stakeholders access information and thus for how the IEC should approach its strategic communication engagement – including what channels it should use – to deliver on its mandate of reaching the voter base as widely as possible with information to empower citizens to make informed decisions during the elections. The critical role that the IEC plays in South Africa has been disrupted by information communication technologies (ICTs), and thus the influence of the digital divide on the organisation's engagement with citizen stakeholders is key to public communication.

The Role of Strategic Communication for Voter Engagement

Since its establishment, the IEC has made many strides over the years in its work to communicate with citizens about electoral matters. From the strategic use of television shows such as *Khululeka*, an edutainment programme (Barnett, 2002) on the importance of voting and the rights of citizens to on-the-ground community engagements and town hall meetings, the IEC in the past has made efforts to reach as many citizens as possible. The discipline of strategic communication emphasises the focus on *all* the communication activities of the organisation, not only those of communication professionals (Falkheimer & Heide, 2018).

The organogram of the IEC divides the communication responsibilities between the Deputy CEO of Corporate Services, who takes care of ICT – i.e. the digital communication tools of the organisation – and the Deputy CEO of Outreach responsible for communications (IEC, n.d.).

The differentiation of the digital communication tools and channels used to disseminate the messages to be carried on such platforms provides insight into the potential challenges of holistic, purposeful communication by the IEC, beyond planned communication at a specific time, such as the 2021 local government elections. The discipline of strategic communication takes a holistic, deliberate and continuous approach to communication by organisations at various stakeholder levels, beyond the communication function (Falkheimer & Heide, 2018).

The IEC has a responsibility to continuously engage citizen stakeholders to:

- educate, inform and involve citizens;
- update the voters' roll; and
- uphold the right to vote for all citizens through deliberate messaging and communication.

The essence of the practice of strategic communication is being purposeful, meaning decisive with the intent to advance an organisation's mission through communicating (Van Ruler, 2018). The purposeful nature of strategic communication is critical (Hallahan et al., 2007) to organisational success. To maintain the integrity of the electoral process, the IEC needs to be deliberate in its stakeholder engagement practices in a multigenerational and geographically dispersed society such as South Africa. The IEC's main vision is "To be a pre-eminent leader in electoral democracy" (IEC, 2022), which requires purposeful communication, especially during the organisational shock of the COVID-19 pandemic.

The COVID-19 Pandemic and the 2021 Local Government Elections

Times of crisis expose acute 4IR inequality challenges. The COVID-19 global pandemic and subsequent response strategies implemented by the South African government were largely reactive to a dynamic health crisis that caught the government underprepared and ill-equipped to cope with its consequences.

The COVID-19 health crisis developed into a socio-economic crisis as the world ground to a halt, nearly crippling economic activity due to lockdowns and movement restrictions (Sitto & Lubinga, 2020). More than half of all South Africans live below the food poverty line, mostly the country's black population (BusinessTech, 2019). The pandemic left the marginalised even more vulnerable as they relied on the government to meet basic needs. Citizens were concerned about meeting their basic needs and the affordability of connectivity slipped further away from the grasp of the majority.

Despite the uncertainty of the direction the COVID-19 pandemic was taking, several political parties and citizens called for the 2021 local government elections to go ahead (Davis, 2020). Local government elections in 2021 were planned to take place in what became the third wave of the COVID-19 pandemic in South Africa. The Constitutional Court's refusal of the IEC's application to postpone the local government elections in 2021 to give them time to prepare for voter education and readiness significantly challenged the strategic communication options of the organisation. With the COVID-19 regulations focusing on the social distancing imperative, the IEC was forced to consider a largely digital-first communication strategy for the 2021 local government elections, using digital communication technologies more heavily than traditional media, including electronic voter registration (PMG, 2021). Thus, many citizens were left behind, not only through the digital divide but also through a generational divide in the use of digital communication as the IEC increased its digital efforts to target younger voters (PMG, 2021). Different generations engage with digital communication technologies in a variety of ways, including avoidance strategies, as the number of platforms for engagement continues to rise (Rossouw, Rautenbach, Pritchard & Sitto, 2018).

Baby Boomers – those born between 1946 and 1964 – Generation X (1965–1979) and Gen Z (2000–2020) are the generations with the least number of registered voters among them, relative to the overall voters' roll. The largest proportion of registered voters reside in Gauteng; geographically the smallest province of South Africa's nine provinces that has the largest share of the national population and is a key economic contributor (South African Government, n.d.). For the IEC, the diversity of citizen stakeholders and the low turnout numbers, particularly in the younger segment of eligible voters, point to a challenge in meaningfully conveying to those stakeholders the importance of registering for voting. The multigenerational society in South Africa allows for numerous communication possibilities – as well as challenges – due to the existence of the technological generational divide (Rossouw et al., 2018). The largest influence of the technological generational divide concerns the different levels of familiarity, skills and knowledge of various communication media. The different generations have unique communication preferences, with millennials – born from 1980 to 1999 – enjoying the most technological integration in their lives (Berkup, 2014). This generational digital divide influences the success of engagement with the citizen stakeholder groups.

The Government Communication and Information System's Annual Report for 2020/21 indicated that during the COVID-19 pandemic the use of traditional broadcast media, specifically community radio, to reach "population segments in rural and far-flung areas" (GCIS, 2022: 9) of the country became critical to information dissemination. The continued pursuit of an e-government strategy, including by public institutions such as the IEC, continues to be challenged by the socio-economic conditions of the country, specifically the rural/urban and generational digital divide, which was also evident in the responses to – and voter turnout for – the 2021 local government elections. Over time, the IEC's observed communication strategy has centred on elections and outside election periods, on the continuous encouragement of voter registration for eligible individuals – those aged 16 or older – with less focus on a sustained communication strategy of voter education (Malada, 2015).

The IEC has increasingly focused on providing resources and information online through its website and social media accounts, relying on voters to access the information themselves – even though many experience internet access constraints. The evaluation of media around the performance of the IEC's communication strategy, through the lens of the 2021 local government elections – admittedly the most technologically advanced elections (Mzekandaba, 2021) – provides some key indicators of the need for reflexivity by this Chapter 9 institution.

Evaluation of Media Coverage of 2021 Local Government Elections

To evaluate the influence of the communication strategy of the IEC during the 2021 local government elections, online searches were conducted specifically considering the keywords 'low voter turnout South Africa 2021' and 'youth vote low in South Africa', yielding nearly 32 million search results. To evaluate the most relevant online results from various sources, the first page of results was considered for each of these search terms. The main sources of information that were qualitatively and thematically analysed are listed in Table 1.

In total, 15 articles were selected for analysis, drawn from various sources, including national research bodies, mainstream media, alternative local press, international press, independent research agencies and political blog sites from key stakeholders. The articles analysed from these various sources were collated to ensure a balance in the views publicised with respect to voter education among South African youth and the role of the IEC. The analysis of the articles' content focused on the communicative issues and challenges to meaningful voter participation in the 2021 elections and the low voter turnout, as outlined by various IEC stakeholders.

The articles were analysed by grouping similar information into codes and developing common themes from the codes. Four main themes were identified, with respect to voter participation, especially among the youth during the 2021 local government elections and the IEC's voter education communication strategies for the local government elections.

The codes and subsequent themes focused primarily on individual voters' challenges, limited knowledge of the voting system linked to limited voter education channels, and under-appreciation of the significance of voting because of low voter education through a digital-first communication strategy by the IEC.

Table 1: Sources for institutional and media analysis (September 2021–June 2022)

Sources		Total
Government reports	GCIS Annual Report 2021/22 (GCIS, 2022)	1
National media	News24 (Dooms, 2021); EWN (Goodall, 2022); Moneyweb (Runciman & Bekker, 2021); Mail & Guardian (Mbanyele & Desai, 2021)	4
Local media	Daily Maverick (Smillie & Payne, 2021; Davis, 2020); The Conversation (Patel & Graham, 2019)	3
International press	Bloomberg (Cele & Vecchiatto, 2021)	1
Research agencies	Institute for Security Studies (Tracey-Temba, 2016); Human Sciences Research Council (Scott, Vawda, Swartz & Bhana, 2012); ResearchGATE (Bekker, Runciman & Roberts, 2022); Konrad-Adenauer- Stiftung (Bekker & Ruciman, 2022)	4
Blogs	My Vote Counts (2021), Freedom Advocacy Network (Zulu, 2022).	2

Discussion

The thematic analysis of the 15 articles selected on strategic voter communication and voters showing up during the local government elections identified four main themes, outlined in Table 2. This table also describes the implications of the main themes for the IEC's digital-first communication strategy for stakeholder engagement.

Theme 1. Lack of service delivery a demotivator for voting

Public sector communication success is influenced by how citizens perceive the basic tenet of government and its agencies – service delivery. A key theme of the analysis was the lack of motivation to vote because citizens have not experienced a marked change in their lives through service delivery. In addition to service delivery, the perceptions of ageing leaders being out of touch with citizens (Lubinga & Sitto, 2021) plays a crucial role in the outlook of voters, especially younger voters.

Chapter 2 of this volume, which discusses municipalities' use of Facebook, emphasises the inextricable link between how public sector communication is received and the quality of the engagement with citizens as key stakeholders. Citizens are disillusioned with the voting system as they have not experienced changes in the basic services received, with some intimating that whether they vote or not, the ruling party will remain in power. The type of thinking expressed demonstrated a limited understanding by citizens of the connection between voting and service delivery. Citizens did not perceive that an increased number of voters turning up at the polls could have changed the election outcome and that by staying away from the polls, they possibly perpetuated the cycle of low service delivery. The IEC has an important role to play in linking the right to vote with the outcomes of free and fair elections, as well as a healthy democracy, through stakeholder engagement.

Theme 2. Individual voter obstacles to participation

The main reasons documented for poor voter turnout in the articles analysed, especially in the 2021 local government

Table 2: Themes from data analysis on local government elections 2021

Theme	Sub-theme	Implication
Lack of service delivery a demotivator for voting	Disillusionment with the voting system Limited understanding of the link between voting and service delivery	Non-party-affiliated citizens cannot connect voting to the outcome of service delivery and their role in changing the outcome.
Individual voter obstacles for participation	Inability to sign up for the voters' roll in time Physical unavailability to vote on election day Lack of relevant paperwork for voting	As citizens in a democracy, voters are unfamiliar with the voting systems available to them through the IEC.
Limited voter education influencing readiness	Lack of understanding of voting processes Limited voter education leading up to elections	There is little information outside election season from the IEC to aid ordinary citizens on actions to take to be ready to vote.
General youth apathy due to ageing leaders	Age disparity between leaders and voters Little direct communication with newly eligible voters Voter turnout as a sign of protest	Young people are unable to connect with older political leaders and have limited motivation to understand the power of their vote against the democratic implications of staying away from the polls.

elections, were individualistic. Obstacles such as employment constraints, not being registered to vote, or not having the proper identification documentation were the leading reasons individuals gave for not voting in 2021. However, these challenges indicate a limited understanding of the voting process and voter rights. The IEC is responsible for communicating to citizens the various options available to them as voters. These options include applying to cast a special ballot, which allows individuals to cast their ballot on a predetermined day other than election day. All registered voters are eligible to apply for a special vote if they are physically unable to go to their voting station to vote (IEC, 2022). The obstacles for participation indicate an obstacle to information access by voters and thus a lack of strategic communication by the IEC to empower citizens for meaningful election participation.

Stakeholder engagement by the IEC has not been meaningful, nor seemingly, as Dawkins (2014) emphasises, done in good faith to balance power inequalities. Citizens are only eligible to vote if they have an official South African identity document, which requires time and money to acquire from the Department of Home Affairs (DoHA), as well as official proof of residence. Obtaining the relevant documentation proved to be another socio-economic obstacle for voters because of the service delivery challenges associated with obtaining identity documents, especially with limited-service provision by DoHA during the COVID-19 lockdown.

Undeniably, the information on the necessary documentation is available online on the IEC's website. However, in a country with a widening digital divide, the imperative is to use converged media to disseminate such critical information more accessibly ahead of elections on a repetitive basis. COSATU has emphasised the importance of the IEC and the DoHA in educating voters ahead of the 2024 elections to ensure they have the relevant identity documents for meaningful participation (Moche, 2023). With citizens facing socio-economic pressures during the COVID-19 pandemic, particularly due to job losses, affordable access to online information became constrained. That individual voters were not ready for the 2021 local elections is also an indication of the limited direct engagement with them, through various channels, to inform, remind and emphasise critical voting information – repeatedly, through various channels and on an ongoing basis, not only during electioneering.

Theme 3. Limited voter education influencing citizen readiness

The limited information voters have is reflected in their limited understanding of how the voting process works. Many citizens turned up at incorrect voting stations or believed their choice of candidates was limited. The education of voters was left largely to political parties in 2021, most of whom were agitating to hold rallies and other public gatherings, as they were constrained by the COVID-19 National Disaster Regulations prohibiting public gatherings. With limited information on voter rights, citizens could not ready themselves for the elections and demonstrated limited appreciation for the power of their vote in the local government elections, especially given the low turnout in 2021.

The youngest voters have not had the benefit of a public service programme, like *Khululeka*, aimed at educating them on the importance of voting in a thriving, healthy democracy, further entrenching their apathetic attitudes toward voting. Older voters may be disillusioned by the outcomes and constrained by various factors such as limited mobility and poor health. However, the 4IR has shifted the communicative power towards stakeholders, away from organisations, requiring institutions such as the IEC to engage more actively online and offline, through dialogue.

Encouraging dialogue in social media use, as Navarro et al. (2017) highlight, may benefit organisations such as the IEC, which may gain insights through user feedback that can inform stakeholder communication. The most prominent political parties can often afford the media coverage to communicate their election campaign messages, leaving the

IEC to come across as a service provider to political parties, and not the authority on preserving democracy through elections. The IEC has experienced continued budget cuts, constraining its ability to spend on voter education and other key strategic communication activities among citizens, relative to political parties. The South African Parliament, in a media statement (2022), outlined some of the key issues of the impact of IEC budget cuts on a healthy democracy, such as:

- the direct impact on the IEC's ability to run free and fair elections;
- only one registration weekend, as opposed to two in previous election cycles;
- not achieving the target set to register 25 960 000 voters on the voters' roll; and
- the dire need to increase electoral education to ensure citizen participation in the electoral process and democratic processes in general.

With limited resources, voter education through strategic stakeholder engagement activities by the IEC has lagged, reducing levels of voter readiness among South African citizens.

Theme 4. General youth apathy due to ageing leaders

The South African political leadership landscape is made up of ageing leaders within the public sector in key positions. The communication norms and competencies differ across generations, influencing the quality of engagement between citizens and leaders. The leadership of the IEC also requires age diversity to develop more relevant, engaging and timely voter information to young voters, especially as citizens become eligible to vote when they turn 18. The age disparity was a key theme for young voters who found it difficult to connect with older political leaders when looking at their needs as young people in a democratic, metropolitan society. In 2018, the Parliamentary Monitoring Group (PMG) estimated that only 6% of members of parliament were under the age of

35. In 2020, the proportion of the population between the ages of 15 and 34 was 63% (Social Progress, 2021).

When considering confidence in the democratic system and young voters' interests, the concerns expressed around the age disparity between leaders and citizens is not unique to South Africa (Lubinga & Sitto, 2021). According to the article analysis conducted for this chapter, young people failed to understand how older leaders would be able to resolve the challenges of young people. This was the case even with leaders who are considered to be 'young'. Without the IEC actively engaging new eligible voters and encouraging them to sign up for the voters' roll, young citizens have limited motivation to understand the power of their vote against the democratic implications of staying away from the polls. Actively engaging new eligible voters cannot happen without targeted strategic communication to young new voters by the IEC as a Chapter 9 institution. However, some of the data indicates that young voters may have remained away from the polls as a form of protest, although that theme was not as prominent as others highlighting shortcomings in voter information and education.

Conclusion

By choosing a digitally led communication strategy, the IEC has, over the years, shifted the responsibility for voter education communication to citizens. This is evident from the IEC's investment in a revamped website and social media channels. The vacuum left by the IEC's voter communication strategy has left citizens largely in the hands of political parties to communicate with them on the ground about elections and voting.

The IEC's pursuit of a digital-first communication strategy, with communication limited to key election periods, and limited stakeholder engagement on the importance of voting in a democracy, leaves large segments of South African citizens – namely Baby Boomers, Generation X and Generation Z – unmotivated to vote. While the COVID-19 pandemic may have threatened the 2021 local government elections, voter turnout has been on the decline for the last decade, with 2021 producing the lowest voter turnout to date. A healthy democracy rests on citizen participation, and for citizens to be active, the IEC is tasked with engaging, educating and informing them; a mandate that is not limited to periods leading up to elections only.

The IEC thus needs to re-evaluate its communication strategy as a Chapter 9 institution to ensure a more converged approach to sustained information dissemination through traditional and digital media to reach diverse citizen stakeholders. Voter education in the digital era in South Africa cannot discard previously successful voter education communication strategies using other traditional/mass mediums of communication, including popular culture, but needs to integrate new with old in a manner that ensures maximum voter reach for the IEC's communication messages.

Citizens are key stakeholders and need to have relevant voter information to participate meaningfully towards upholding a healthy democracy in South Africa through various strategic communication efforts. The IEC is a key public institution and needs to adopt strategic communication principles to build up a stronger reputation among voters and improve stakeholder relationships for improved sustained engagement to deliver on its mandate as a pivotal public sector organisation. To reach geographically dispersed citizens of different generations and diverse socio-economic circumstances, the IEC needs to revise its communication strategy to a more converged media approach to ensure good faith and balancing of stakeholder power by purposefully placing stakeholders at the centre of all communication activities.

References

Bachoo S, Hlakanyane L, Thompson S & Harmacek J. (2021). Youth Progress Index 2021: Toward Greater Impact for our Youth. Social Progress. https://www.socialprogress.org/static/ebd8cf65080c9100450f78e5754a7617/Youth_Progress_Index_2021_0.pdf

Barnett C. (2002). More than just TV: Educational broadcasting and popular culture in South Africa. In: C von Feilitzen & U Carlsson (Eds). *Children, Young People and Media Globalisation*. Goteberg, Sweden: Unesco International Clearinghouse on Children, Youth and Media.

Bekker M & Runciman C. (2022). *The youth vote in the 2021 local government elections within five metropolitan municipalities*. Konrad-Adenauer-Stiftung/Centre for Social Change. https://doi.org/10.31235/osf.io/57twh

Bekker, M., Runciman, C., & Roberts, B. (2022). Beyond the binary: examining dynamic youth voter behaviour in South Africa. *Politikon*, 49(4): 297-317. https://doi.org/10.1080/02589346.2022.2151687

Berkup SB. (2014). Working with Generations X and Y in Generation Z period: Management of different generations in business life. *Mediterranean Journal of Social Sciences*, 5(19): 218. https://doi.org/10.5901/mjss.2014.v5n19p218

BusinessTech. (2019). *More than half of South Africans are living on less than R41 a day*. 8 October. https://businesstech.co.za/news/lifestyle/345026/more-than-half-of-south-africans-are-living-on-less-than-r41-a-day/

BusinessTech. (2021). *The biggest and most popular social media platforms in South Africa, including TikTok*. 1 July. https://businesstech.co.za/news/internet/502583/the-biggest-and-most-popular-social-media-platforms-in-south-africa-including-tiktok/

Cele S & Vecchiatto P. (2021,). *South African voter turnout slumps in municipal elections*. Bloomberg. 1 November. https://www.bloomberg.com/news/articles/2021-11-01/voter-turnout-slumps-in-south-african-municipal-elections

Davis R. (2020,). *2021 local government elections likely to go ahead – and they could be the most contested ever*. Daily Maverick. 28 September. https://www.dailymaverick.co.za/article/2020-09-28-2021-local-government-elections-likely-to-go-ahead-and-they-could-be-the-most-contested-ever/

Dawkins CE. (2014). The principle of good faith: Toward substantive stakeholder engagement. *Journal of Business Ethics*, 121(2):283–295. https://doi.org/10.1007/s10551-013-1697-z

Dooms T. (2021). *Low voter turnout - Voter apathy or party apathy?* News24. 2 November. https://www.news24.com/news24/opinions/analysis/analysis-tessa-dooms-low-voter-turnout-voter-apathy-or-party-apathy-20211103

Falkheimer J & Heide M. (2018). Strategic Communication: An Introduction. London: Routledge. https://doi.org/10.4324/9781315621555

Freeman RE. (1984). *Strategic Management: A Stakeholder Approach*. Boston, Massachusetts: Pitman.

Freeman RE, Wicks AC & Parmar B. (2004). Stakeholder theory and "the corporate objective revisited". *Organization Science*, 15(3):364–369. https://doi.org/10.1287/orsc.1040.0066

Gerber J. (2021). *Constitution doesn't allow for postponement of elections – IEC tells Parliament*. News24. 7 April. https://www.news24.com/news24/southafrica/news/constitution-doesnt-allow-for-postponement-of-elections-iec-tells-parliament-20210407

Goodall K. (2022). *Why do so many South Africans choose not to vote?* [EWN?] 7 November. https://www.702.co.za/articles/459019/why-do-so-many-south-africans-choose-not-to-vote

Hallahan K, Holtzhausen D, Van Ruler B, Verčič D & Sriramesh K. (2007). Defining strategic communication. *International Journal of Strategic Communication*, 1(1):3–35. https://doi.org/10.1080/15531180701285244

Harrisberg K & Mensah K. (2022). *As young Africans push to be online, data cost stands in the way.* Thomson Reuters Foundation. 14 June. https://news.trust.org/item/20220614123128-f5ske/

Human Sciences Research Council. (2021). Election Indicators Report: National. 10 April. file:///C:/Users/kasit/Downloads/IEC%20Election%20Indicators%20National%20Report%202021.pdf

Scott D, Vawda M, Swartz S & Bhana A. (2012). Punching below their weight. Young South Africans' recent voting patterns. *HSRC Review*, 10(3). https://hsrc.ac.za/uploads/pageContent/2842/HSRC%20review%20Sept%20recent%20voting%20patterns.pdf

Tracey-Temba L. (2016). Do you want my vote? Understanding the factors that influence voting among young South Africans. Institute for Security Studies (ISS). 26 July. https://issafrica.org/about-us/press-releases/new-study-reveals-reasons-for-low-voter-turnout-among-sa-youth

Internet World Stats. (2022). *Internet users' statistics for Africa.* Internet World Stats. 25 May. https://www.internetworldstats.com/stats1.htm

Kahla C. (2019). *Report: South Africa has the most expensive internet* [infographic]. *The South African.* 18 December. https://www.thesouthafrican.com/technology/south-africa-most-expensive-internet-infographic/

Kayembe C & Nel D. (2019). Challenges and opportunities for education in the Fourth Industrial Revolution. *African Journal of Public Affairs*, 11(3):79–94.

Koko K. (2021). *Distrust of politicians the reason for low voter turnout, but voters saw elections as free and fair – HSRC.* Mail & Guardian. 3 November. Available from: https://mg.co.za/politics/2021-11-03-distrust-of-politicians-the-reason-for-low-voter-turnout-but-voters-saw-elections-as-free-and-fair-hsrc/

Lewis C. (2023). *A step closer to achieving a connected South Africa where no one is left behind.* Independent Communications Authority of South Africa (ICASA). 31 March. https://www.icasa.org.za/news/2023/a-step-closer-to-achieving-a-connected-south-africa-where-no-one-is-left-behind

Lubinga E & Sitto K. (2021). Health communication in Africa. In: W Mano & V Milton (Eds). *Routledge Handbook of African Media and Communication Studies*. Abingdon, UK: Routledge. 217–233. https://doi.org/10.4324/9781351273206-16

Malada B. (2015). Voter education in post-apartheid South Africa. In: M Ndletyana (Ed). *Institutionalising Democracy: The Story of the Electoral Commission of South Africa: 1993–2014*. Pretoria: Africa Institute of South Africa. 161–178.

Mbanyele S & Desai P. (2021). *Getting back the elusive youth vote.* Mail & Guardian (M&G). 30 October. https://mg.co.za/opinion/2021-10-30-getting-back-the-elusive-youth-vote/

Moche T. (2023). *COSATU calls on IEC, Home Affairs to ensure 2024 elections run smoothly.* SABC News. 18 April. https://www.sabcnews.com/sabcnews/cosatu-calls-on-iec-home-affairs-to-ensure-2024-elections-run-smoothly/

Mokoena S. (2021). *COVID-19 pandemic poses constitutional dilemma for local government elections.* Parliament of the Republic of South Africa. 3 August. https://www.parliament.gov.za/news/covid-19-pandemic-poses-constitutional-dilemma-local-government-elections

Mudau P. (2021). *2021 local government elections, voter education and COVID-19 in South Africa*. AfricLaw. 28 October. https://africlaw.com/2021/10/28/2021-local-government-elections-voter-education-and-covid-19-in-south-africa/

Mwareya R & Simango A. (2023). *South Africa's poorest are staying up all night for cheaper internet rates*. Rest of World. 7 February. https://restofworld.org/2023/south-africa-internet-access/

My Vote Counts. (2021). *A look at youth apathy: Why the low youth voter turnout?* 2 February. https://myvotecounts.org.za/a-look-at-youth-apathy-why-the-low-youth-voter-turnout/

Mzekandaba, S. (2021). *New tech 'catapulted' electoral management, says IEC*. ITWeb. 5 November. https://www.itweb.co.za/article/new-tech-catapulted-electoral-management-says-iec/JN1gP7OYgWwqjL6m

Navarro C, Moreno A & Al-Sumait F. (2017). Social media expectations between public relations professionals and their stakeholders: Results of the ComGap study in Spain. *Public Relations Review*, 43(4):700–708. https://doi.org/10.1016/j.pubrev.2016.12.008

Njilo N. (2021). *LISTEN | IEC says it's not to blame for poor voter turnout, set to release final results on Thursday*. TimesLive. 2 November. https://www.timeslive.co.za/politics/2021-11-02-iec-says-its-not-to-blame-for-poor-voter-turnout-set-to-release-final-results-on-thursday/

Overton-de Klerk N & Verwey S. (2013). Towards an emerging paradigm of strategic communication: Core driving forces. *South African Journal for Communication Theory and Research*, 39(3):362–382. https://doi.org/10.1080/02500167.2013.837626

Parliamentary Monitoring Group (PMG). (2018). *Youth Day – How many of our MPs qualify?* 14 June. https://pmg.org.za/blog/Youth%20Day

Parliamentary Monitoring Group (PMG). (2021). State of readiness for 2021 local government elections: engagement with DCoG, SALGA & IEC; with Deputy Minister. 10 April. https://pmg.org.za/committee-meeting/32692/

Parliamentary Monitoring Groups 9PMG). (2022). *Report on the 2021 Municipal Elections.* 10 April. https://pmg.org.za/files/220520Report_on_the_2021_Municipal_Elections_to_Portfolio_Committee_on_Home_Affairs_April_2022.pptx

Patel L & Graham L. (2019). *Study shows young South Africans have no faith in democracy and politicians.* The Conversation. 11 June. https://theconversation.com/study-shows-young-south-africans-have-no-faith-in-democracy-and-politicians-118404

Republic of South Africa. GCIS. (2022). Government Communications (GCIS) Annual Report 2021/22. https://www.gcis.gov.za/sites/default/files/docs/gcis/GCIS_Annual%20Report%202021.pdf

Republic of South Africa. Government. (n.d.). *South Africa's provinces.* https://www.gov.za/about-sa/south-africas-provinces#:~:text=Gauteng%20is%20the%20smallest%20of,of%20the%20South%20African%20population

Republic of South Africa. IEC. (2022). *About special vote.* https://www.elections.org.za/pw/SpecialVotes/About-Special-Vote

Republic of South Africa. IEC. (n.d.). *FAQ: Voter registration.* https://www.elections.org.za/content/For-Voters/FAQ--Voter-registration/

Republic of South Africa. Parliament. (2022). *Media statement: Home Affairs Committee concerned by impact of budget cuts on IEC operations.* 4 May. https://www.parliament.gov.za/press-releases/media-statement-home-affairs-committee-concerned-impact-budget-cuts-iec-operations

Republic of South Africa. Parliament. (n.d.). *How our democracy works*. https://www.parliament.gov.za/storage/app/media/EducationPubs/how-our-democracy-works.pdf

Rossouw S, Rautenbach E, Pritchard M & Sitto K. (2018). Essential digital business tools for organisations. In: M Pritchard & K Sitto (Eds). *Connect: Writing for Online Audiences*. Cape Town: Juta. 291–306.

Runciman C & Bekker M. (2021). *Here are five factors that drove low voter turnout in South Africa's 2021 elections*. The Conversation. 8 December. https://theconversation.com/here-are-five-factors-that-drove-low-voter-turnout-in-south-africas-2021-elections-173338

Salway D. (2020). *United Nations: Broadband Access is a Basic Human Right*. Lifewire. 6 March. https://www.lifewire.com/united-nations-broadband-access-is-a-basic-human-right-436784

Shenton AK. (2004). Strategies for ensuring trustworthiness in qualitative research projects. *Education for Information*: 22(2):63–75. https://doi.org/10.3233/EFI-2004-22201

Sitto K & Lubinga E. (2020). A disease of privilege? Social representations in online media about COVID-19 among South Africans during lockdown. *Papers on Social Representations*, 29(2): 6.1–6.29. https://doi.org/10.18820/24150525/Comm.v24.9

Sitto, K., Lubinga, E., Chiumbu, S., Sobane, K., & Mpofu, N. (2022). Evaluating South African and Namibian governments' use of digital media during Covid-19. *World Medical & Health Policy*, 14(2): 325–342. https://doi.org/10.1002/wmh3.507

Smillie S & Payne S. (2021). *Dismal voter turnout at South Africa's municipal polls a blow to democracy*. Daily Maverick. 2 November. https://www.dailymaverick.co.za/article/2021-11-02-dismal-voter-turnout-at-south-africas-municipal-polls-a-blow-to-democracy/

Statistics South Africa (StatsSA). (2019). *General Household Survey: 2018*. http://www.statssa.gov.za/publications/P0318/P03182018.pdf

Van Ruler B. (2018). Communication theory: An underrated pillar on which strategic communication rests. *International Journal of Strategic Communication*, 12(4):367–381. https://doi.org/10.1080/1553118X.2018.1452240

Worldometers. (2022). *South African population* (LIVE). https://www.worldometers.info/world-population/south-africa-population/

Xing B & Marwala T. (2017). Implications of the fourth industrial age on higher education. (In press.) *arXiv*:1703.09643. https://doi.org/10.25073/0866-773X/87

Zulu S. (2022). *South Africa's low voter turnout is no laughing matter: 5 crucial takeaways*. Freedom Advocacy Network. 6 June. https://freedomadvocacy.net/media/south-africas-low-voter-turnout-is-no-laughing-matter-5-crucial-takeaways

Chapter 5

Public Sector Communications and Institutionalised Bureaucracy

Margaret L. Dingalo

"I believe that a guarantee of public access to information is indispensable in the long run for any democratic society ..."
Swedish philosopher, Sissela Bok, 1982

In democratic societies, the right to access information is critical for public participation processes. Transparency, accountability and trust are closely associated with how public institutions openly and honestly engage communities on decisions that affect their lives (Hyland-Wood, Gardner, Leask & Ecker, 2021). The role that public sector communicators play in enabling participation and enables citizens to judge the work of public institutions (Canel & Sanders, 2012). Public sector communicators are tasked with facilitating communications between the public institutions and the citizens they serve (Ruijer, 2013). Communicators that work in public institutions make a valuable contribution in facilitating transparency, participation and engagement in policy-making processes, according to the Government Communications and Information Service of South Africa (GCIS, 2019).

Despite public sector communications importance to 21st century politics as a distinct area of research, it is not yet well understood its . The complexity of public sector communications and its unique environment wherein it is practised has become a subject of interest for many public sector investigations (Dingalo, 2020; Mbhele, 2016; Mukhudwana, 2014). Researchers tend to focus on communication systems (Dingalo, 2020), processes (Mbhele, 2016) and how communication is practised in public sector institutions (Mukhudwana, 2014). This chapter argues that the uniqueness of the environment within which public institutions operate – in particular, institutionalised bureaucracy – has a bearing on their communication practices.

Public Sector Institutions

Public sector institutions operate in highly regulated environments and have a responsibility to diverse stakeholders, often with divergent and competing interests. This means public institutions are under constant scrutiny, more so than their private sector counterparts. Public administration scholars advocate for the need to distinguish between public and private sector organisations particularly when conducting organisational communication research, because of the distinct differences in their operating environments (Dingalo, 2020; Mukhudwana, 2014). When compared to corporate communication, public sector communication is considered more complex because it must deal with significantly broader issues in managing the evolving expectations of different constituencies (Fairbanks, 2005). Scholars like Morudu and Halsal (2017), Allan and Heese (2017) as well as Khale and Worku (2013) lament the effects of bureaucratic systems of public institutions on the pace of implementing policy and service delivery. (;;.

Bureaucratic Theory and Its Influence on the Public Sector

The bureaucratic approach provides valuable insight into the public institutions operational environment and influences how people communicate within these organisations (Weber, 1947; Waters & Waters, 2015). Bureaucracies are large-scale organisations, which are commonly found in both the public and private sectors (Olsen, 2008). Weber's theory of bureaucratic management is the basis for the most widely recognised system of public administration (Sager & Rosser, 2021). Weber (1978) describes a bureaucracy as a highly structured, formalised organisation with defined hierarchical structures with clear rules and regulations and clear lines of authority, which govern it.

Dahlström, Lapuente and Teolle (2010) refer to bureaucracy as any large organisation of appointed officials whose primary function is to implement the policies of decision-makers. The rules that govern procedures within bureaucratic organisations, whether formal or informal, largely influence how public institutions operate (Hyden, Court & Mease, 2003). According to Weber (1947), bureaucracy plays a critical role in ensuring effective as well as efficient execution of policies. Weber (1947) highlighted three important characteristics of bureaucracies in his definition:

1. a well-defined hierarchy within the organisation;
2. a formal set of rules and regulations; and
3. clear lines of authority.

These clearly specified sources of control and decision making facilitate supervision, competency and accountability in large, complex organisations.

While scholars consider the concept of bureaucracy differently, the common point of departure among their different interpretations involves the understanding of how rules and regulations, hierarchal structures and lines of authority are used in large organisations to ensure effectiveness and efficiencies during the implementation and execution of policies (Dhalström et al., 2010; Hyden et al., 2003; Sager & Rosser, 2021). Organisations cannot always be considered as entirely bureaucratic, thus it is important to understand which bureaucratic rules and processes matter in defining bureaucracy. Among the many rules that matter, and which are relevant to this chapter are rules that govern accountability, communications and transparency. Transparency refers to the ability to guarantee information access to within the realm of accountability that public officials possess (Jaeger & Bertot, 2010). Public officials, by virtue of being serving in the public service, are accountable to constituencies they serve (Olsen, 2008). Section 32(1) of the South African Constitution, Act 108 of 1996 enshrines the right to access information on the work of public institutions, and serves as the basis for holding public officials accountable.

Bureaucratic theory makes vital assumptions about the role of hierarchical structures and regulations in managing large institutions. Weber (1947) believed that a well-defined hierarchy and clear lines of authority are crucial for effective and optimal functioning of large organisations. Establishing a set of rules that serve to codify regulations for everyone to follow not only seeks to guarantee achievement of organisational goals, it also ensures discipline and consistency in implementation.

Although these standard rules are viewed as implicitly positive, they may have unintended consequences. Weber (1978) reflected on the prospect of more red tape, that is, bureaucracy being put in place when rules get in the way of immediate goals. Weber's theory was based on his conception of rational and efficient organisations in private and public sectors, bearing in mind that scholars like Graham (1994) Kaplan (2009) highlight that there exist distinct differences in how bureaucratic principles are applied in public and private organisations;. Public sector institutions operate within a complex and highly regulated environment thus making them inflexible and unresponsive compared to their private sector counterparts (Liu & Levenshus, 2008).

Early 20th century literature on the role of bureaucracy, particularly during a period of rapid growth in Asian economies, asserts the view that the bureaucratic organisation became a key contributor to the success of many public institutions (Dahlström et al., 2010; Evans & Rauch, 1999). While scholars argue that bureaucracies differ structurally from across countries because of historical factors and administrative traditions, they acknowledge that the institutional features and the framework that guide the relationship between the state and society remain largely the same (Olsen, 2008; Peters, 2008).

African countries adopted bureaucratic models later on in their development, with the hope of reaping the benefits provided by the regularity and certainty of a system, thus enabling consistency in service provision of public institutions. Some African scholars believed initially that the bureaucratic approach had the potential to improve the social and economic conditions of African citizens (Goldsmith, 1999; Olowu, 1988; Okoli, 2010). Although this was the initial belief of providing improvement, it is notable that during the period of colonisation in Africa, bureaucratic practices that were subsequently inherited from colonial states, centred not on issues of governance and administration as expected, but rather around issues of belonging and identity. In the colonial context, bureaucracy was used to define traditional systems of governance, which in South Africa referred to an early form of government system, focused more on the protecting culture, traditions and customs (SA History, 2019). When the concept of bureaucracy started gaining traction in the industrialised world in the 19th century that the term was used universally to describe a system of public administration (Sager & Rosser, 2021).

African countries began adopting western models of governing and post-colonial African countries began viewing the concept of bureaucracy differently, appreciating its potential to enhance the effectiveness of the public sector (Olowu, 1988; Okoli, 2010). It is interesting to note that, the latest literature on African bureaucracies is characterised by increased stereotypes related to inefficient governance and poor service delivery, contrary to the original intentions of its implementation (Masuku & Jiu, 2019; Schrire, 2007; Evans & Rauch, 2000). Numerous scholars lament the negative impact of bureaucratic systems in Africa on policy implementation and service delivery (Khale & Worku, 2013; Mamogale, 2016; Allan & Heese, 2017; Morudu & Halsal, 2017).

Rules And Regulations that Govern Public Sector Institutions and Unintended Consequences on Information Dissemination and Service Delivery

South Africa has experienced an unparalleled rise in public protests over the past 10 years due to the public sector's failure to deliver services, blamed in part on process inefficiencies in public institutions (Morudu & Halsal, 2017). Morudu and Halsal (2017) establish a strong link between service delivery levels and the number of protests in South Africa. Khale and Worku (2013) point to public institutions' lack of transparency and accountability as some of the contributing factors, citing inefficient bureaucratic systems as responsible for the slow pace of service delivery in many instances.

In spite of these challenges, bureaucratic theorists continue to defend bureaucratic systems in public institutions and argue that bureaucratic rules and regulations that govern most of these institutions are necessary because they enable certainty in policy making and implementation (Cornell, Knutsen & Teorell, 2020). These scholars believe that these rules make it possible to hold public officials to account (Cameron & Milne, 2011). Public institutions need the bureaucracy to turn laws into rules in line with political intentions (Acs, 2015). This seemingly undesirable system of organisation has managed to weather relentless criticism over the years and bureaucratic theorists still see value in the system (Baekgaard, et al., 2018; Boushey & McGrath, 2017; Cornell et al., 2020).

Although public institutions still view bureaucracy as necessary to retain control and ensure consistency in policy implementation of, balanced against the unintended consequences of rigid processes on service delivery (Sager & Rosser, 2021). Public administration scholars are still convinced that regulated systems in public institutions are necessary because they directly influence efficient implementation and achievement of stated goals (Baekgaard, Mortensen & Seeberg, 2018).

The latter alludes to the importance of bureaucracy in the policy-making agenda of governments, considering the scope and scale of the work they do. The issues they deal with are broad and diverse and therefore require some level of discipline, which the use of bureaucratic rules allows (Baumgartner & Jones, 2015).

Public Sector Communication Adapting to the Changing Environment

Public sector communication

Literature on public sector communication uses different terms to refer to the exchange of information between state, its institutions and diverse stakeholders. These are terms such as *public information* (Weiss, 2002); *public sector communications* (Graber, 1992); *administrative communication* (Garnett & Kouzmin, 1997); *government public relations* (Lee, 2008); or *government communications* (Grunig, 2008; Liu, Horsley & Levenshus, 2010). To understand the concept of public sector communications requires reflecting on the term 'government' and its role as an institution in society.

Public sector communication scholars consider a government or a state as an institution through which enforcement of policies happen and people are governed (Canel & Sanders, 2012; Sanders, Canel & Hotlz-Bacha, 2011). Society inherently needs to create entities that manage shared resources and exercise authority on its behalf; in other words, people need to assign "agency or co-opt institutions that act on their behalf" (Canel & Sanders, 2012). People need to be confident that the government they choose will always act in their best interests and appoint relevant institutions to do so. The responsibility these institutions have, and their accountability to those who elected the government, is always assumed (Graber, 2003). A responsible government is regarded as one that always consults and confers powers on its public institutions to share information on how a public mandate is being executed (Sanders et al., 2011). Canel and Sanders

(2012) posits that governments are typically constituted based on people's direct or indirect consent, irrespective of political realities. That means that even the most authoritarian regimes may be regarded as a 'government' since they are also expected to govern on their people's behalf.

The term government broadly to refers to the legislative, executive and judiciary branches of the state, or more narrowly, to refer to public institutions who act on behalf of a government to execute its mandate across different spheres (Grunig & Jaatinen, 1999). In the South African context, the government is responsible for crafting legislative frameworks, which are used to regulate the work of public sector institutions and monitor implementation of its policies across different sectors (GCIS, 2018).

An effective government, through these institutions, is one that engages constantly with citizens on its policies and decisions, educating them on how the policies will impact their lives (Morudu & Halsal, 2017; Sanders et al., 2011). GCIS (2018) emphasises that government's responsibility is to provide a framework to ensure that public sector institutions constantly keep citizens informed of government implementation of its mandate. Governing is an ongoing act of communication between those that govern and those governed (Heinze, Schneider & Ferie, 2013).

Scholars offer varied perspectives on the role of public sector communications in this context. Canel and Sanders (2012: 86) define governance as "the practice of communication by public officials in order to effect change in people's lives".

Yudof (1979) focused more on the public sector communication's role in promoting democratic values in society and empowering people to make rational choices about issues that matter to them. On the other hand, Ruijer (2013) focuses on public sector's communication's constitutive role in promoting transparency and accountability, important foundational principles in a democracy. In this regard, public sector communicators play an societal important role and that public sector communication is central to a functioning democracy; that is, it cannot be separated from the act of governing (Canel & Sanders, 2012).

Literature generally assumes an automatic link between transparency in public sector communications and trust (Fairbanks, Plowman & Rawlins, 2007; Grimmelikhuisjen, 2012; Ruijer, 2013; Hyland-Wood et al., 2021). To understand what their government is up to citizens need information including how their government makes decisions that affect them (Meijer, Curtin & Hillebrandt, 2012). There is a connection between transparency of public sector communications and effective public participation in democratic societies, according to the Open Government Directive (Orszag, 2009).

Transparency in public sector communications refers to institutions enabling access to information for interested stakeholders, enabling them to participate and contribute to decision-making (Hyland-Wood et al., 2021). However, legal and regulatory controls, which public institutions rely on to regulate their operations, unfortunately tend to stand in the way of enabling access and transparency within the public sector (Pandey & Garnett, 2006). Public administration scholars including Khale and Worku (2013) as well as Dingalo (2020), highlight the complexity of public sector policies and rules, which is often blamed for delays in information sharing with citizens – as one of the challenges public sector communicators faces.;.

While positive organisational outcomes such as improved productivity, effectiveness and consistency in the execution of policies are associated with bureaucratic processes , , bureaucratic systems may also impact negatively on communication practices in public institutions (Dingalo, 2020). Despite some of these challenges, public sector communicators have a legal and moral obligation for to keep the public informed about the policies and decisions, along with their implications.

Public institutions and communicators still have to meet expectations of stakeholders who often rely on them to access information about public services (Khale & Worku, 2013; Morudu & Halsal, 2017). It is in this context that public sector communication researchers suggest that factors influencing communication practices in government institutions cannot be ignored when looking to understand public sector communications (Montsho, 2013; Mukhudwana, 2014; Dingalo, 2020). Scholars recommend, in particular, the need to recognise the uniqueness of public institutions (Mukhudwana, 2014; Dingalo, 2020). Montsho (2013) considered the influence of leadership and culture in public institutions, supporting the notion that public sector communications are complex and nuanced and must be considered with a separate lens from other communicative practices (Canel & Sanders, 2012).

Public institutions operate in a unique environment, , and in particular their institutionalised bureaucratic frameworks, have a bearing on their communication practices. Bureaucratic systems not only inhibit public sector communicators' ability to adapt but impede their flexibility to respond appropriately to changing dynamics in their environment.

Public employees who participated in the author's study raised concerns about official channels of communications, perceived as slow, outdated and irrelevant, partly due to bureaucratic processes (Dingalo, 2020). Although bureaucratic systems were perceived positively in terms of ensuring the credibility of the information they received, the employees noted that bureaucratic practices hampered their ability to obtain information needed to communicate timeously with their stakeholders.

Weberian principles of centralised control are key to the management of communications within public institutions as they are accountable to a range of stakeholders that expect public institutions to provide accurate and reliable information. Thus, the bureaucratic perspective emphasises the significance of hierarchies and centralised control, in that those in authority have to vet information before it can be released to the public. In Weber's view on bureaucracy, although the vetting of information might cause delays, gatekeeping by management is pivotal to lend credibility to communications (Weber, 1978). The institutional configuration of hierarchies symbolises the centralisation of decision-making powers and organisational planning in these institutions, and the positionality of organisational authority (Weber, 1947).

The environment is changing: Public sector communicators' adapt to the digital information age

The communication environment is changing faster than organisations as well as researchers can adapt. Public sector organisations have begun to realise that what worked during the industrial age is no longer relevant in the 21st century. The 4IR is here and new media technologies have brought about far-reaching implications for public sector communications (Davis, 2019; Murphy, 2015). Employees who work for public institutions, and citizens who traditionally rely on public sector communicators for information, can now access information about policies and their intentions from different online sources, such as websites or social media channels any time, from anywhere. Some of these online sources may not be credible because of the ability for anyone to publish content, posing a risk as institutions can potentially lose control over the narrative.

The proliferation of misinformation on some digital platforms can compromise public sector communications (Waszak, Kasprzycka-Waszak & Kubanek, 2018). On the other hand, new media technologies do offer citizens new ways of engaging with government.

These challenges and opportunities enjoin public sector communicators and researchers to review their approaches and methods as they seek to understand changing dynamics in the environment and the implications of these on the work they do (Zerfass & Viertmann, 2016; Winkler & Etter, 2018; Davis, 2019). The traditional top-down and one-to-many communication approaches that organisations relied on in the past to control the narrative about their organisations have been replaced by many-to-many approaches (Falkheimer & Heide, 2015). Managing control over organisational messages is becoming more and more difficult (Murphy, 2015; Winkler & Etter, 2018) because of the interactivity of new media channels. Seeking to understand organisational communication is no longer about understanding only the deliberately planned and controlled communication processes; it is also about understanding all forms of communications, including communication processes over which organisations have no control (Winkler & Etter, 2018). In their analysis, public sector communicators and researchers thus need to look beyond formalised communications to consider conversations that take place outside organisations (Schafer & Fahnrich, 2020).

Given that new media technologies have opened new spaces for citizen participation, the pace of these shifts and the disruptions they bring – whether beneficial or destabilising – means it is no longer business as usual for public sector communications (Davis, 2019; Schafer & Fahnrich, 2020). The implications for emerging digital technologies on public sector communications and public participation processes need to be explored further (Burgess & Green, 2018; Dunan, 2020).

Methodology

The study sought to explore employee experiences with the communications in a state institution. An explanatory sequential mixed-method design was employed. First, online questionnaires – to explore employee perceptions and attitudes towards communication, as well as to test the association between their personal view of communications, and how it affects their ability to do their jobs – were administered to 109 selected individuals. In the second phase, semi-structured qualitative interviews with nine purposefully selected individuals were conducted, and participants were made up of public sector communicators of three lower-level employees, three middle managers and three senior managers. The aim was to provide more in-depth insights.

Findings indicate that 90% of survey respondents had a degree or higher qualification, while 75% had six years' experience in the organisation and 63% were on a management or higher level.

All nine employees who participated in the interviews had degrees or higher qualifications, seven had more than six years' experience and all three job levels were equally represented. In short, they all had sufficient experience and understanding to provide credible input to the study.

Discussion

The survey and interviews findings indicate that employees could identify 17 official methods used by their organisation to communicate with employees. When testing for general awareness and use of the various methods, survey and interviews data suggests that while employees are generally aware of – and use most of – these sources to access information, it takes time for the information disseminated through these channels to reach them, because of bureaucratic systems. This delay explains why they often rely on the grapevine or other informal channels of communication to access information necessary to carry out their work. 93% of survey respondents indicated reliance on communication with co-workers for work-related information ($n=4.03$). Interview participants explained that they trust information received from co-workers because they consider it useful as some of the participants articulated:

> "I consider information I receive from colleagues useful because, in most cases, information that is shared with us on official platforms is old news; we hear about these things in the corridors before we hear about them from official channels." (Participant 5, lower-level employee)

"It takes a while for a newsletter, which we use to update staff on important matters, to be compiled and distributed." (Participant 6, senior manager)

Interview participants expressed dissatisfaction with information received from their official channels for different reasons. Notwithstanding that they are not regularly updated, and official channels are slow in disseminating information, in some instances they carry content that is considered irrelevant to the work they do, further explaining reliance on unofficial channels as another participant intimated:

"Newsletters like 'KM' newsletter, are not relevant. It is as if they use these platforms just to tick the boxes without putting thought to it. The information they share is not relevant to me personally." (Participant 1, middle manager)

It is expected to have this type of result in institutions where communication is hierarchical as a norm as the information has to go through various levels within the organisation to be vetted before it can be shared with employees, according to Dahlström (2009). Literature highlights the unintended consequences of bureaucratic systems on internal communications function in state institutions and by extension, the negative impact it has on service delivery (Allan & Heese, 2017; Morodu & Halsal, 2017; Khale & Worku, 2013). Results from the survey and interviews data indicate that informal communications in this instance carries greater credibility. Wagner (2013) concludes that particularly in public sector organisations informal networks tend to be more popular because of their bureaucratic systems. Informal networks enable employees to support one another in executing their duties, and they help them make sense of the world around them by providing them much needed relief from their day-to-day challenges of work (Conrad & Poole, 2002).

When probed about the reliability of official channels of communication, results show that all survey respondents $n=40(100\%)$ identified departmental and staff meetings as most reliable compared to other channels. Interview participants offered more clarity on why that is the case. Employees consider these two platforms as more reliable in conveying important information about their work in particular. Interview participants further reveal that when it comes to information that has to be shared with external stakeholders, they trust information received from the meetings convened by the relevant minister, director general (DG) and departmental heads because of their position in the organisation. This finding highlights a culture equating rank and position with trust, especially in bureaucratic organisations. People higher up in the organisation are considered as an authority on communication matters. This supports Weber's (1978) notion that emphasises the important role those in authority play in lending credibility to communications in bureaucratic organisations. The gate-keeping role they play in vetting information before it can be shared with the public means that employees can trust that it is credible.

Interview participants find staff addresses from the minister, DG or heads of departments as constructive as they are often used to share information about the organisational vision as indicated in the following comments:

> "As a staff member, I sometimes get information through interactions with the DG or the minister. I consider them reliable because most often some of the information we receive is referenced from existing government policies, and one would know about them already." (Participant 2, lower-level employee)

> "I find staff addresses by the minister every year where she communicates her plan and what is expected from us very useful." (Participant 3, middle manager).

> "We also have directorate and staff meetings, where we address all work-related stuff and issues that affect people working in that directorate." (Participant 4, senior manager)

These findings indicate that the bureaucracy is viewed as holding some benefit and is appreciated by the participants when it comes to ensuring credibility of the information received from the organisation. GCIS (2018), as the officially recognised coordinator of public sector communications in South Africa, emphasises the importance of ensuring that information shared with stakeholders on behalf of state institutions is not only credible but can be trusted. Dissatisfaction occurs when the bureaucracy impedes employees' ability to access timely information in order to be able to carry out their duties (Allan & Heese, 2017; Khale & Worku, 2013). The bureaucratic processes are often blamed for the delay in updating and disseminating required information, which, in essence, nullifies the notion of its credibility or usefulness.

The levels of employee satisfaction with communication generally was also explored. Evidence shows that employees enjoy varying degrees of satisfaction with various aspects of communication in their organisation. In this context, four constructs were assessed:

1. communication climate;
2. quality of communications;
3. communication with supervisors; and
4. communication with co-workers.

The participants' greatest area of satisfaction indicated was with co-worker communications ($n=3.99$). This finding underscores the importance of the relationships employees have with one another, and how these relationships affect their perceptions of their organisations. The bureaucratic nature of public institutions forces employees to seek alternative ways of accessing information, especially on work-related matters where decisions have to be made on the spot, as Wagner (2013) suggested. Colleagues are often viewed as knowledgeable about what is going on in their own organisation. Muller, Bezuidenhout & Jooste (2006: 305) suggest – arguably – that communication between co-workers is just as important to organisations as 80% of information communicated this way contains business-related politics, and is considered to be 90% correct on detail. Conrad and Poole (2002: 74) suggest that this form of employee communication is considered more accurate, and is more trusted because it is voluntary, uninhibited and uninfluenced by organisational power relations.

Results overall indicate that survey respondents expressed the most satisfaction with co-workers ($n=3.78$), with the least satisfaction expressed with immediate supervisors ($n=3.11$). This finding is particularly interesting, although communication from authority figures such as the minister, the DG and heads of departments is valued, communication with immediate supervisors, not so much. Interview participants explained that it is because of the one-directional nature of communications from supervisors that limits their ability to give input on issues that matter to them, or more importantly, their involvement in decision-making as aptly articulated here:

> "Communication is typically one way; people are not given an opportunity to give input ... as individuals were treated as objects." (Participant 7, lower-level employee)

> "I think, having more engagements with staff where they are given an opportunity to ask questions will help a lot." (Participant 8, middle manager)

> "The concern I have is when staff in the lower levels do not engage with their supervisors." (Participant 9, senior manager)

This finding is in line with the top-down nature of communications in bureaucratic organisations. In bureaucracies a top-down structure creates logical lines of reporting. Communication flows from the top to the bottom with vetting of information occurring at every step, so as to ensure credibility as Weber (1978) proposed. Public sector entities in South Africa, like other bureaucracies, are expected to operate within the prescribed framework on communication matters; observing protocols is one such measure (GCIS, 2018). Sebastiaõ, Zulato and Trindade (2017) highlight the influence of culture and leadership styles on communication processes in public sector institutions.

Conclusion

State institutions operate in a unique environment which cannot be ignored when seeking to understand public sector communications. Of particular importance is the influence of the bureaucratic systems on the effectiveness of the institutions' internal communication practices. The complexity of government communication, and the context within which it is practised, will continue to be a subject of interest for many public sector researchers given its importance for 21st century politics.

The advent of the 4IR and the innovations brought about by new media technologies have shattered stereotypes about the need for bureaucracy in state institutions as employees and citizens become exposed to alternative ways of sourcing information, some of which might not be credible. The fragmented multimedia environment and the culture of social media are forcing researchers to review their assumptions and approaches and experiment with new theories, conceptualisations and methods.

References

Acs A. (2015). Which statute to implement: Strategic timing by regulatory agencies? *Journal of Public Administration Research and Theory*, 26(3):493–506. https://doi.org/10.1093/jopart/muv018

Allan K & Heese K. (2017). Understanding why service delivery protests take place and who is to blame. Municipal IQ. https://www.municipaliq.co.za/publications/articles/sunday_indep.pdf

Baekgaard M, Mortensen PB & Seeberg HB. (2018). The bureaucracy and the policy agenda. *Journal of Public Administration Research and Theory*, 28(2):239–253. https://doi.org/ 10.1093/jopart/mux045

Baumgartner FR & Jones BD. (2015). The Politics of Information: Problem Definition and the Course of Public Policy in America. Chicago, USA: University of Chicago Press.

Bok S. (1982). *Secrets: On the Ethics of Concealment and Revelation.* New York, USA: Oxford University Press

Boushey GT & McGrath RJ. (2017). Experts, amateurs and bureaucratic influence in the American States. *Journal of Public Administration Research and Theory*, 27(1):85–103. https://doi.org/10.1093/jopart/muw038

Burgess J & Greene J. (2018). *YouTube: Online Video and Participatory Culture.* 2nd Edition. Digital Media and Society Series. Cambridge, UK: Polity Press.

Cameron R & Milne C. (2011). Representative bureaucracy in the South African public service. *African Journal of Public Affairs*, 4(2):12–32.

Canel MJ & Sanders K. (2012). Government communication: An emerging field of communication research. In: HA Semetko & M Scammel (Eds). *The SAGE Handbook of Political Communication.* London, Thousand Oaks, New Delhi, Singapore: SAGE Publications

Conrad C & Poole MS. (2002). Strategic Organizational Communication in a Global Economy. Orlando, USA: Harcourt.

Cornell A, Knutsen CH & Teorell J. (2020). Bureaucracy and growth. *Comparative Political Studies*, 53(14):2246–2282. https: doi.org/10.1177/0010440209I226

Dahlström C. (2009). The bureaucratic politics of the welfare state crisis: Sweden in the 1990s. *Governance*, 22(2):217–238. https://doi.org/10.1111/j.1468-0491.2009.01433.x

Dahlström C, Lapuente V & Teolle J. (2010). Dimensions of bureaucracy: A cross-national data set on the structure and behaviour of public administration. Gothenburg, Sweden: University of Gothenburg. Paper presented, 13 October.

Davis A. (2019). *Political Communication: A New Introduction for Crisis Times*. Cambridge, UK. Polity Press.Dingalo ML. (2020). Understanding Communication Experiences and Job Satisfaction of Employees at a State Institution. Master's thesis. Pretoria: University of South Africa.

Dunan A. (2020). Government communications in digital era: Public relations and democracy. *Jurnal Pekommas*, 5(1):71–80. https://doi.org/10.30818/jpkm.2020.2050108

Evans P & Rauch JE. (1999). Bureaucracy and growth: A cross-national analysis of the effects of "Weberian" sates structure and economic growth. *American Sociological Review*, 64(4):748–765. https://doi.org/10.1177/000312249906400508

Evans P & Rauch JE. (2000). Bureaucratic structure and bureaucratic performance in less developed countries. *Journal of Public Economics*, 75(1):49–71. https://doi.org/10.1016/S0047-2727(99)00044-4

Fairbanks J. (2005). Transparency in the Government Communication Process: The Perspective of Government Communicators. PhD thesis. Hawaii, USA: Brigham Young University.

Fairbanks J, Plowman DK & Rawlins BL. (2007). Transparency in government communication. *Journal of Public Affairs*, 7(1):23–37. https://doi.org/10.1002/pa.245

Falkheimer J & Heide M. (2015.) Strategic communication in participatory culture: From one-and two-way communication to participatory communication through social media. *The Routledge handbook of strategic communication*. New York, NY: Routledge. 337–347.

Garnett JL & Kouzmin A. (1997). *A Handbook of Administrative Communication*. New York, USA: Marcel Dekker.

Gelders D & Ihlen O. (2010). Mending the gap: Applying a service-marketing model into government policy communications. *Government Information Quarterly*, 27(1):34–40. https://doi.org/10.1016/j.giq.2009.05.005

Goldsmith A. (1999). Africa's overgrown state reconsidered: Bureaucracy and economic growth. *World Politics*, 51(4):520–546. https://doi.org/10.1017/S0043887100009242

Graber DA. (1992). The Power of Communication: How Organizations Manage Information. Washington DC, USA: CQ Press.

Graber DA. (2003). The Power of Communication: Managing Information in Political Organisations. Washington, DC, USA: CQ Press. https://doi.org/10.4135/9781483329949

Graham P. (1994). Marketing in the public sector: Inappropriate or merely difficult? *Journal of Marketing Management*, 10(5): 364–537. https://doi.org/10.1080/0267257X.1994.9964284

Grimmelikhuisjen S. (2012). Transparency and trust: An experimental study of online disclosure and trust on government. Master's thesis. Netherlands: Utrecht University.

Grunig JE. (2008). Public Relations Management in Government and Business. New York, USA: CRC Press. https://doi.org/10.1201/b15784-4

Grunig JE & Jaatinen M. (1999). Strategic, symmetrical public relations in government: From pluralism to societal corporatism. *Journal of Communication Management*, 3(3):218–234. https://doi.org/10.1108/eb026049

Heinze J, Schneider H & Ferie F. (2013). Mapping the consumption of government communication: A qualitative study in Germany. *Journal of Public Affairs*, 13(4): 370–383. https://doi.org/10.1002/pa.1483

Hyden G, Court J & Mease K. (2003). The bureaucracy and governance in 16 developing countries. New York, USA: United Nations. World Governance Survey Discussion paper, 7 July.

Hyland-Wood B, Gardner J, Leask J & Ecker UKH. (2021). Toward effective government communication strategies in the era of COVID 19. *Humanities and Social Sciences Communications*, 8(30). https://doi.org/10.1057/s41599-020-00701-w

Jaeger PT & Bertot JC. (2010). Transparency and technical change: Ensuring equal and sustained public access to government information. *Government Information Quarterly*, 27(4):371–376. https://doi.org/10.1016/j.giq.2010.05.003

Kaplan AM. (2009). The increasing importance of public marketing: Explanations, applications and limits of marketing within public administration. *European Management Journal*, 27(3):197–212. https://doi.org/10.1016/j.emj.2008.10.003

Khale S & Worku Z. (2013). Factors that affect municipal service delivery in Gauteng and North West provinces of South Africa. *African Journal of Science, Technology, Innovation and Development*, 5(1):61–70. https://doi.org/10.1080/20421338.2013.782143

Lee M. (2008). *Government Public Relations: A Reader*. Boca Raton, USA: Taylor & Francis Group.

Liu BF & Levenshus AB. (2008). Testing the government communication decision wheel: Toward a new theory of government public relations. *58th Annual International Communication Association Conference*. Montreal, Canada. Paper presented, 22–26 May.

Liu BF, Horsley JS & Levenshus AB. (2010). Government and corporate communication practices: Do the differences matter? *Journal of Applied Communication Research*, 38(2):189–213. https://doi.org/10.1080/00909881003639528

Mamogale MJ. (2016). Examining Bureaucratic Performance of South African Local Government: Local Municipalities in Limpopo Province. PhD thesis. Johannesburg: Witwatersrand University.

Masuku M & Jiu N. (2019). Public service delivery in South Africa: The political influence at local government level. *Journal of Public Affairs*, 19(4): e1935. https://doi.org/10.1002/pa.1935

Mbhele S. (2016). Internal Communication in Achieving Employee Engagement Within a South African Government Department. Master's thesis. Pretoria: University of Pretoria.

Meijer AJ, Curtin DM & Hillebrandt M. (2012). Open government: Connecting vision and voice. *International Review of Administrative Sciences*, 78(1):10–29. https://doi.org/10.1177/0020852311429533

Montsho RK. (2013). Exploring Internal Communication within the Government Communication and Information System. Master's thesis. Pretoria: University of Pretoria.

Morudu HD & Halsal J. (2017). Service delivery protests in South African municipalities: An exploration using principal component regression and 2013 data. *Cogent Social Sciences*, 3(1):1–15. https://doi.org/10.1080/23311886.2017.1329106

Mukhudwana RF. (2014). Investigating Communication Management by Government Departments in the Kwazulu-Natal Province in South Africa. PhD thesis. Pretoria. University of Pretoria.

Muller ME, Bezuidenhout MC & Jooste K. (2006). *Healthcare Service Management*. Cape Town: Juta.

Murphy P. (2015). Contextual distortion: Strategic communication versus the networked nature of nearly everything. In: DR Holtzhausen & A Zerfass (Eds). *The Routledge Handbook of Strategic Communication*. New York and London: Routledge: 113–126.

Okoli F. (2010). An overview of conventional contract system and private public partnership. *Workshop organized by the Department of Public Administration and local government*. Enugu, Nigeria. Paper presented. 15–17 November.

Olowu D. (1988). Bureaucratic morality in Africa. *International Science Review*, 9(3):215–229. https://doi.org/10.1177/019251218800900306

Olsen JP. (2008). The ups and downs of bureaucratic organization. *Annual Review of Political Science*, 11:13–37. https://doi.org/10.1146/annurev.polisci.11.060106.101806

Orszag PR. (2009). *Open government directive.* https://obamawhitehouse.archives.gov/open/documents/open-government-directive

Pandey SK & Garnett JL. (2006). Exploring public sector communication performance: Testing a model and drawing implications. *Public Administration Review*, 66(1):37–51. https://doi.org/10.1111/j.1540-6210.2006.00554.x

Peters BG. (2008). The Napoleonic tradition. *International Journal of Public Sector Management*, 21:118–132. https://doi.org/10.1108/09513550810855627

Republic of South Africa. Government Communication and Information System (GCIS). (2018). Government Communication Policy. https://www.gcis.gov.za/sites/default/files/government%20Communication%20policy% Cabinet%20/Approved%20Oct%202018.pdf

Republic of South Africa. Government Communication and Information System (GCIS). (2018a). About us. https://www.gcis.gov.za

Republic of South Africa. Government Communication and Information System (GCIS). (2018b). Government Communication Policy. https://www.gcis.gov.za/sites/default/files/government%communication%20policy%online%20cabinetapproved.pdf

Republic of South Africa. Government Communication and Information System. (GCIS). (2019). Government Communicators Handbook. https//: www.gcis.gov.za/docs/pdf.

Ruijers HJM. (2013). *Proactive transparency and government communication in the USA and the Netherlands*. PhD thesis. Richmond, USA: Commonwealth University of Virginia.

Sager F & Rosser C. (2021). Weberian bureaucracy. In: WR Thompson (Ed). Oxford Research Encyclopedia of Politics. Oxford University Press. https://doi.org/10.1093/acrefore/9780190228637.013.166

Sanders K, Canel MS & Hotz-Bacha C. (2011). Communicating government: A three country comparison of how governments communicate with citizens. *The International Journal of Press and Politics*, 16(4):523–547. https://doi.org/10.1177/1940161211418225

Schafer MS & Fahnrich B. (2020). Communicating science in organisational contexts: Toward an organizational turn in science communication research. *Journal of Communication Management*, 24(3):137–154. https://doi.org/10.1108/JCOM-04-2020-0034

Schrire R. (2007). South Africa: Bureaucracy and the process of reform. *Journal of Contemporary African Studies*, 5(1-2):145–164. https://doi.org/10.1080/02589008608729458

Sebastiaõ SP, Zulato G & Trindade A. (2017). Internal communication and organisational culture interplay in the view of the Portuguese communication consultant. *Public Relations Review*, 43(4):863–871. https://doi.org/10.1016/j.pubrev.2017.05.006

SA History (2019). *The role of traditional leaders during apartheid*. https://www.sahistory.org.za/article/role-traditional-leaders-during-apartheid

Wagner JD. (2013). *Communication Satisfaction of Professional Nurses Working in Selected Public Health Care Services in the City of Johannesburg*. Master's thesis. Pretoria: University of South Africa.

Waszak PM, Kasprzycka-Waszak W & Kubanek A. (2018). The spread of media fake news on social media: The pilot quantitative study. *Health Policy Technical*, 7(2):115-118. https://doi.org/10.1016/j.hlpt.2018.03.002

Waters T & Waters D. (2015). *Weber's Rationalism and Modern Society*. New York, USA: Palgrave MacMillan. https://doi.org/10.1057/9781137365866

Weber M. (1947). *Theory of Social and Economic Organisation*. New York, USA: Oxford University Press.

Weber M. (1978). *Economy and Society: An Outline of Interpretive Sociology*. Berkeley, USA: California University Press.

Weiss JA. (2002). Public information. In: LM Salamon (Ed). *The Tools of Government: A Guide to the New Governance*. Oxford, UK: Oxford University Press. 611–645.

Winkler P & Etter M. (2018). Strategic communication and emergence: A dual narrative framework. *International Journal of Strategic Communication*, 12(4):382–398. https://doi.org/10.1080/1553118X.2018.1452241

Yudof MG. (1979). When governments speak: Towards a theory of government expression and the first amendment. *Texas Law Review*, 57: 865–917.

Zerfass A & Viertmann C. (2016). Multiple voices in corporations and the challenge for strategic communication. In: M Brown, K Alm & S Royseng (Eds). *Communication and Freedom of Expression in Organizations*. Oslo, Norway: Capperen Damm. 44–63.

Chapter 6

The Public Sector Communication of Development Programmes for Small Businesses: An Implementation Challenge in South Africa

Maphelo Malgas *and Andiswa Mrasi*

According to Canel and Luoma-aho (2018), communication is the exchange of information through symbols; when that information is arranged into a body of thinking, it becomes knowledge that enables a clear understanding of a specific circumstance. Furthermore, public sector functions within their cultural and/or political environments are made possible by goal-oriented communication within, between, and with their stakeholders. Essentially, public sector communication is aimed at establishing and maintaining public good, as well as ensuring trust between communities with various channels that promote public participation. The authors do, however, caution that effective communication necessitates engagement with stakeholders, and the value of the engagement is derived from its capacity to facilitate participation and comprehend dialogic dynamics. As a concept, engagement should be viewed as a tool of achieving greater equality in the relationship between the public and government agencies (Canel & Luoma-aho, 2018). Additionally, public sector entities exist to ensure the effective functioning of society in accordance organisations with government-established principles, according to Vuori, Aher, and Kylänen, (2020). The authors further suggest that public sector entities that organisations public sector entities must strike a balance between democratic communication goals and, in the case of public institutions tasked with small business development, involve these enterprises as their primary stakeholders in their communications (Vuori et al, 2020).

Canel and Luoma-aho (2018) further noted that public sector communication should be viewed as a tool that offers a long-term view of the organisation and its functions, giving stakeholders a comprehension of the context and environment and ultimately leading to the creation of cooperative and realistic attitudes. Also, the authors stated that public sector communication has been largely regarded as inefficient, resulting citizens frequently disregarding government and public sector behaviour guidelines on various issues such as waste management, safety, and health. Consequently, public sector entities must comprehend the evolving needs of stakeholders for public sector communication to succeed (Canel & Luoma-aho, 2018).

Vuori, et al (2020) stated that public sector entities responsibility for the promotion of small enterprises is to create an enabling environment that will empower them to realize their goals. The author also emphasizes the fact that there is no one definition of "good public sector communication", as the messaging sent by public sector entities reflects the cultural and historical legacy of the society in which they operate. Since models typically work well in one social context but not another, we offer a public sector communication model in this chapter that can be utilized by public sector entities responsible for the development of small businesses in South Africa. According to Kaidi Aher (2020), successful public sector communication is a challenge on a worldwide scale, as such, developing a model that is specific to a given environment requires a deeper understanding of that setting.

This chapter aims to provide a comprehensive, setting-specific view of current public sector communication focusing on entities charged with the development of small business in South Africa, such as the Small Enterprise Development Agency (SEDA) and Small Enterprise Finance Agency (SEFA).

We focus on public sector entities tasked with the development of small businesses in South Africa after considering the country's extensive public sector communication system. Next, we provide an overview of the small business environment in South Africa, emphasizing the challenges that these businesses face, particularly in the wake of the COVID-19 pandemic. In addition, we examine how the central government supports the growth of small, medium, and micro enterprises (SMMEs) in South Africa, referring to a case study that reveals how public sector entities failed to communicate with small businesses about support programmes during the COVID-19 pandemic. The chapter concludes with a proposed public sector communication framework that can assist in communicating support programmes for small businesses in South Africa.

Methodology

Using a case study design and a qualitative research methodology, this study aimed to provide a comprehensive knowledge of the settings of township SMMEs in South Africa and the ways in which public sector communication failed to support these businesses both during and after COVID-19. Additionally, the study sought to identify key stakeholders and their roles when the post-COVID-19 relief programmes for SMMEs. Lastly, the study, through a qualitative desktop data collection method, the study explored public sector communication during COVID-19 and how SMMEs regarded the programmes meant to support them.

Public Sector Communication Framework

According to Luoma-aho and Canel (2020), public sector entities are supported by the lawful authority of the central government and are dependent on the consent of the public, in a democratic environment to function. Operating at several levels—national, provincial, and local in South Africa, for example—these public sector entities offer services that are paid for by taxes and other public funds.

Since public sector entities and the media work together to promote their programmes and occasionally get unfavorable media coverage, there is a constant demand for transparency from these bodies (Luoma-aho & Canel, 2020). In addition to being subject to public scrutiny and being more restricted by legal and regulatory frameworks, public sector entities are expected to be highly accountable.

In South Africa, public sector entities charged with the advancement of small businesses account to a parliamentary portfolio committee that has oversight on all entities falling under the Department of Small Business Development (DSBD). The portfolio committee monitors and evaluates the effectiveness of public sector entities' communication about programmes through public engagement with individual and small business representative bodies, community engagement programmes in various local municipalities, and parliamentary committee meetings in parliament.

A communication framework (Table 3) was devised by the parliamentary committee of the DSBD with the intention of visually delineating the intended initiatives pertaining to the small business development programmes. Furthermore, the framework analysing both the current status quo and the desired outcomes.

Though the framework is relevant, it is too generic to work in communicating development programmes targeted at small businesses. For instance, a framework ideally represents an approach diagrammatically. Thus, the DSBD parliamentary committee framework lacks detail on the most critical aspect, which is "the main channel for communicating SMME development programmes". We must reflect often on the role of the DSBD, which is to support the development, growth, and sustainability of SMMEs, as they are known to be key economic drivers.

Government and development partners should work together to better coordinate the development of inclusive SMMEs, relevant policies, and the methods of delivery, utilizing an impactful model. A methodology that enables

Development Programmes for Small Businesses

Table 3: Communication framework (DSBD parliamentary committee)

Outcome: Programmeme areas	Outputs: Programmeme areas	Project activities to achieve outputs	Target groups	Institution Responsible (implementing Agency – Lead and Support)	Current situation and risks
Partnerships outreach for SMME growth	Strengthen partnerships to identify new projects and investments for SMME growth and competitiveness	Establish a business and government working group at national and provincial levels	Small enterprises; Entrepreneurs	DSBD; Relevant agencies; Organised business	The trust deficit between business and government
Intergovernmental and business dialogue to assist the delivery of the NISED master plan and the National Summits objectives		Improve coordination to support the implementation of Presidential Summit resolutions	SMMEs and cooperatives	DSBD; Government; Private sector; Organised business	Failure of parties to engage
		SMMEs and cooperatives, and private sector	DSBD; New Agency; Government; Private sector; Organised business	The trust deficit between business and government	

(Source: Adapted from DSBD, 2022: 73)

DBSD to collaborate with small company forums for enhanced service synergy and more efficient resource use for expanded outreach is necessary for the organisation to have a significant impact. Improved coordination of SMME support should also result from significant involvement in the biannual national presidential summits and provincial conferences. To this end, we recommend a model that public sector entities under DBSD can use to effectively communicate their developmental programmes aimed at supporting SMME growth and sustainability.

The Small Business Landscape in South Africa

In South Africa, small businesses are defined as companies with fewer than 200 employees under the National Small Business Act (NSBA) 102 of 1996. The Act aims to establish favourable conditions for small enterprises to function better. In addition to Act 102, the South African government has established several small business-supporting entities and agencies including SEDA, SEFA, the Industrial Development Corporation (IDC), and the Centre for Small Business Promotion (CSBP).

Bvuma and Marnewick (2020) noted that SMMEs in South Africa face particular contextual issues because they operate in a variety of contexts, including cities and townships. The authors also point out that SMMEs' significance and the part they play in spurring economic progress are recognized by economies all over the world. Additionally, SMMEs can be extremely helpful in reducing some of the economic challenges facing South Africa, such as unemployment, poverty, and inequality, as stated in the country's National Development Plan (NDP) (National Planning Committee, 2011).

However, Makwara (2022) notes that globally, and in South Africa, there is yet to be a commonly agreed definition of a small business because of the ambiguities of how and what dimensions are appropriate for measuring business size. Furthermore, Makwara (2022) states that "in South Africa, a small business is officially defined as a separate and distinct business entity, including cooperative enterprises and non-governmental organisations, managed by one owner or more, including its branches or subsidiaries, if any, and is predominantly carried on in any sector or subsector of the economy". Adding complexity to the South African situation is that an SMME is regarded as either a formal or an informal business. The difference is that while formal businesses are monitored, protected, and taxed by the government, informal SMMEs are not government-regulated (Bvuma & Marnewick, 2020).

Formal SMMEs are complex, well-established, licensed firms that are primarily found in urban areas. In comparison to informal SMMEs, they are typically more technologically advanced, especially when it comes to those who operate in township and rural areas (Bvuma & Marnewick, 2020). The many ICT adoption frameworks that are currently in place will not be effective for township SMMEs due to their unique characteristics, as there are limited insights on ICT adoption frameworks for these businesses (Bvuma & Marnewick, 2020).

Agbobli, Oni, and Fatoki (2017), however, believe that a drastic strategy is necessary given the study's findings on the significant incidence of unofficial small enterprises in South Africa. They add that a great deal of work needs to be put into the SMME sector to transform the largely unofficial and necessity-driven small businesses into sustainable and profitable businesses. Serviço Brasileiro de Apoio às Micro e Pequenas Empresas (SEBRAE), the Brazilian counterpart of SEDA, has demonstrated remarkable success in assisting small businesses in formalizing their operations and transforming them into thriving, economically sustainable enterprises. To move most the nation's small enterprises into the commercial sphere, the South African government should tenaciously pursue a formalization policy in collaboration with NGOs that support small businesses.

Other SMME issues such not having access to bank credit financing will be resolved by entering the commercial sector (Agbobli, Oni & Fatoki, 2017). Furthermore, as formalization has many advantages, registered SMMES may also be eligible for state guarantees for lending facilities and formalized training in a range of business-related subjects. It is a definite way to boost the small business sector's efficiency and, in the end, address the persistent challenges of poverty, inequality, and unemployment (Agbobli et al., 2017). The goal of provincial governments, municipal and provincial SMME departments, as well as other entities is to assist small business operations; however, small businesses continue to perform appallingly and have not significantly improved South Africa's economic challenges despite the government's elaborate interventionist efforts (Agbobli et al., 2017).

According to SEFA, SMMEs and cooperatives are facing compounding challenges, and the COVID-19 pandemic had a severe impact on them, the full extent of which is still becoming apparent (SEFA, 2022). SEFA has further noted that the number of SMMEs in South Africa declined by 11% (or 289 000) year-on-year, from 2.61 million to 2.33 million in the first quarter of 2021, while "jobs declined by 6.2% over the same period" (SEFA, 2022). SEFA has stated that "The South African economy recovered somewhat in 2021, growing at 4.9% after the previous year's contraction of 6.4%" (SEFA, 2022). However, SEFA has also observed that the pace of recovery has slowed with the war in Ukraine and related global volatility and supply chain disruptions, and oil and food price inflation (SEFA, 2022).

Wegerif (2022) claims that the agriculture sector's robust macroeconomic performance in 2020 and the first part of 2021—along with robust export growth—covered the difficulties that many farmers were experiencing because of COVID-19. The special circumstances of black farmers and the production and distribution networks they are a part of were not sufficiently considered by the government's COVID-19 actions or the support programmes implemented to lessen the disease's detrimental consequences. Notably, the official sector frequently ignores the informal sector of small businesses, even though they play a critical role in food systems (Wegerif, 2022).

Undoubtedly, the advent of COVID-19 took the entire global economy by surprise. The lockdowns that followed caused significant disruptions to the networks of SMMEs, which persisted in showing up as a lack of effective support to address the impacts faced by black farmers (Wegerif, 2022) and informal SMMEs in general. After the devastating effects of the COVID-19 pandemic, it is more important than ever to devise strategies aimed at supporting SMMEs. To guarantee the revival and long-term viability of the SMME sector in the nation, strong plans based on efficient public sector communication must be created.

Informal SMME Post-COVID-19 Study in Delft and Mfuleni Townships

The importance of government development entities communicating about development programmes to small businesses cannot be overanalysing. However, there seems to be poor communication about government programmes designed to improve small business in South Africa. To stimulate economic recovery, the South African government made a commitment to help SMMEs that have been severely impacted by the pandemic to foster economic expansion and generate employment opportunities.

Amidst the COVID-19 lockdown period, the DSBD announced a collaboration with Nedbank to help SMMEs under SEFA's Credit Guarantee Scheme. The initiative exclusively focused on helping SMMEs owned by South African citizens, enabling them to endure the challenging lockdown period where all businesses were required to close as mandated by government.

In one project, we partnered with SEDA in the Western Cape to implement the post-COVID-19 relief grant project in the areas of Delft and Mfuleni, working with 52 small business owners. None of these business owners benefited from the COVID-19 relief funds because either they did not meet the criteria set by the government or they were not aware of the relief funds because of limited communication.

As for those who were aware, they were not able to submit the required documents because of the cumbersome nature of the documentation – including language barriers. Battersby (2020) argued that the South African government's lockdown regulations demonstrated a considerable bias which favoured the well-established formal businesses, while pushing towards formalisation of the informal sector through the conditions set as to who was allowed to benefit as well as conditions placed on the relief measures communicated.

As such, even though the communicated objective of the SEDA project was to assist informal SMMEs in completing the required documentation, the project itself was clearly not designed for informal businesses as some of the requirements included company certification documents, business bank accounts, and South African Revenue Service (SARS) income tax. To date, none of the 52 informal businesses received support or communication, even after all documentation was submitted. Instead, these informal businesses are now dealing with credit collections from various banks because of business accounts that are overdrawn or not in use.

The conclusion drawn from this case study is that there was a failure on the part of the public entities to communicate the relief grant to small businesses, and the government failed informal businesses by excluding them from the grant criteria.

SMME Representative Bodies in South Africa

Facilitating the establishment of a conducive atmosphere for the informal economy stakeholders to exercise the freedom of the right to association is regarded as vital in the quest for shaping the regulatory landscape that ultimately transforms informal economy workers and businesses at large (Berrett, 2003). According to the Parliamentary Monitoring Group (PMG), the South African environment has seen a rise in representative bodies, from worker's unions to various industry, sector, and market bodies (PMG, 2022). PMG has provided an overview of some of these bodies, with a particular focus on the informal market.

The South African National Taxi Council (SANTACO) is by far the largest informal representative body for informal businesses operating in the public transport sector. SANTACO's primary purpose is to be the voice of the sector, more especially as far as regulations are concerned, and to bridge the communication gap between government and taxi operators (Berrett, 2003). PMG (2022) has further observed that the South African National Apex Cooperative (SANACO) continues to foster solidarity among cooperatives in South Africa, acting as a representative of cooperatives at the International Cooperative Alliance (ICA). Similarly, the National Cooperative Association of South Africa (NCASA) represents the character, nature, and purpose of cooperatives locally (PMG, 2022). More recently, the South African Informal Traders Alliance (SAITA) was formed to represent informal traders and was created within the legislation that covers the informal sector industry (PMG, 2022).

The Informal Economy Development Forum (IEDF) connects the informal and formal sectors of South Africa's economy to integrate the former into the mainstream economic system (PMG, 2022). All these bodies should work with public sector entities tasked with implementing programmes for small business development in South Africa.

The existence of representative bodies has been one of the avenues used to create a universal voice to make known needs and concerns across the various sectors or markets. If the relationship with the representative bodies is well established, the government can partner with them to ensure the successful implementation of regulations governing the sectors and offer relevant support. Several countries have invested in the establishment of representative and statutory bodies to support the SMME sector. These bodies are regarded as key elements in organising SMMEs and the informal sector.

In China, for example, one organisation that was established with the sole mandate of connecting international buyers and SMMEs is Alibaba (Alibaba, n.d.). The organisation, although operated as a private company, was established with the primary objective of assisting SMMEs in China that lacked resources and knowledge in trading with international buyers. On the other hand, Alibaba created a trustworthy platform for international buyers seeking to procure products from China-based suppliers. Thus, the company's success and rapid growth can be attributed to the role it played in simplifying international trade regulations, being the voice for SMMEs, and ultimately benefiting its members.

Similarly, the India SME Forum was established with the aim of "building a neutral platform and voice to small and medium entrepreneurs of India". It "has been at the forefront of demanding a radical change in the way the country is led and committed to a paradigm shift in the mindset of the people of the country, towards its entrepreneurs" (India SME Forum, n.d.).

Parameters for Crisis Communication

According to Coombs (2010), crisis communication is the process of gathering, analysing, and disseminating information needed to handle a crisis. The author also points out that gathering data on crisis risks, deciding how to handle possible crises, and preparing those who will participate in the crisis management process are the main activities of pre-crisis, crisis communication. Post-crisis communication also includes analysing the crisis management endeavour, informing people of any adjustments that are required, and sending out follow-up crisis messages as required.

The Situational Crisis Communication Theory (SCCT), created by Coombs (2010), is shown in Figure 5. The theory's premise is that crises—like the global epidemic caused by COVID-19—are always perceived as unfavourable occurrences. Affected parties' interactions with the organisation during a crisis are influenced by the attributions they make about crisis culpability. Nonetheless, according to Coombs (2010), SCCT is audience-oriented since it aims to shed light on how people view crises, how they respond to crisis management plans, and how the public responds to the organisation that is experiencing a crisis.

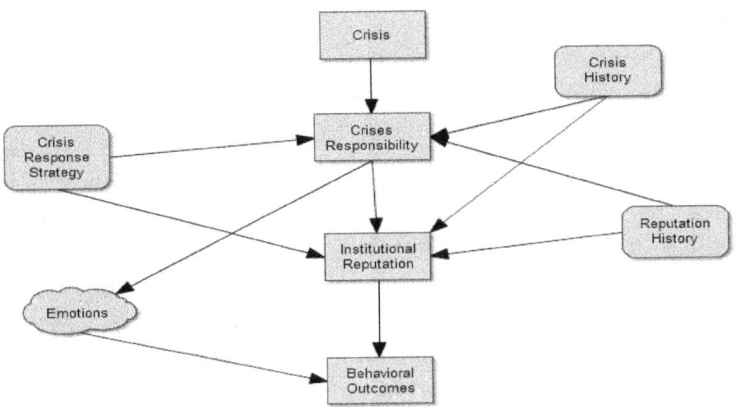

Figure 5: Model for the situational crisis communication theory variables (Source: Coombs, 2010)

According to Coombs' (2010) SCCT, there are three main crisis response strategies: (i) deny; (ii) diminish; (iii) reconstruct; and one supplemental strategy: reinforce. While diminish strategies aim to lessen the perceived importance of the issue and minimize the organisation's role for it, deny strategies try to show that the organisation was not at fault for the crisis. Conversely, rebuild methods are thought to be highly accommodating and aim to enhance the organisation's reputation by offering compensation and/or an apology (Coombs, 2010). Furthermore, by complimenting others—a tactic known as ingratiation—and/or bolstering—a technique known as reminding people of the organisation's previous good deeds—reinforcing tactics are employed to add positive information about the organisation.

According to Lovari, D'Ambrosi, and Bowen (2020), communication in public sector entities was formerly thought of as a simple transmitting function that was primarily focused on a vertical, bipolar, hierarchical, and unidirectional relationship between administrations and citizens, who were frequently seen as passive recipients of the messages generated by institutions. But in recent years, organisations in the public sector have encouraged citizens to participate in public communication policy by giving them access to pertinent information as well as by implementing targeted communication tactics to make experiences and initiatives—like integrated policies, area plans, programme agreements, and service conferences—easier to access.

Additionally, Coombs and Holladay (2022) view a crisis as a disruptive phenomenon that involves the violation of salient stakeholder expectations, which can create harm for stakeholders and organisations. Furthermore, they claim that to varied degrees, crisis communication, like all forms of communication, acknowledges the social construction component of communication (Coombs & Holladay, 2022).

Adept strategic communicators, which include crisis managers, work to establish common understandings between organisations and their stakeholders to spot significant patterns in meaning in communication. Crisis communication theories vary in how strongly they explicitly analysing social construction (Coombs & Holladay, 2022). Sometimes a disaster such as COVID-19 triggers a crisis and public sector institutions must communicate through such a crisis in a way that is understandable to all the stakeholders.

COVID-19 crisis communication

Lovari et al. (2020) argued that COVID-19 pandemic and its effects on socio-political variables at the international, national, and local levels put pressure on the key elements of public sector communication. Following the World Health Organisation's (WHO) declaration of COVID-19 as a pandemic following its discovery in Wuhan, China, public sector entities faced pressure to engage with all stakeholders using digital and social media platforms. Following this, there was an informational pandemic known as an "infodemic" (Lovari et al., 2020) that had a significant impact on media systems, public sector communication initiatives, and individuals' information-seeking behaviours. The infodemic was characterised by a combination of facts, fears, rumours, and guesses.

Thus, governments and organisations in the public sector have encountered unforeseen difficulties that have brought to light certain crucial elements of institutional communication that were already in place (Lovari et al., 2020). Chunxia, Fei, and Wei (2022) contend, however, that governments worldwide have been confronted with enormous obstacles as a direct result of COVID-19, ranging from need for robust health care and income to support severely affected businesses. A state's capacity to manage such a crisis is based on the total amount of money it has invested in its capacity for governance and management (Chunxia et al., 2022).

The necessity to create a challenge-based policy framework became more pressing with the advent of the new coronavirus outbreak (Chunxia et al., 2022). The pandemic also highlighted the importance of the public sector's capacities, as it is believed that this sector will be able to handle emergencies and have the necessary skills to address social problems and challenges. Many voices emerged from various nations because of the uncertainty surrounding COVID-19, which was made worse by social and economic ramifications. Government and institutional communication were frequently out of step with the mass media, which tended to sensationalise the virus while also incorporating contradictory medical and scientific viewpoints into their reporting (Lovari et al., 2020). The public's mistrust increased because of these voices becoming shareable content on digital platforms, where they were frequently politicised or linked to false information and conspiracy theories (Lovari et al., 2020).

In South Africa, the advent of COVID-19 revealed the level at which sectors, industries, and markets are organised – or not. Ntimane, Mugobo and Mrasi (2022) observe that, globally, countries implemented various economic restrictions as a means of curbing the spread of COVID-19, such as permitting only the operation of essential services and imposing curfews, total liquor bans and restricted liquor sales.

While some industries and markets were more organised, making it possible to mobilise government and business support, this was not the case for the South African liquor trader market (Ntimane et al., 2022). Consequently, liquor traders suffered great financial loss, and full recovery for some remains unclear as they were not included in the priority list of businesses benefiting from the various government initiatives to support business (Ntimane et al., 2022).

The establishment of National Liquor Traders Council in 2020, a representative structure for informal liquor traders, once again proved to be the most effective way to represent the voice of the said businesses (BIZ community, 2020). Though these informal businesses did not receive any financial support from the government, the establishment of the representative structure resulted in their voice being represented in calls for some relaxation of liquor license regulations during covid-19 lockdown (Magubane, 2021; BIZ community, 2020).

Chunxia et al. (2022) also argued that enterprises made a concerted effort to supply their stakeholders with resources to mitigate the effects of the pandemic following the introduction of COVID-19. To build confidence among stakeholders, however, companies required good communication from public entities tasked with helping them weather the COVID-19 pandemic. This was achieved through the practice of empathy and transparency.

Organisations and companies may play a crucial role in fostering trust and hope among their stakeholders and helping them adjust to difficult situations like the COVID-19 pandemic by implementing efficient crisis response methods (Chunxia et al., 2022). In addition, the communicators worked to create crisis communication plans that would link stakeholders, workers, and communities to lessen the COVID-19 pandemic's destructive consequences on industry.

Chunxia et al. (2022) propose the following crisis communication response strategy:

- Offer information that could assist stakeholders in mitigating the crisis's negative effects.

- Make use of the material at your disposal regarding crisis management as well as the forms and causes of crises.
- Consider the causes and reasons for the crisis, which need to be promptly communicated to the relevant parties.

Lovari et al. (2020) stated that research on the diversity of opinions and the improvement of communication tactics and procedures both before and after the COVID-19 pandemic is necessary. The writers also emphasise the importance of considering the public sector voice, concentrating on the offline and digital communication strategies used by public sector entities, and looking into the ethical, social, and political ramifications. According to Lovari et al. (2020), the inquiry should also pay attention to the perspectives of the public, looking into grassroots communication strategies and the dynamics of participation through traditional and nontraditional means. The COVID-19 epidemic undoubtedly marked a sea change in public sector communication regarding connections with various publics, including the small business sector (Lovari et al., 2020).

According to Lovari et al. (2020), public sector entities should prioritise the enhancement of their digital presence while simultaneously allocating resources towards a multichannel approach that considers the diverse needs and abilities of their various audiences, as well as the moral implications of the uneven effects of COVID-19.

Removing certain segments of the populace from public sector communication channels might exacerbate social and digital divides. Additionally, according to Lovari et al. (2020), public sector entities should enlighten and listen to the public equitably as well as provide voice to all voices, especially those of minorities. On the other hand, communication that is rigid, closed, and solely focused on the organisation without any active or responsive listening to the demands of the public runs the risk of propagandising and repeating post-communication rhetoric (Macnamara, 2018). The breakdown of trust undermines credibility, undermines social cohesiveness, upsets the delicate balance that underpins relationships within society, and may even cause public institutions to become closed off to their constituents.

According to Lovari et al. (2020), ethics is the new, main force behind communication in the public sector. Additionally, the authors assert that public sector entities have an even higher obligation to be trustworthy because of their duty to the public. To emphasise this duty and the necessity of sincere, open, and authentic engagement and communication to foster trust, we center ethics around public sector communication. Furthermore, because choices in the public sector are based on reason, these organisations can uphold their ethical obligations in a world where pandemics, crises, and upheavals provide constant challenges. Thus, by employing strategic communication initiatives to sustain accountable connections with citizens, stakeholders, the public, and the international community would benefit public sector entities in strengthening relations with these key stakeholders.

Lovari et al. (2020) note that public sector communication should have a strategic role in this time of uncertainty, which is characterised by the spread of misinformation and by economic and social crises. There is a need to add new words to the public sector's communication language, such as 'openness', 'flexibility', 'resilience', 'reliability', 'authenticity', 'honesty', 'interdependencies' and 'dialogue'. Communication professionals in public entities should be given more authority in their jobs, both inside and outside institutions, and should work to enhance their image of being trusted by top management, journalists, and the public. Meeting these new challenges calls for a major investment in communication professionals' new technical, technological, managerial, and strategic skills and knowledge (Lovari et al., 2020).

Proposed communication framework

Governments should inform its stakeholders in a way that makes communication easier and more efficient, according to Mishaal and Abu-Shanab (2015). Additionally, often governments struggle with communication since they have limited funding and don't prioritise communicating with stakeholders (Mishaal & Abu-Shanab, 2015). However, governments should take input from small business owners in the form of feedback, participation, and discussion (Mishaal & Abu-Shanab, 2015). Government and public sector entities should be open to collaboration by asking small business owners to co-create and co-design for a specific output.

However, we caution that this task is complex and requires collective intelligence. For this reason, the government could use a shared document to engage the public's participation in designing government applications. Howlett (2009) argues that although there are many types of government communication, there are very few contextually based frameworks to guide government and public sector communication with small businesses. Therefore, we propose the following communication framework for government to engage with small businesses about its development programmes.

We propose using the framework depicted in Figure 6 for communicating government development programmes to small businesses. The framework is founded on a set of proposed factors that may lead to communication success:

Small business owners should participate when government develops support programmes. At this stage, the government – through public business development agencies – should conduct a needs analysis survey to make sure that the programmes they develop are in line with the needs of small business owners.

The government should then consider the feedback from small business owners' participation and incorporate that feedback into the development of the proposed development programmes.

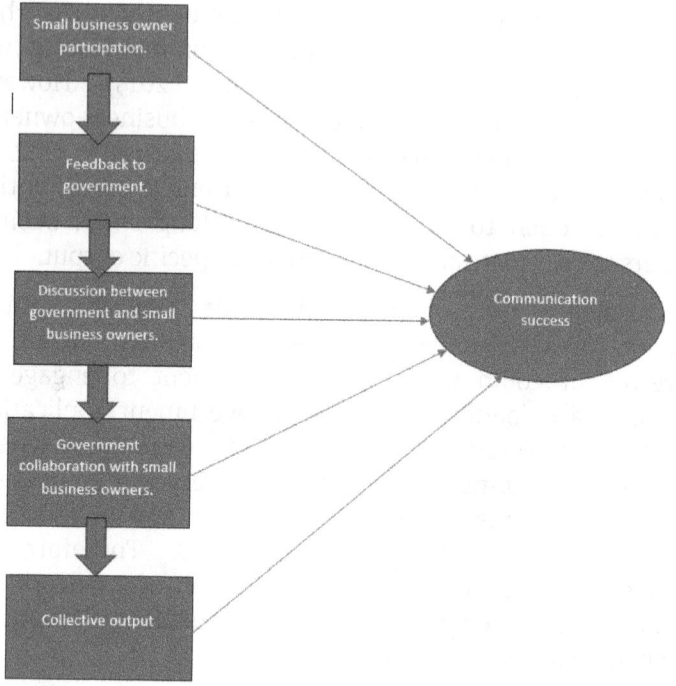

Figure 6: Framework for government communication with small businesses

Once the draft programme for small business development has been completed based on inputs from owners, public agencies and the government, there should be a discussion between small business owners and government development agencies on the feasibility of the programme and its implementation plan.

Furthermore, the implementation plan should be a collaboration between the public development agencies of government and forums for small business owners.

In this way, the communication will be a product of collective efforts and some of the stumbling blocks will be dealt with during the collaboration phase.

The next step is to measure the impact of the development programmes using various survey methods, based on agreed-upon success measures by small business owners and the public sector. Also, the communication success should be measured based on the reach of the programmes and an evaluation of whether the intended outcomes have been achieved.

Conclusion

SMMEs are undoubtedly important drivers of economic growth globally, and South Africa is no exception (The World Bank, 2019). While the South African government has developed various programmes aimed at supporting SMMEs and informal businesses (Rogerson, 2004; Ligthelm, 2005), more must still be done, as these initiatives have not yielded the desired results of supporting small businesses financially to successfully weather the COVID-19 crisis effects. The South African government and its development agencies need to provide all the necessary assistance to start-up entrepreneurs as a way of promoting and encouraging an entrepreneurial culture (Affendy, Asmat-Nizam & Farid, 2015).

Singh and Belwal (2008: 121) also add that "the development of SMEs is seen as accelerating the achievement of wider economic and socio-economic objectives, including poverty alleviation in developing countries".

This study explored the literature to better understand the small business environment in South Africa and the role of government in developing and communicating support programmes for small businesses. The framework proposed in this chapter includes five major predictors of government communication success: participation, feedback, discussion, collaboration, and collective output. Furthermore, government development agencies should use social media communication strategies to reach small businesses, especially those businesses operating in the townships and rural areas of South Africa.

As such, we recommend that the South African government, through the DSBD, should involve small business forums when considering initiating development programmes for small businesses. Then, once a programme has been drafted in consultation with small business owners, a proper communication plan should be formulated so that it may reach the intended beneficiary. Lastly, according to Adisa, Abdulraheem, and Mordi (2014), the South African government ought to support its development finance organisations' capacity for effective communication and urge them to provide conferences, workshops, and training sessions for small business owners on how to take advantage of developmental programmes.

References

Adisa TA, Abdulraheem I & Mordi C. (2014). The characteristics and challenges of small businesses in Africa: An exploratory study of Nigerian business owners. *Economic Insights: Trends and Challenges*, III (LXVI)(4):1–14.

Affendy A, Asmat-Nizam AT & Farid MS. (2015). Entrepreneurial orientation effects on market orientation and SMEs business performance: An SEM approach. *Review of Integrated Business Economic Research*, 4(3):259–272.

Agbobli EK, Oni O & Fatoki O. (2017). Market orientation and performance of small businesses in South Africa. *Journal of Economics and Behavioural Studies*, 9(5):135–143. https://doi.org/10.22610/jebs.v9i5(J).1915

Alibaba (n.d.). *More Than Two Decades of Track Record of Innovation*. https://www.alibabagroup.com/en-US/about-alibaba [accessed on 11 April 2024]

Battersby, J. (2020). South Africa's lockdown regulations and the reinforcement of anti-informality bias. *Agriculture and Human Values*, 37: 543–544. https://doi.org/10.1007/s10460-020-10078-w

Berrett, J. (2003). Organizing in the Informal Economy: A Case Study of the Minibus Taxi Industry in South Africa. Geneva, International Labour Office, 1–59.

BIZcommunity (2020). *Easing of alcohol sales restrictions a welcome relief for* industry. https://www.bizcommunity.com/Article/196/307/210317.html [accessed 09 April 2024]

BIZcommunity (2020). National Liquor Traders Council created to transform tavern industry. https://www.bizcommunity.com/Article/196/785/205394.html. [accessed 09 April 2024]

Bvuma S & Marnewick C. (2020). An information and communication technology adoption framework for small, medium and micro-enterprises operating in townships South Africa". *Southern African Journal of Entrepreneurship and Small Business Management*, 12(1): a318. https://doi.org/10.4102/sajesbm.v12i1.318

Canel MJ & Luoma-aho V. (2018). Public Sector Communication: Closing Gaps Between Citizens and Public Organizations. John Wiley & Sons. https://doi.org/10.1002/9781119135630

Chunxia Z, Fei W & Wei F. (2022). Exploring the antecedents to the reputation of Chinese public sector organizations during COVID-19: An extension of situational crisis communication theory. *Frontiers in Psychology*, 13. https://doi.org/10.3389/fpsyg.2022.818939

Coombs, W.T., 2010. Parameters for crisis communication. In. *The Handbook of Crisis Communication*. Chichester, UK: Blackwell Publishing. 17-53. https://doi.org/10.1002/9781444314885.ch1

Coombs WT & Holladay SJ. (Eds). (2022). *The Handbook of Crisis Communication*. Wiley-Blackwell. https://doi.org/10.1002/9781119678953

Howlett M. (2009). Government communication as a policy tool: A framework for analysis. *Canadian Political Science Review*, 3(2):23–37. https://doi.org/10.24124/c677/2009134

India SME Forum (n.d).

Ligthelm A. (2005). Informal retailing through home-based micro-enterprises: The role of spaza shops. *Development Southern Africa*, 22(2):199–214. https://doi.org/10.1080/03768350500163030

Lovari A, D'Ambrosi L & Bowen SA. (2020). Re-connecting voices. The (new) strategic role of public sector communication after the COVID-19 crisis. *Partecipazione econflitto*, 13(2):970–989.

Luoma-aho V & Canel MJ. (Eds). (2020). *The Handbook of Public Sector Communication*. John Wiley & Sons. https://doi.org/10.1002/9781119263203

Macnamara J. (2018). A review of new evaluation models for strategic communication: Progress and gaps. *International Journal of Strategic Communication*, 12(2):180–195. https://doi.org/10.1080/1553118X.2018.1428978

Magubane, K. (2021). Liquor traders request Ramaphosa's audience over Covid-19 restrictions, News24, 23 May. Available at https://www.news24.com/fin24/economy/liquor-traders-request-ramaphosas-audience-over-covid-19-restrictions-20210523 [accessed: 09 April 2024]

Makwara T. (2022). Large firms as threats to small business survival in South Africa: An exploratory literature review. *Journal of Management and Entrepreneurship Research*, 3(1):14–25. https://doi.org/10.34001/jmer.2022.6.03.1-25

Mishaal DA & Abu-Shanab E. (2015). The effect of using social media in governments: Framework of communication success. *The 7th International Conference on Information Technology (ICIT 2015)*. Amman, Jordan: Al-Zaytoonah University. May 12–15.

Ntimane LJ, Mugobo VV & Mrasi AP. (2022). Business recovery, renewal and resilience strategies for township taverns in South Africa: A post-COVID-19 prognosis. *International Journal of Business and Management Studies*, 3(10):60–67. https://doi.org/10.56734/ijbms.v3n10a5

Parliamentary Monitoring Committee. (2022). 'National Cooperative Association of South Africa (NCASA)'. *Informal Traders & Cooperatives Associations engagement session 30 November 2022.*

Parliamentary Monitoring Committee. (2022). "The South African Informal Trades Alliance". *Informal Traders & Cooperatives Associations engagement session 30 November 2022.*

Parliamentary Monitoring Committee (2022). 'The South African National Apex Cooperative (SANACO)'. *Informal Traders & Cooperatives Associations engagement session 30 November 2022.*

Republic of South Africa. Department of Small Business Development (DSBD). (2022). National Integrated Small Enterprise Development (NISED) Masterplan: Final Draft (Executive Summary). Pretoria: Department of Small Business Development. https://www.gov.za/sites/default/files/gcis_document/202205/nised-masterplan.pdf

Republic of South Africa. National Planning Commission. (2011). National Development Plan 2030. Pretoria: National Planning Commission.

Republic of South Africa. Small Enterprise Finance Agency (SEFA). (2022). SEFA Annual Report. Centurion: Small Enterprise Finance Agency. https://www.sefa.org.za/uploads/files/files/SEFA-Annual-Report-2022.pdf

Rogerson CM. (2004). The impact of the South African government's SMME programmes: A ten-year review (1994–2003). *Development Southern Africa*, 21(5):765–784. [Retrieved 31 July 2012] https://doi.org/10.1080/0376835042000325697

Singh G & Belwal R. (2008). Entrepreneurship and SMEs in Ethiopia. *Gender in Management: An International Journal*, 23(2):120–136. https://doi.org/10.1108/17542410810858321

The World Bank (2019). Small and medium enterprises' (SMEs) finance: Improving SMEs' access to finance and finding innovative solutions to unlock sources of capital. https://www.worldbank.org/en/topic/smefinance

Vuori, J., Aher, K. and Kylänen, M., 2020. The Influence Of Weber And Taylor On Public Sector Organizations' Communication. *The handbook of public sector communication*, pp.115-125. https://doi.org/10.1002/9781119263203.ch7

Wegerif M. (2022). The impact of COVID-19 on black farmers in South Africa. *Agrekon*, 61(1):52 –66. https://doi.org/10.1080/03031853.2021.1971097

Chapter 7

Public Health Communication in South Africa: Concepts, Contemporary Issues and Challenges

Elizabeth Lubinga

Communication, in general, is core to the existence of human beings, representing our way of accomplishing mutual meaning through exchanging information that signifies our symbolic capability (Rimal & Lapinski, 2009). The importance of public health communication is increasingly being driven by numerous environmental, social and psychological factors that affect human behaviours and how these behaviours affect human health. The COVID-19 pandemic that swept through the world from the end of 2019 is testament to how environmental factors not only affect human health, but also have a bearing on socio-economic aspects – and others – concerning individuals, organisations and societies as a whole.

Public health communication contributes to the wellbeing and health of human beings through crucial communicative acts ensuring disease prevention and upholding a good quality of life, using health promotion and education for behaviour change among societal publics (Rimal & Lapinski, 2009). The World Health Organisation (WHO) (n.d.) recognises wellbeing as a positive state not only experienced by individuals but societies as a whole, a resource of necessity for daily life, determined by social, economic and environmental conditions. Wellbeing encompasses numerous aspects including physical and mental health as well as emotional wellbeing (NHS, 2017). Public health communication thus becomes a pivotal ingredient in ensuring individual, community and, ultimately, societal wellbeing. An unhealthy populace places a great burden on the financial resources of a country, among other services.

In resource-constrained countries such as South Africa, where various public government services compete for resources, it is important to manage the financial burden wrought by public health systems. For the 2022/23 financial year, for instance, the government budget for health increased to R64.5 billion (Landu, 2022), up from the R62.5 billion (Mkhize, 2021) allocated for the previous financial year. This R2 billion budget increase emphasises the increasing health needs of South Africans. The health budget reduced to R60.1 billion in the 2023/2024 budget (Parliamentary Monitoring Group, 2024). Additionally, since most common societal health problems, both communicable and non-communicable, can be prevented, the increase in the health budget underscores how critical it is to use public health communication as a tool to educate and develop a health-literate populace. Using public health communication campaigns to emphasise prevention can be the most cost-effective strategy to ensure good health through positive behaviour and to control expensive and debilitating chronic health problems such as cancer (WHO, 2022).

This chapter provides a working conceptualisation and examines how public health communication is aligned in South African contexts. It examines some theoretical perspectives that underpin public health communication and outlines some public health communication successes in South Africa. Furthermore, this chapter critiques selected challenges to public health communication, including health literacy, and looks at how communication around public health problems has been prioritised and, in turn, how this prioritisation has affected the quality of past and recent health campaigns in South Africa.

Access to comprehensible health information is critically assessed, premised on the fact that South Africa is a largely rural country with media access disparities. Also discussed are tactics currently being used for public health communication, which, while they have apparently been effective, exclude certain segments of the population, inadvertently creating health disparities. Examples are given of how public health communication has been applied to health crises such as HIV/AIDS, COVID-19 and teenage pregnancy in South Africa.

Conceptualising Public Health Communication

The scientific study of health communication is recent, having emerged during the 1970s (Thompson, 2014), by distinguishing itself as a distinct scholarly field that achieves more than mere dissemination of information through combining scientific research with communication. Public health communication has been defined as the scientific development, strategic dissemination, and critical evaluation of relevant, accurate, accessible and understandable health information communicated to, and from, intended audiences to advance the health of the public (Bernhardt, 2004).

Public health communication is an interdisciplinary field of study which, in addition to public health, straddles journalism, health promotion, health education, informatics and big data, as well as psychology, among other disciplines. Public health communication does not only apply to individual members of the public responsible for fostering the advancement of societal health; other participants such as communities, organisations, health systems and policymakers are all affected.

Theoretical perspectives to public health communication

Various theories guide the construction of messages and health campaigns that intend to change the health behaviour of individuals and societies in general. These include change-oriented theories, culture-centred theories (Dutta, 2007; 2011; Dutta & Bergman, 2004a & 2004b) and, as WHO (2008) proposed, the Communication for Behavioural Impact (COMBI) approach to health communication, developed in response to existing theories that do not seem to create impact upon implementation. However, this chapter will focus on ecological models.

Ecological models to public health acknowledge that the health of people in societies is affected by several factors, including social, political, environmental and behavioural, among others (Bernhardt, 2004). Sallis and Owen (2015) emphasise that environmental and policy contexts of health are simultaneously aligned to social and psychological contexts as key influencers of behaviour that enable the construction of comprehensive health communication interventions targeting multiple levels of influence.

The core argument for following ecological models is that designing effective health communication interventions requires the comprehension of multiple and interacting health behaviour determinants. These determinants operate at intrapersonal, interpersonal, community, organisational and public policy levels (Rural Health Information Hub, 2024).

The determinants may be applied at various levels, including the intrapersonal or individual level. When COVID-19 vaccines were introduced in South Africa, the country faced the problem of low vaccination uptake due to vaccine hesitancy, with only 60% of the population vaccinated by November 2022. The 60% of vaccinated people equates to 63 doses per 100 people, compared to the 203 doses per 100 people in Seychelles, which had the highest vaccination rates in Africa (Saleh, 2022).

South Africa's vaccination rate placed the country 18th in Africa, even though it was most affected by COVID-19 infections and deaths. By the end of March 2022, South Africa had 25 million COVID-19 vaccine doses in stock; however, the low uptake led to over 100 000 Pfizer doses reaching expiry and having to be destroyed (Rédaction Africanews, 2022). If applied to the ecological model, it would be relevant to understand individual knowledge about the benefits and risks of vaccination, for instance, in order to design messages intended to improve uptake and minimise hesitancy.

In South Africa, framed from an ecological perspective, health communication campaigns were designed to encourage young people to help older people to access COVID-19 vaccination. Numerous global studies have indicated that elderly people and those with comorbidities such as cardiovascular disease, diabetes and obesity, had the highest risk of dying from COVID-19 (Mueller, McNamara & Sinclair, 2020; Ge et al., 2021). Older people were therefore encouraged to go for COVID-19 vaccines because of the high disease risk and weaker immune systems. These public health campaigns were framed for the social good, with the intention to convince younger people to protect older members of society.

Regarding public policy factors, South Africa, according to President Cyril Ramaphosa, had set a target of vaccinating 70% of all adults by December 2021. By 26 December 2021, on 39% of adults were fully vaccinated and 6% partially vaccinated (Alexander & Xezwi, 2021). These authors argue that data from Round 5 of the COVID-19 Democracy Survey of the University of Johannesburg/Human Sciences Research Council, showed that in November 2021, only a quarter of adults could be regarded as hesitant. In other words, they were definitely not going to be vaccinated, would probably not be vaccinated or did not know whether they would get vaccinated. Alexander and Xezwi (2021) posited that government did not do enough to persuade the population through social-media-driven public education campaigns and that the campaigns used were ineffective.

Figure 7 shows the types of messages often used for public health communication at the different levels.

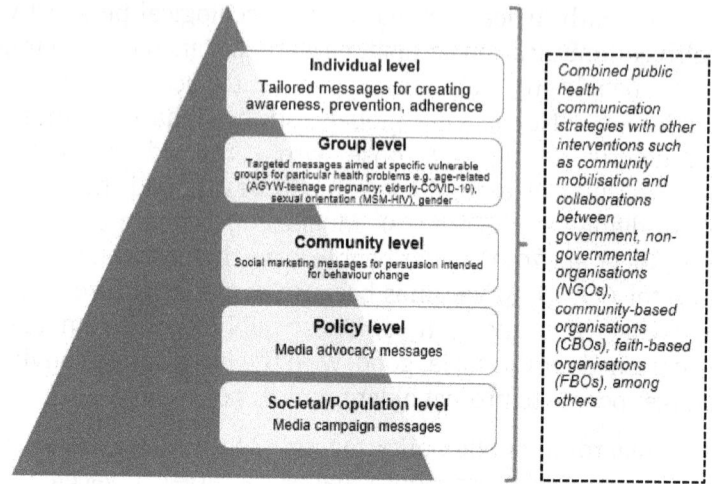

Figure 7: An illustration of an ecological perspective with multi-level health messaging (Source: Bernhardt, 2004)

Combined Public Health Communication Using an Ecological Multisectoral Lens

Public health communicators in South Africa

In South Africa, public health communication typically occurs at three tiers of government: national, provincial and local. Health policies are formulated at national government level and are mostly communicated to the public through national health campaigns and cascaded to the provincial and local levels. The National Department of Health (NDoH) coordinates national and provincial levels of public health communication efforts. The local public health communication level has a multisectoral approach and is mostly dominated by community-based organisations (CBOs) and non-governmental organisations (NGOs). These organisations are familiar with the challenges of the communities in which they are based and play a crucial role in terms of communicating tailored health messages to their specific communities.

Using community-based workers for grassroots public health communication

The South African government notably, has successfully utilised community-based workers to enable grassroots communication of public health matters, as well as public compliance. Community health workers, typically members of the community, deliver healthcare services in communities and are trained for specific health interventions, even though they may have no formal professional or academic health-related education. Since the 1970s, these workers have been tasked with improving public access to primary healthcare through spreading health information and raising awareness about disease through health promotion (Magingxa, 2011). In many rural areas of South Africa, community workers have boosted communication health interventions by bridging the gap in health communication through door-to-door campaigns.

An example is the HIV project, Bending the Curves, run by Doctors without Borders – *Médecins Sans Frontières* (MSF) – in Eshowe, KwaZulu-Natal, which was a multisectoral plan responding to HIV, tuberculosis and sexually transmittable infections in the province between 2017 and 2022. The plan exceeded an important milestone set by UNAIDS in 2013 when MSF announced in 2019 that it had exceeded the 90-90-90 target one year ahead of the target of 2020 by achieving 90-94-95. The aim was to ensure that by 2020, 90% of people living with AIDS knew their status, 90% were using antiretrovirals and 90% achieved a suppressed viral load. The Eshowe HIV project proved that community-level interventions can successfully reach and support communities that have limited access to health communication.

Conversely, the effectiveness of public health communication using community health workers is negated if they are not trained on the information they are expected to disseminate. Such was the case at the outset of the COVID-19 pandemic where training was not provided to community leaders and outreach community workers who were expected to educate communities (Goldstein, Coulson & Pillay, 2021). Apart from the lack of training, a risky situation arose during the pandemic where community health workers had to interact with the public to communicate prevention methods, yet the government did not have sufficient personal protective equipment (PPE) for medical personnel in healthcare facilities or for door-to-door campaigns involving community workers.

Traditional healers: A potential mouthpiece for public health communication

The COVID-19 pandemic, as well as previous and ongoing epidemics such as HIV/AIDS, among others, underscored prevailing gaps and opportunities for public health communication using alternative communicators such as traditional leaders and healers. Traditional healers hold historical influence in the communities where they are based, built on decades of ongoing interpersonal consultations. The effectiveness of word-of-mouth communication is widely acknowledged in traditional healing. Thus, the effectiveness of traditional healing is sustained through clients who share their experiences with others, creating a positive reputation in communities.

Research shows that in sub-Saharan African countries, 80% of the population are reported to initiate their health-seeking behaviour in traditional medicine (Renckens & Dorlo, 2013). Furthermore, the interactions between traditional healers and their clients are perceived to be more holistic as they take a socio-cultural approach towards health and wellness, making them more desirable as a first point of contact among community members. However, during the COVID-19 pandemic, stakeholders such as traditional healers, who are basic health providers, were largely excluded from participating in government activities designed to combat the spread of the virus (Beyers, 2020).

Public Health Communication Message Content and Quality

Message strategies

In interpersonal public health settings, such as during doctor-patient interactions, the language used is not always mutually understandable and, in some instances, medical doctors use medical jargon when interacting with patients. Given that medical doctors mostly achieve a higher level of education than, for example, members of the public in rural areas, jargon renders health communication ineffective. In many rural hospitals in South Africa, for example, Cuban doctors who could not speak English or local languages were employed. Even interpretation through nurses to patients became difficult (Lubinga & Sitto, 2021). In addition, in some cases where health messages have been translated into local languages with the goal of reaching wider audiences, the essence of the messages has sometimes been lost in translation because African languages are ambiguous in comparison to English.

Past public communication campaigns have used innovative message strategies to communicate about health problems. NGOs in particular have used a variety of message strategies to stimulate behaviour-changing conversations. In Limpopo Province during the late 1990s and early 2000s, the Ndlovu Medical Trust, founded in 1994 by Dr Hugo Tempelman and his wife Liesje, offered health services to the communities of Elandsdoorn, Bushbuckridge and the surrounding townships. The trust created memorable HIV/AIDS messages, such as "Don't be a fool, put a condom on your tool".

Furthermore, in the early 2002's, loveLife South Africa created cryptic public health HIV messages that provoked conversations with their audiences. However, as several studies revealed, some of these cryptic messages do not appear to have been understood by members of the public. In the case of sensitive HIV messages, some African languages have employed metaphors to avoid offending audiences, with the result of disseminating indirect, less effective messages.

Channels used for public health communication

Public health communicators have commonly used mass media, including broadcast (television and public and community radio), print (newspapers, posters, brochures and pamphlets) and digital and social media platforms. COVID-19 was accompanied by a rise in the use of digital and social media platforms for public health communication. However, critics point out that the use of various digital and social media platforms mostly involved the repurposing of health messages across various media of communication (Sitto et al., 2022). Moreover, while national and provincial health departments were commended for widely employing digital and social media, given the number and geographic spread of South Africans with access to internet-enabled smartphones, these health messages likely reached a mostly peri-urban and urban audience, excluding citizens in rural communities (Aruleba & Tere, 2022; Kemp, 2022; Ostrowick, 2018). On the other hand, the use of text messages by the government during COVID-19 for public health communication ensured that many messages reached everyone who has a South African mobile phone, irrespective of internet connectivity. During the COVID-19 pandemic, national public health communication in South Africa often made use of mass media in combination with interpersonal message sources such as health professionals in clinics and community-based workers. This strategy ensured that messages reached most of the population through multiple channels of communication.

A shortcoming of using digital and social media during the COVID-19 pandemic was that the platforms were largely for informational purposes only, with limited engagement. These media hold great potential for interaction, and this was the expectation of the users of public health officials. A case in point was the Tweet sent by the late businessman Shonisani Lethole, who allegedly died in hospital after receiving no food at Tembisa Hospital for two days. His Tweet to the then

Minister of Health, Dr Zweli Mkhize, in June 2020, attracted a flurry of communication, yet received no response from the Twitter account to which it was sent (Ngqakamba, 2020; Tlou, 2020).

Successes for Public Health Communication in South Africa

Focused and effective HIV health campaign collaborations

Well-known collaborations between the government and NPOs have led to successful campaigns such as the Khomanani campaign on HIV, AIDS, STIs and TB (2001–2008) and loveLife on HIV prevention among young people (1999). Soul City (1994) and Soul Buddyz (2013) were instrumental in increasing knowledge about HIV/AIDS, challenging social norms about health and other social problems such as gender-based violence, and supporting behaviour change. The success of these campaigns appears to have been due partly to the fact that they were tailored to target specific audiences. *Soul Buddyz* focused on children aged 8 to 12 years and *loveLife* targeted teenagers and youth aged 10 to 24 years.

These four national HIV/AIDS communication programmes are credited with crucially increasing public knowledge about antiretroviral therapy (ART) and prevention of mother-to-child HIV transmission in South Africa, among other achievements. These programmes used a combination of mass media and interactive strategies that were community-based, involving community theatre, door-to-door engagements and activities at youth groups, schools and universities. As part of HIV/AIDS prevention, these campaigns are recognised for having increased consistent condom use among young men from 11% in 1995 to 84% in 2012 (Goldstein, Coulson & Pillay, 2021).

For example, in the 2000s, loveLife South Africa initiated the *mpintshi* programme, a peer education initiative meant to influence youth sexual behaviour at the height of the HIV/AIDS epidemic. The programme attracted youth between the ages of 12 and 17 for in-school *mpintshis*, while out-of-school *mpintshis* were aged between 17 and 24 years old. Annually, about 1 800 youth were recruited into the programme to implement outreach programmes in schools, communities, loveLife Y-Centres, adolescent and youth-friendly clinics, as well as youth groups, to influence health lifestyles among their peers (loveLife, n.d).

The South African 2006 National HIV/AIDS Communication Survey indicated that 92.5% of the population was reached through national HIV/AIDS communication programmes (Kincaid et al., 2008). Research on the effects of exposure to communication indicates a direct contribution to AIDS-related knowledge, as well as indirect effects on increasing condom use, HIV testing and helping people who were sick with AIDS (Shisana et al., 2009: 5).

Functional health information systems in South Africa

The COVID-19 pandemic demonstrated that South Africa has functional health information systems (HIS) at local, provincial and national levels. HIS fall under the field of medical informatics and are created and necessary for managing healthcare data. They may include systems that collect, store, manage and transmit patient records, inform hospital management or support healthcare policy decisions. Good quality HIS are important to inform decision-making and policies and, as Haux (2006) argues, they are important for high-level quality of care because they enable access to data, enabling diagnostic and therapeutic decisions. There is a link between good quality HIS and public health communication.

Previously, these systems publicly and visibly operated at hospital or clinic level where the personal files of an individual visiting the facility would be retrieved to commence with medical assistance. To undiscerning members of the public, it would appear that the HIS in South Africa demonstrated a level of efficiency when the pandemic broke out, judging from the speed with which COVID-19 patient information was collected daily, locally and provincially, and shared relatively swiftly at a national level. For the first time, members of the public were exposed to, and primed towards, looking out for and monitoring daily COVID-19 statistics at provincial and national levels, as published on traditional, digital and social media platforms.

Daily statistics from HIS shared by the various provincial and national departments of health, as well as other health organisations such as the National Institute for Communicable Diseases (NICD), played a critical role in persuading public health behaviour change during COVID-19. Public persuasion was facilitated through access to up-to-date information that individuals could use to monitor increases in COVID-19 cases and deaths at provincial and national levels in order to engage in protective measures. In addition, these daily statistics provoked unprecedented levels of public discussions about health, specifically about the state of COVID-19 and other related matters in the country, inadvertently improving communication about the disease among the public. Research indicates that interpersonal discussions about health issues increases knowledge and awareness, as well as feelings of self-efficacy, ultimately contributing to the adoption of healthy lifestyles (Lubinga, Maes & Jansen, 2016; Donné, Jansen & Hoeks, 2017).

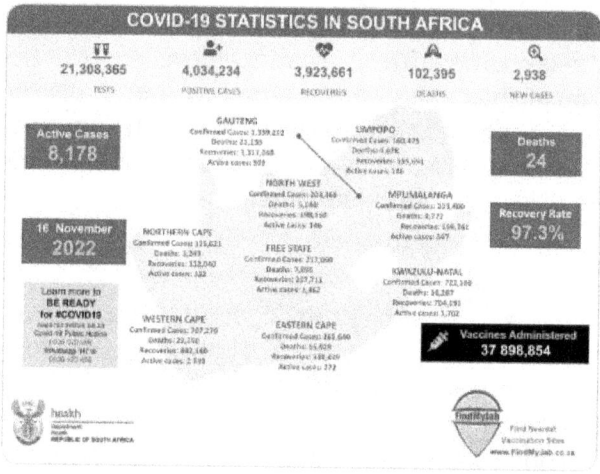

As of 16 November the cumulative number of #COVID19 cases identified in SA is 4 034 234 with 2 938 new cases reported. 24 deaths have been reported bringing the total to 102 395 deaths. The cumulative number of recoveries now stand at 3 923 661 with a recovery rate of 97,3%

Figure 8: Example of daily tweets from the national Department of Health's Twitter account indicating daily COVID-19 statistics (Source: https://twitter.com/HealthZA/status/1593278355754942468)

Intensive use of digital and social media health communication: COVID-19

The COVID-19 pandemic drove the use of digital and social media platforms for public health communication in South Africa and globally. The nature of the pandemic, specifically the speed with which the virus spread, required agility in communicating preventative behaviour to contain contagion. The speed with which COVID-19 spread among populations and the required communication to ensure relevant behaviour, necessitated the use of various media of communication, but digital and social media offered instant communication. In South Africa, government immediately harnessed daily text messages with fear-inducing slogans such as 'Coronavirus kills'. More than 100 million unsolicited daily text messages were sent via service providers to every person in the country who owned a functional device (Kemp, 2021). The South African government spent R43 million to run multimedia campaigns to communicate COVID-19 (Maqhina, 2020).

Farao (2020) notes that COVID-19 digital communication was partly credited with ensuring timely, essential health communication necessary for curbing the spread and shifting behaviours and perceptions. Digital platforms were central in communicating authoritative information, as required by WHO, and by 2021, the then Minister of Health Dr Zweli Mkhize had almost 600 000 followers on Twitter (Sitto et al 2022).

The provinces, the NDoH, President, Presidency, Premiers and Provincial MECs of Health, among others, communicated via dedicated websites, social media and video streaming platforms, thus, ensuring a concentration of coordinated health information. By 20 November 2022, the NDoH's Twitter account had almost 400 000 followers, the Gauteng DoH 97 000 and the Western Cape DoH 54 000, indicating that the public regarded these accounts as reliable sources of COVID-19 health information and messages.

Challenges for Public Health Communication in South Africa

Health (il)literacy

Health literacy is important for public health communication at several levels. The discussion about health literacy focuses on the individual level, although it can operate at organisational and societal levels. Health literacy at the individual level entails the ability of an individual to obtain and translate knowledge and information in order to maintain and improve health in a way that is appropriate to the individual and system contexts (Liu et al., 2020). Healthy individuals in a state of positive wellbeing relieve the burden on health systems, and, as Pleasant (2014) argues, health literacy is dynamic and its current definitions do not take into consideration health systems and policymakers, for example.

Behavioural theories predict that individuals' health behaviour is greatly influenced by communication, accenting, for instance, that perceptions of self-efficacy by individuals enable them to engage in and sustain positive health behaviour change. In order for individuals to engage in certain behaviour, they need to understand and effectively use communication through knowledge and awareness about health problems, as well as how to prevent them or how to manage them if they are sick. Health literacy can be functional, interactive and critical (Nutbeam, 2000) and should be perceived as an outcome of health education, with functional health literacy developing from the communication of factual information leading to improved knowledge of health risks, health systems and adherence to positive behaviour.

Health literacy and individual empowerment using communication

The focus of functional health literacy is individual empowerment through improvement of knowledge leading to the capacity to act on knowledge and adherence to positive behaviour. Nutbeam (2000) summarises health literacy as a range of outcomes to health education and communication. When access to factual knowledge is negated in health communication, adverse effects may arise. For instance, the WHO reported that TB increased in countries such as South Africa in 2020 when resources, including communication resources, for addressing such diseases were deflected to focus on fighting COVID-19.

The WHO estimated that the diversion of resources during the COVID-19 pandemic could lead to 6 million new

TB infections and 1.4 million deaths between 2020 and 2025 globally, especially among 8 countries, including South Africa (AFP, 2020). By mid-2020, the South African government had committed R43 million to health promotion for COVID-19 related communication campaigns, according to the then Health Minister Zweli Mkhize (Maqhina, 2020).

Interactive health literacy and the development of skills occurs in a supportive environment and involves community involvement and the development of skills for public benefit, in addition to benefiting the individual (Nutbeam, 2000). Improving health literacy as part of public health is more than basic communication or a mere transmission of information. Health literacy is a complex but crucial construct that relates to public health communication, especially in developing contexts such as South Africa.

Digital health literacy (or eHealth literacy) is defined as "the ability to seek, find, understand and appraise health information from electronic sources and apply the knowledge gained to addressing or solving a health problem" (Norman & Skinner, 2006: 2). It is such matters of access, as well as digital literacy, that raise questions about digital health exclusion when large volumes of health communication campaigns and messages are conducted using digital media. Lubinga, Sitto and Molebatsi (2021) concluded that for greater effectiveness, government communication strategies need to match healthcare interventions to the levels of ICT access of citizens, especially those most in need.

It can be argued that developing health literacy doubles as both a function and an outcome of effective public communication through health promotion and education. Communication as a driver of health education and promotion lies at the core of health literacy. Health literacy not only benefits individuals in society but influences public health and the sustainability of healthcare systems, because when people take more responsibility in managing their own health, they also use health services more effectively (Liu et al., 2020). The WHO recognises the importance of health literacy by recommending it as an instrument for achieving various key targets listed in the Sustainable Development Goals.

Conversely, individuals with insufficient health literacy experience difficulties in comprehending health information, have a limited knowledge of diseases and lower medication adherence. These factors, in turn, worsen already poor health, pose a high risk of mortality and lead to insufficient and ineffective use of healthcare while increasing costs and health disparities (Sheridan, Halpern & Viera, 2011). Links exist between low levels of education, literacy in general, health literacy and poor health, poor healthcare utilisation, increased barriers and early death globally (Pleasant, 2014). Furthermore, low health literacy is associated with adverse health outcomes across many health domains and contexts (Gilder, Moo & Hashmi, 2019).

From 2020 to 2022, in terms of literacy levels, South Africa's adult literacy rates declined to 87% ranking lower than other developing countries such as Brazil and Mexico, with lower child literacy rates; about a third of South African children are illiterate (Naidoo, 2022). Health messaging is generally rendered inaccessible to people who have low to no literacy, depending on message formats.

For example, South African public health communication relies greatly on the use of printed verbo-visual communication materials, specifically posters and pamphlets with a combination of visuals and text. Visual communication has generally been found to be effective for health promotion among populations with low literacy. However, in India, posters were often misinterpreted because of specific local understandings of the images, meaning that images have the potential to hold multiple meanings (Meppelink, Smit & Buurman, 2015). Gilder et al. (2019) recommend that images used on public health posters should be piloted before implementation in mass communication campaigns. Piloted poster images can identity and negate the potential for unintentional negative perceptions that often emerge from using such posters and are common but difficult to overcome.

Negative perceptions may arise due to reasons ranging from cultural taboos and complex, enigmatic images to indistinct or elusive concepts leading to misunderstanding of visuals.

Besides, in a multiracial and multilingual country such as South Africa, with diverse demographic populations, poster images may be subject to racial (mis)interpretations, leading to message resistance. Research has indicated that during public health education campaigns, if educational materials such as brochures, posters, pamphlets and websites use photographs that match the demographics of the target population, the messages communicated are more effective. This is because demographically matched messages improve message attractiveness, the ability to capture audience attention and heighten comprehension, message relevance and persuasiveness (Buller, Bettinghaus & Liu, 2010).

Prioritising public health communication's limited resources

In resource-constrained countries, like South Africa, questions arise regarding the prioritisation of public health communication of health problems. Financial constraints lead to cost-cutting measures that affect crucial communicative aspects of public health communication, such as the quality of campaigns and their messaging, as well as the quantity of public health communication, resulting in fewer campaigns. In South Africa, a constrained budget for public health communication has compounded public health communication prioritisation challenges, leading to minimal mass media health promotion characterised by unfocused, multi-layered health campaigns. Limited resources also often mean that for public health communication, countries will focus communicative efforts on media campaigns for the most significant health crises that arise.

However, prioritisation does not only pertain to contemporary health problems or crises that have hit the country. In general, financial resources committed to health promotion by NPOs in South Africa have reduced over a decade

(Goldstein, Coulson & Pillay, 2021). Previously, during the late 1990s and early 2000s, collaborations between the South African government and NPOs led to successful public health communication campaigns, as discussed.

Within the past decade, the NDoH has run less prominent national public health campaigns (excluding the COVID-19 pandemic) that appear to have been characterised by vague campaign messages, a move down from the previous audience-specific, tailored campaigns. These public health campaigns appear to have been framed based on cost savings, with formulated preventative messages simultaneously covering multiple health problems and targeting multiple audiences. Such campaigns include Phila, launched in 2017 to encourage healthy living. The campaign was so broad that it addressed infant vaccination, breastfeeding, non-communicable diseases such as TB, HIV and AIDS, obesity, violence, trauma and contraception use (Mkize, 2017).

In 2018, another national wellness communication campaign, *Cheka Impilo*, was conceived, with the aim of "testing and treating people who have HIV, TB, sexually transmitted infections and non-communicable diseases such as diabetes and hypertension". The campaign targeted several populations with the aim of providing comprehensive health and wellness services targeted at men, adolescent girls and young women, as well as key and vulnerable population groups (Myeni, 2018). There is thus a stark difference between previous campaigns under the collaboration of the NDoH and NPOs, which were tailored and audience specific, and which were evaluated as effective.

Minimised face-to-face interpersonal health communication

The hard lockdown in the country in 2020 and various other lockdown levels made it difficult to deploy some of the alternative effective means of ensuring health communication, such as through community health workers. During the hard lockdown phases of COVID-19, when human contact and movement was restricted, they could not operate. Had this not been the case, these workers could have played an invaluable role in communicating within communities and enhancing the credibility of communication, especially among rural populations.

In 2021, research by the South African Medical Research Council (SAMRC), the Human Sciences Research Council (HSRC) and the Sarraounia Public Health Trust revealed that possible vaccine hesitancy could have been negatively influenced by the absence of a credible voice of authority from the Ministry of Health about COVID-19 in communities (Goldstein, Coulson & Pillay, 2021).

Community health workers who would normally have provided the necessary communicative boost to educate communities about COVID-19 were not trained, and instead, relied on information from the media and from presidential 'family meetings' to respond to questions from the public (ibid.). A 2020 study conducted among disadvantaged communities in the Northern Cape and Gauteng provinces revealed that during the hard lockdown, 68% of 1 760 participants received their COVID-19 relief information from news in the mass media (Lubinga et al., 2021).

Conclusion

This chapter has attempted to provide insight into the South African public health communication landscape, based on the basic communication processes. The starting point was to provide a working definition of health communication, which is a relatively new field of study but one that combines a number of disciplines with the intention of providing support for health and wellness among the public. The successes of public health communication in South Africa were acknowledged, along with its limitations.

References

Agence France Presse (AFP). (2020). *Coronavirus threatens to reverse progress in TB fight: WHO*. France24. 14 October. https://www.france24.com/en/20201014-coronavirus-threatens-to-reverse-progress-in-tb-fight-who

Alexander K & Xezwi B. (2021). *Dose of discrimination: Why the government failed to reach its vaccination targets*. Daily Maverick. 28 December. https://www.dailymaverick.co.za/article/2021-12-28-dose-of-discrimination-why-the-government-failed-to-reach-its-vaccination-targets/

Aruleba K & Jere N. (2022). Exploring digital transforming challenges in rural areas of South Africa through a systematic review of empirical studies. *Scientific African*, 16:e01190. https://doi.org/10.1016/j.sciaf.2022.e01190

Bernhardt JM. (2004). Communication at the core of effective public health. *American Journal of Public Health*, 94(12):2051-2053. https://doi.org/10.2105/AJPH.94.12.2051

Beyers J. (2020). Who may heal? A plea from traditional healers to participate in treating Covid-19. *HTS Teologiese Studies/Theological Studies* 76(1):a6169. https://doi.org/10.4102/hts.v76i1.6169

Buller M, Bettinghaus E & Liu X. (2010). Availability of effective photographs for public health education materials: Public health practitioners' need for diversity. *138th APHA Annual Meeting and Expo Conference*. Denver, USA: Colorado Convention Center. Presentation, 8 November. https://www.researchgate.net/publication/266791899_Availability_of_effective_photographs_for_public_health_education_materials_Public_health_practitioners'_need_for_diversity

Donné L, Jansen C & Hoeks J. (2017). Uncovering factors influencing interpersonal health communication. *Global Qualitative Nursing Research*, 4:1–10. https://doi.org/10.1177/2333393617711607

Dutta MJ. (2007). Communicating about culture and health: Theorizing culture-centred and cultural sensitivity approaches. *Communication Theory*, 17(3):304–328. https://doi.org/10.1111/j.1468-2885.2007.00297.x

Dutta MJ. (2011). *Communicating social change: Structure, culture and agency.* New York: Routledge. https://doi.org/10.4324/9780203834343

Dutta-Bergman MJ. (2004a). The unheard voices of Santalis: Communicating about health from the margins of India. *Communication Theory*, 14(3):237–263. https://doi.org/10.1093/ct/14.3.237

Dutta-Bergman MJ. (2004b). Poverty, structural barriers and health: A Santali narrative of health communication. *Qualitative Health Research*, 14(8):1107–1122. https://doi.org/10.1177/1049732304267763

Farao J. (2020). Digital Health Communication in South Africa during COVID-19. *Global Health Innovation*, 3 (1): 1. DOI 10.15641/ghi.v3i1.891. https://doi.org/10.15641/ghi.v3i1.891

Ge E, Li Y, Wu S, Candido E & Wei X. (2021). Association of pre-existing comorbidities with mortality and disease severity among 167,500 individuals with COVID-19 in Canada: A population-based cohort study. *PLOS ONE*, 16(10):e0258154. https://doi.org/10.1371/journal.pone.0258154

Gilder ME, Moo P, Hashmi A, Praisaengdet N, Wai K, Pimanpanarak M, Carrara VI, Angkurawaranon C, Jiraporncharoen W & McGready R. (2019). "I can't read and don't understand": Health literacy and health messaging about folic acid for neural tube defect prevention in a migrant population on the Myanmar-Thailand border. *PLOS ONE*, 14(6):e0218138. https://doi.org/10.1371/journal.pone.0218138

Goldstein S, Coulson N & Pillay N. (2021). *How South Africa dropped the ball on health communication*. University of the Witwatersrand, Johannesburg. 28 May. https://www.wits.ac.za/covid19/covid19-news/latest/how-south-africa-dropped-the-ball-on-health-communication.html

Haux R. (2006). Health information systems: Past, present, future. *International Journal of Medical Informatics*, 75(3-4):268–281. https://doi.org/10.1016/j.ijmedinf.2005.08.002

Kemp S. (2021). Digital 2021: South Africa. DataReportal. 11 February. https://datareportal.com/reports/digital-2021-south-africa

Kemp S. (2022). Digital 2022: South Africa. DataReportal. 15 February. https://datareportal.com/reports/digital-2022-south-africa

Kincaid DL, Parker W, Johnson S, Schierhout G, Kelly K, Connolly C & Pham VHT. (2008). *AIDS Communication Programmes, HIV Prevention and Living with HIV and AIDS in South Africa, 2006*. Pretoria: JHHESA.

Landu Y. (2022). *Minister of Health concerned about decrease in health budget in medium term*. Parliament of the Republic of South Africa. 16 May. https://www.parliament.gov.za/news/minister-health-concerned-about-decrease-health-budget-medium-term

Liu C, Wang D, Liu C, et al. (2020). What is the meaning of health literacy? A systematic review and qualitative synthesis. *Family Medicine and Community Health*, 8(2):e000351. https://doi.org/10.1136/fmch-2020-000351

loveLife. (n.d.). MPINTSHI'S. https://lovelife.org.za/en/programmes/mpintshis/

Lubinga E, Maes A & Jansen C. (2016). How peer conversations about HIV/AIDS media messages affect comprehension and beliefs of young South African women. *SAHARA-J: Journal of Social Aspects of HIV/AIDS*, 13(1):68–80. https://doi.org/10.1080/17290376.2016.1197146

Lubinga, E. & Sitto, K. 2021. Health Communication in Africa. In: Routledge Handbook of African Media and Communication Studies,. W. Mano & v.C.Milton (eds,) 1st edition. (pp. 217-233). New York: Routledge.Lubinga E, Sitto K & Molebatsi K. (2021). Health disparities and the digital divide within South African disadvantaged communities during the COVID-19 pandemic. *Catalan Journal of Communication & Cultural Studies*, 13(2):285–302. https://doi.org/10.1386/cjcs_00054_1

Magingxa N. (2011). Community Health Workers: A Brief Description of the HST Experience. February. https://www.hst.org.za/publications/HST%20Publications/CHWs_HSTexpo22011.pdf.

Maqhina M. (2020). *Taxpayers paid R11.2m to Resort to accommodate repatriated South Africans from China.* IOL. 8 June. https://www.iol.co.za/news/politics/taxpayers-paid-r112m-to-resort-to-accommodate-repatriated-south-africans-from-china-49110643

Meppelink CS, Smit EG, Buurman BM & Van Weert JC. (2015). Should we be afraid of simple messages? The effects of text difficulty and illustrations in people with low or high health literacy. Health Communication, 30(12):1181–1189. https://doi.org/10.1080/10410236.2015.1037425

Mkhize Z. (2021). Minister Zweli Mkhize: Health Department budget vote 2021/22. Speech, 13 May. https://www.gov.za/news/speeches/minister-zweli-mkhize-health-dept-budget-vote-202122-13-may-2021

Mkize V. (2017). *What you need to know about Department of Health's Phila campaign.* IOL. 20 November. https://iol.co.za/lifestyle/health/what-you-need-to-know-about-department-of-healths-phila-campaign-12079443

Mueller AL, McNamara MS & Sinclair DA. (2020). Why does COVID-19 disproportionately affect older people? *Aging*, 12(10):9959–9981. https://doi.org/10.18632/aging.103344

Myeni G. (2018). *'Cheka Impilo' campaign launched*. Zululand Observer. 22 October. https://zululandobserver.co.za/181223/cheka-impilo-campaign-launched/

Naidoo T. (2022). *Decline in literacy levels in SA attributed to COVID-19*. SABC News. 9 September. https://www.sabcnews.com/sabcnews/decline-in-literacy-levels-in-sa-attributed-to-covid-19/

National Health Service (NHS). (2017). *The Care Act: Wellbeing*. Hertfordshire Partnership NHS. 19 January. https://www.hpft.nhs.uk/information-and-resources/care-act-2014/the-care-act-wellbeing/

Ngqakamba S. (2020). *Covid-19: 'Why did he not eat for 48 hours?': Father wants answers after son dies in hospital*. News24. 4 December. https://www.news24.com/news24/southafrica/news/covid-19-why-did-he-not-eat-for-48-hours-father-wants-answers-after-son-dies-in-hospital-20200702

Norman CD & Skinner HA. (2006). eHealth literacy: Essential skills for consumer health in a networked world. *Journal of Medical Internet Research*, 8(2):e9. https://doi: 10.2196/jmir.8.2.e9

Nutbeam D. (2000). Health literacy as a public health goal: A challenge for contemporary health education and communication strategies into the 21st century. *Health Promotion International*, 15(3):259–267. https://doi.org/10.1093/heapro/15.3.259

Ostrowick J. (2018). Empowering teachers to use ICTs in South Africa. *Global Dialogue on ICT and Education Innovation*. Moscow, Russia. Presentation, 18-19 April. https://iite.unesco.org/wp-content/uploads/2018/05/John-Ostrowick-Teachers-and-ICTs-in-South-Africa.pdf

Parliamentary Monitoring Group. (2024).*The Budget Vote Report of the Portfolio Committee on Health, dated 03 May 2023*. https://pmg.org.za/files/230505pchealthreport.docx#:~:text

Pleasant A. (2014). Advancing health literacy measurement: A pathway to better health and health system performance. *Journal of Health Communication*, 19(12):1481–1496. https://doi.org/10.1080/10810730.2014.954083

Rédaction Africanews. (2022). *South Africa to destroy 100,000 covid 19 vaccines by end of March?* africanews. 4 March. https://www.africanews.com/2022/03/04/south-africa-to-destroy-100-000-covid-19-vaccines-by-end-of-march//

Renckens CN & Dorlo TP. (2013). *Please, let not Western quackery replace traditional medicine in Africa. Tropical Medicine & International Health*, 18 (2):242–244. https://doi.org/10.1111/tmi.12037

Rimal RN & Lapinski LK. (2009). Why health communication is important in public health. Bulletin for World Health Organisation, 87(4):247–247a. https://doi.org/10.2471/BLT.08.056713

Rural Health Information Hub. (2024. *Ecological models*. RHIhub. https://www.ruralhealthinfo.org/toolkits/health-promotion/2/theories-and-models/ecological

Saleh M. (2022). *Number of COVID-19 vaccination doses administered in Africa, by country*. Statista. 17 November. https://www.statista.com/statistics/1221298/covid-19-vaccination-rate-in-african-countries/

Sallis, J. F., & Owen, N. (2015). Ecological models of health behavior. In K. Glanz, B. K. Rimer, & K. "V." Viswanath (Eds.), Health behavior: Theory, research, and practice (5th ed., pp. 43–64). Jossey-Bass/Wiley.

Sheridan SL, Halpern DJ, Viera AJ et al. (2011). Interventions for individuals with low health literacy: A systematic review. *Journal of Health Communication*, 16(3):30–54. https://doi.org/10.1080/10810730.2011.604391

Shisana O, Rehle T, Simbayi LC et al. (2009). *South African National HIV Prevalence, Incidence, Behaviour and Communication Survey 2008: A Turning Tide among Teenagers?* Cape Town: HSRC Press.

Sitto K, Lubinga E, Chiumbu S, Sobane K & Mpofu N. (2022). Evaluating South African and Namibian governments' use of digital media during Covid-19. *World Medical & Health Policy.* 14(2):325–342. https://doi.org/10.1002/wmh3.507

Thompson TL. (2014). Health communication, History of. In: TL Thompson (Ed). *Encyclopedia of Health Communication,* Thousand Oaks, USA: SAGE Publications. 568–572. [Retrieved 15 November 2022] https://doi.org/10.4135/9781483346427

Tlou G. (2020). *Businessman fighting Covid-19 dies after complaining of not being fed for two days.* IOL. 4 December. https://www.iol.co.za/the-star/news/businessman-fighting-covid-19-dies-after-complaining-of-not-being-fed-for-two-days-50284953

World Health Organisation (WHO). (2008). *Framework and Standards for Country Health Information Systems.* 2nd Edition. Geneva, Switzerland: World Health Organisation

World Health Organisation. (WHO). (2022). *Preventing cancer.* World Health Organization. https://www.who.int/activities/preventing-cancer

World Health Organisation (WHO). (n.d.). *Promoting well-being.* World Health Organization. https://www.who.int/activities/promoting-well-being

Chapter 8

Analysing Public Policies and Communication Strategies in Zimbabwe's Eye Healthcare Industry

Vincent Tshuma *and Sibongile Mpofu*

Public health is defined as "the science and art of preventing disease, prolonging life and promoting, protecting and improving health through the organised efforts of society" (Acheson, 1988: 1). Its functions, among many, include developing policies and plans that support individual and community health efforts and also health promotion.

Eye health, specifically, is important because vision is the most valued of the five senses and plays a crucial role in every facet of human lives (WHO, 2019). Among the sighted, vision is integral to interpersonal and social interactions in face-to-face communication where information is conveyed through non-verbal cues such as gestures and facial expressions (WHO, 2019). It is for this reason that efforts by countries, organisations and communities to improve eye health contribute to the advancement of several United Nations' SDGs, including those not exclusively eye-health-related (Zhang et al., 2020). As such, Zhang et al. (2020) argue that eye health promotion is an essential part of improving universal access to improve livelihoods.

From this premise, communication policies and strategies towards eye healthcare promotion are therefore important processes in the attainment of the SDGs. This study therefore assesses how public health communication policies and strategies contribute towards public awareness of eye and vision health in a particular community. This is because the wellbeing of an eye for an individual determines how one accesses education and employment, how they contribute to economic growth, and how they are affected by poverty (Zhang et al., 2020).

Similarly, Chen (2021) argues that eye health is essential for achieving the SDGs as poverty is both a cause and consequence of poor eye health. Statistics reveal that, globally, women and girls are 12% more likely to have vision loss and experience additional barriers to eye care services, thus contributing to gender inequality (Chen, 2021). Therefore, improved eye health can increase household income, which, in turn, reduces hunger and promotes inclusive economic growth, employment and improved living standards.

The IAPB further posits that, being driven by social, financial and political inequality, eye health promotion requires a holistic approach, and we argue that this should not be the preserve of governments alone, but of all stakeholders in the eye and vision healthcare industry. Therefore, this study critically assesses communication policies, activities and strategy frameworks by analysing the policy documents of eye health regulatory bodies in Zimbabwe, including the Pharmacists Council of Zimbabwe (PCZ), Health Professions Authority of Zimbabwe, Zimbabwe Optometric Association and Zimbabwe Ophthalmologists Association.

Further, strategy documents, social media activity, communications and stakeholder relationship and community engagement initiatives during the period January 2020 to July 2022 are analysed. The choice of the time frame, pre-COVID-19 and during the COVID-19 period, is relevant to identify health communication practices before and during the pandemic, including digital communication strategies in eye health promotion. The study is limited to optometry/optical practitioners, policymakers and strategy developers.

Overview of Public Health Communication in Zimbabwe

Communication within the public health sector in Zimbabwe is governed overall by Chapter 15:17 of the Public Health Act of 2018. Section 3 of the Act stipulates that the Ministry of Health and Child Care (MoHCC) is responsible for informing, educating and empowering the population about health issues, and for taking measures to prevent, limit and suppress infectious, communicable and non-communicable diseases. Chapter 37 of this Act stipulates that the duty to disseminate information lies with the Health Services Board – which the Government of Zimbabwe later declared should work jointly with the Health Services Commission. The Health Services Board ensures that appropriate, adequate and comprehensive information is disseminated on health services.

The Public Health Act states who can be delegated to release such information. Generally, governments have used health marketing targeting whole communities, entire populations or segments of society to disseminate public health communication messages (Schiavo, 2014: 37). It is important to note that in Zimbabwe's public health system, the Health Services Board is the key regulatory authority for health matters and practice, but that there are numerous regulatory subsets in the form of healthcare professional regulatory bodies, outlined in Chapter 27: 19, Part II, Section 5 of the Health Professions Act, which also outlines the major responsibilities of the Health Professions Authority – to register and control health institutions and to regulate the services provided at, or from, them, as well as to conduct inspections in all health institutions throughout Zimbabwe. The authority is the coordinating umbrella body for the seven health professional councils that regulate health practitioners in Zimbabwe. Thus, the public health ecosystem in Zimbabwe is subject to heavy regulation and operational scrutiny.

The eye health industry in Zimbabwe, with which this study is concerned, has been characterised by very low levels of communication, public relations, stakeholder engagement and community engagement for more than a decade (MoHCC, 2014). International eye calendar events such as World Sight Day and World Optometry Day, among other international health commemorations, are barely recognised in Zimbabwe, while other conditions such as cancer, diabetes, HIV/AIDS, tuberculosis and other communicable diseases receive national attention from the Ministry of Health and Child Care and its stakeholders (MoHCC, 2014).

Literature and Theoretical Approach

Health communication is an evolving and increasingly prominent field of public health and healthcare, both in the non-profit and private sectors (Schiavo, 2014). Schiavo further posits that when analysed, the various definitions of health communications:

> "... point to the role that health communication play[s] in influencing, supporting, and empowering individuals, communities, healthcare professionals, policymakers, or special groups to adopt and sustain a behaviour, or a social, organisational, and policy change, that will ultimately improve individual, community, and public health outcomes." (2014: 37)

This illustrates how communication, and health communication in particular, plays a pivotal role in shaping, directing and contesting narratives and behaviours in public health discourses, be it behaviour change, policymaking or increasing knowledge and awareness among societal groups. Therefore, health communication is a fundamental part of public health practice, whether in the context of clinical practice, community-based healthcare services or health behaviour change and awareness building (Schiavo, 2014: 37). It is of note that communication is a critical important component of healthcare and is worth investing in (Kreps, 1993; Pandit et al., 2017). Schiavo (2014) further adds that health communication creates the right organisational mindset and capacity that should lead to the successful use of communication approaches to reach group, stakeholder and community-specific goals. From this premise, one can argue that health communication is vital not only for health practice, but also in contributing towards the promulgation of national health policies that empower, inform, engage and influence individuals and communities on matters regarding their health.

However, scholars such as Kreps (1993: 56) further lament the lack of attention to the dynamics of communication generally in public health research, especially as strategic communication directed at specific constituencies in communities can contribute to improved quality healthcare for the citizens of any country. He argues: "However, it [communication] is often taken for granted, its complexities and subtleties are overlooked, and it receives little attention in the literature on healthcare."

Much of the scholarly focus has been on interpersonal communication, especially the practitioner-to-patient communication, thus overlooking other communication dynamics and the influence of the environment. As Schiavo (2014) further observed, in contemporary society, health communication practice takes place in an open system environment, where the healthcare consumer (client) is in the centre of the system where he or she is surrounded by, and interacts with, service providers. In such instances, the client is usually the initiator of healthcare. Kreps and Thornton, (1992: 42-45) further concur that both clients and health professionals interact with the healthcare settings and external environment from where necessary and sometimes vital information is obtained. We therefore argue that it is critical for private healthcare professionals and policymakers to understand the key dynamics of how communication works outside the health institution. We further argue that there is a lack of appreciation and understanding that health communication, and communication in its raw form, exists at community, stakeholder and macro levels, which arguably contributes to high levels of ignorance, myths, misconceptions and misinformation on health matters, including eye care across the world today. National Academies of Sciences, Engineering, and Medicine (2016) argue that eye and vision health remain absent as a priority in the overarching public health and healthcare systems globally, and thus is underrepresented in strategic plans that address the impact of chronic diseases in economies.

Further, critiques of health communication models, for example, Lupton (1994), have argued that communication in the health context is traditionally conceptualised as a top-down approach with communication flowing from centres to peripheral locations. Health communication is, therefore, according to Dutta-Bergman (2005: 106) a "political process marked by power relations that determine the relationship between the bourgeoisie and the subaltern classes". Thus, health communication has the ability to shape social contexts (Wilkins & Mody, 2001: 198). From this premise, to achieve the intended health outcomes, there is a need for broader health communication strategies, tools and methods of communication – especially in view of new technologies – that take into account the social contexts and specific needs of communities. The social context in particular is critical: scholars such as Teutsch, Masur and Trepte (2018) remind us that the social, economic and health conditions of a country, community or society largely affect the outcome of eye health, hence the connection between eye health and economic, socio-cultural and health development. As such, one can argue that eye health is a catalyst to universal health equity for individuals and communities, hence contributing immensely to the achievement of the SDGs.

This leads the study to address the following questions:

1. Do the national policies guiding the eye health industry in Zimbabwe integrate communication for public awareness on eye health?
2. What strategies are utilised by service providers in the eye health industry to communicate with their various stakeholders?

3. Who are the key audiences for eye health communication messages, and what are the key messages?
4. How do these communication policies and strategies contribute to the attainment of SDGs in the Zimbabwean context, if at all?

This study utilises the critical theory, integrative strategic communication management and health communication theories as well the Precede-Proceed model to identify and analyse the communication policies and strategies within Zimbabwe's eye health industry.

Critical theory

Critical theory is a normative approach that is based on the judgment that domination is a problem, and that a domination-free society is needed (Fuchs, 2016). According to Fuchs (2016), there are six dimensions of critical theory:

1. critical ethics;
2. critique of domination,
3. exploitation and alienation;
4. dialectical reason;
5. ideology critique; and
6. struggles and political praxis.

According to the critical theory of communication, communication is one of the crucial foundations of the economy (Habermas, 1987). Habermas (1987) further notes that in capitalism, communication – such as technology, the media, ideology or labour – is an instrument that is used by the dominant system to defend its rule. Critical theory is relevant for this study to effectively identify, analyse and interpret the hidden underpinnings of politics, domination and inequities inherent in the communication policies and strategies employed by regulatory bodies and service providers in the eye health industry in Zimbabwe.

The overall goal of using critical theory for this study is to assess whether the communication policies and strategies encompass the needs of every Zimbabwean. In addition, through its diverse thematics of communication and power, critical theory allowed us as researchers to analyse the existing communications policies, strategies and activities in the eye healthcare industry, determine and decipher whom the policies favour, against whom they discriminate, and what eye health industry stakeholders are communicating to the public regarding eye health.

Integrative strategic communication management theory

Strategic communication broadly explores the capacity of all organisations – not only corporations, but also for not-for-profit organisations (including advocacy and activist groups) and government – to engage in purposeful communication (Hallahan et al., 2007). Further, strategic communication emphasises the strategic application of communication and how an organisation functions as a social actor to advance its mission (Hallahan et al., 2007).

The integrative strategic communication management approach therefore emphasises a holistic, collaborative and intentional communication approach, where key stakeholders have an impact on the communication process (Steyn & De Beer, 2012). One of the key tenets of this integrative approach to strategic communication is that the value of communication is added at the strategic level, taking into account the changing environment, within a context – this to ensure sustainability and governance (Steyn & De Beer, 2012). Thus, health communication should be strategic and cognisant of the socio-cultural, economic and political environment for messages to have desired outcomes.

Another key characteristic relevant for this study is the differentiation between "strategic communication management" and "communication management" taking place on different levels in an organisation (De Beer, Steyn & Rensburg, 2013). While this paradigm was initially applied to corporate settings, it is relevant for government public affairs, which serve a critical function of meeting public expectations and societal developmental goals. This paradigm is relevant as it will help identify the levels of decision-making and strategy-making within the eye health sector in Zimbabwe, and how these different structures and levels of regulation contribute, if at all, towards the communication strategy within the sector. The paradigm could also assist in assessing whether, in the formulation of eye health messages, there is integration among the relevant stakeholders in the eye health sector, such as private players, individuals, community and wider society.

Precede-Proceed model

The Precede-Proceed model of Green and Kreuter (1999), posits that the approach to planning health communication should take into account the factors that contribute to behaviour change. The model further postulates that sustainable change is determined by the individual's motivation to become directly involved with the process of social change, and that individuals need to feel empowered to change their quality of life (National Cancer Institute cited in Schiavo, 2014). The model outlines three factors influencing behaviour change, two of which are relevant for this study: predisposing factors – i.e. individual knowledge, beliefs and values – and enabling factors – i.e. factors in the environment of an individual that enable or impede change (Schiavo, 2014: 53). This model helps us to assess health communication messages and especially the target audiences.

Further, because the model considers the individual as part of the social environment, it allows for the analysis and integration of Zimbabwe's socio-cultural, economic and political environment into understanding the importance of eye and vision health. The model further supports the notion of individual empowerment and capacity building at both the individual and community levels (Schiavo, 2014: 53). Thus, the model is applicable in the identification and analysis of the communication strategies used in the eye health sector in Zimbabwe.

Methodology

This study utilises a qualitative research approach, enabling a deeper exploration of the social phenomenon of interpretation and sense construction (Corbin & Strauss, 2007). Within the context of the COVID-19 pandemic, in-depth interviews were conducted utilising online technologies/platforms, in particular Zoom and Skype, as well as email. Informed consent was sought from the participants and the organisations concerned, and the interviews were recorded with the participants' consent. Ten eye healthcare practitioners participated in the study. Observations were used to monitor social media pages of at least 10 optometry/optical organisations/practices and the online activity of ophthalmologic practitioners was monitored as well to assess the characteristics of this activity on the sites concerned.

Document analysis was utilised to analyse Chapters 27:19 and 15:17 of the Health Professions Act, as well as the Optometrists and Dispensing Opticians Professional Conduct Regulations of 2010. Document analysis was conducted to analyse power dynamics in eye health governance especially the power structures, hidden meanings and intended meanings in the communications policies and strategies implemented by eyecare service providers in Zimbabwe.

Discussion

National and organisational policies guiding communication in the eye health industry in Zimbabwe

Our findings demonstrate that the policies governing the eye health industry are not drafted by the country's eye healthcare service providers, but are developed, enforced and enacted by the Pharmacists Council of Zimbabwe and Health Professions Authority of Zimbabwe. Furthermore, Chapter 27:19 of the Health Professions Act is the primary reference point for all regulations drawn up by industry regulators who craft policies to govern professions such as optometry, ophthalmology, opticianry, pharmacies and other health professions. With regards to communication, Section 4, subsection (1) of the Optometrists and Dispensing Opticians Professional Conduct regulations (PCZ, 2010), limits promotional communication and states that:

> "... no optometrist or dispensing optician shall advertise or give publicity to his/her practice or business ..."

Furthermore, subsection (2) of the regulation states that:

> "Any advertising undertaken by optometrist or dispensing optician, and which is permitted under these regulations, shall be of a dignified and restrained character, and free from any reference to the efficiency of him/her, or the facilities offered by other optometrists or dispensing opticians."

The clause is in line with section 145 of the Health Professions Act, Chapter 27:19.

Therefore advertising, which is defined on page 3 of the policy document as "including any advertisement contained in a print media publication or as a production in the electronic media or by loudspeaker or public address system", is disallowed by law. In addition, the policy document further adds that the term "publication" includes:

> "(a) any newspaper, book periodical, pamphlet, poster, playing card, calendar or other printed matter; or (b) any writing or typescript which has in any manner been duplicated or exhibited or made available to the public or any section of the public".

Thus, within this industry, there are considerable restrictions on communication as a whole imposed on private eye health providers by the government's health professions authority function. This conforms to other findings by Lupton (1994) and

Dutta-Bergman (2005) that health communication is largely top-down from the centre to peripheral locations, and marked by relations of power between the elite and subaltern classes.

Another finding reveals that there are legislative restrictions on stakeholder communications and public relations activities by eye healthcare practitioners/service providers. Section 6, subsection 2 of the regulations enacted by the PCZ on eye health service providers/eye health industry stipulate that:

> "An optometrist or a dispensing optician may take part, in relation to his practice or business, in—
>
> (a) trade shows or exhibitions which are **not open to the general public** and **are wholly or mainly related to the display of optical appliances and parts thereof, or of fittings, appliances, apparatus and instruments intended for use or sale by opticians or medical practitioners**; [bold is for emphasis by the authors]
>
> (b) other shows or exhibitions with **the consent of the local association and subject to any conditions which the association may impose.**"

From the forementioned, we argue that such policies restrict stakeholder communications as exhibitions are typically a platform where multiple stakeholders are addressed simultaneously. What can be inferred is that the policies in the eye healthcare industry are not conscious of the need for strategic public relations practices in promoting eye healthcare services and information to the public. Because of the limitations imposed by the government, they thus create a gap in public knowledge about eye and vision health, which, arguably, negatively affects the pace at which SDGs are being achieved in Zimbabwe. This argument is supported by the World Health Organization (2017), which argues that communication is an integral part of promoting and achieving the SDGs for every community as it bridges the gaps in knowledge, information and education about healthcare, economic, political and socio-cultural narratives of members of society. The findings from the document analysis previously mentioned correspond with those from the interviews, in which the health practitioners confirmed the consequences of the restrictions imposed by the public sector on their eye health promotion activities.

Furthermore, section 7 of the Professional Conduct regulations (2010) restricts tools of communication within the industry to trade or professional periodicals, and not mass media. The regulation policy document states that:

> "An optometrist or dispensing optician may publish advertisements, or other matter relating to his practice or business, in periodicals circulating wholly or mainly among optometrists, medical practitioners, ophthalmologists, pharmaceutical chemists or members of ancillary professions to medicine, or to manufacturers of or dealers in optical appliances and employees of optometrists or dispensing opticians".

From this premise, one can argue that there is a dearth of knowledge on eye health education and awareness among the public communities in Zimbabwe, owing largely to restrictive regulations. It is for this reason that we argue that there is a de-prioritisation of public eye health education and awareness in Zimbabwe and this, according to the Precede-Proceed model (Green & Kreuter, 1999), disempowers individuals and communities. Since advertisements and exhibitions are forms of communication, we argue their restriction is a direct impediment to the practice of public health communication in Zimbabwe, specifically in relation to the furthering and promotion of eye health communication and education information. The effect of this is lower prioritisation of eye and vision health in the country. Further, the restriction of mass media tools in communicating eye health is indicative of the lack of an integrative strategic communication management approach proposed by Hallahan et al. (2007) and Steyn and De Beer (2012). We therefore argue that by communicating through trade and professional periodicals, such eye health communication negates wider society, as these trade shows are prevalently done in urban setups and neglect the wider population living in peri-urban and rural areas. Thus, such policies can also be argued to be largely discriminatory as far as promoting access to health communication and knowledge are concerned.

The country's eye healthcare policy as stipulated by the Zimbabwe Optometric Association (2021) also states how practitioners in the industry should communicate with their existing clients/patients, stating that such communication should be in the form of print communication material such as pamphlets and flyers. Zhang (2020) argues that health communication campaigns can play a central or supportive role in health education and social marketing; hence, as the findings of this study attest, advertising and marketing efforts aimed at increasing awareness and access to eye healthcare services could promote positive eye healthcare choices, attitudes and behaviours in Zimbabwe. Section 10 (1) of the Professional Conduct regulations (2010: 7) states that:

> "An optometrist or dispensing optician may send to a person who has had an eye examination or been supplied with optical appliances in the course of his practice or business, a notice informing them of –
>
> a change of address or telephone number of the premises where their eyes were examined or where they were supplied with optical appliances, or of closing those premises, or the changes in hours of opening or closing of the premises, or of the name under which the practice or business is carried on at those premises ...

And that:

> An optometrist or a dispensing optician may send circular letters, booklets, leaflets or pamphlets, relating to optical appliances and of an informative nature, by—
>
> making them available at his premises;

sending them to persons who have had their eyes examined or have been supplied with optical appliances in the course of his practice or business,

sending them to any person who has specifically requested that they should be sent to him."

What we deduce from the forementioned is that there are also restrictions on what should be contained in the printed communication material such as pamphlets and circulars. The findings therefore highlight that the policies regulating the industry only allow specific communication to a particular type of stakeholder – i.e. only a client who has accessed eye healthcare services, and not the general public, who may need such information. As such, there is no consideration for the prospective or potential client/patient out in the community or workplace and the general community member who is not aware of eye health or the importance of eye healthcare, and hence this also contradicts one of the core principles guiding public health in Zimbabwe. Specifically, Chapter 15:17, Part III, Section 31(d) of the Public Health Act stipulates that public health plays/should play a role in the promotion of health and of access to the social determinants of health. Therefore, the lack of consideration given to the sharing and dissemination of eye health communication with people who are not existing patients of an eye health facility affects the extent to which public health information and awareness fundamentals are attained in Zimbabwe. A representative of the Pharmacists Council of Zimbabwe stated:

> "Practitioners are allowed only to advise the public of their practice's location and trading hours."

And that:

> "The profession has noted that advertising of professional services has to continue to be regulated to ensure that the public is not misinformed and there is no unhealthy competition which will end up harming the public" (Practitioner 1, 2022).

Thus, we argue there is no strategic intention to create public awareness on eye healthcare through public policy. The major weakness of the policy is that it is not sustainable as far as promoting eye healthcare and services to individuals in the community is concerned. This is because these policies specifically do not allow an eyecare service provider to inform other members of society who have not received eye health services and products either about the importance of eye health or on various issues to do with eye health, as also argued by Lederman, Kreps and Roberto (2017). Thus, one can argue that the policies on eye health in Zimbabwe do not favour the advancement of the SDGs as they do not extend their reach to communities and individuals in much need of eye health education and services. Therefore, we posit that eye health communication does not take into context the specific needs of communities in Zimbabwe. As Teutsch et al (2016) remind us, there is a connection between eye health and socio-cultural as well as overall health development. Not taking cognisance of the specific needs of societies regarding eye health may arguably be detrimental to the attainment of SDGs, not only for healthcare but for the entire betterment of society socially, economically and physically (WHO, 2019).

In addition, the restrictive policies in the eye health industry arguably present an obstacle to eye and vision health as little information filters through to individuals and communities on the importance of eye health. Eye health is an integral part of individual healthcare and can affect large parts of the population if neglected (Teutsch et al., 2016: 4; Burton, Faal & Ramke, 2019). Therefore, the restrictions imposed upon eye health practitioners in Zimbabwe make the promotion of public health messages in the context of promoting eye health very difficult, negatively affecting the overall extent to which public health as a national health thematic is achieved and adequately promoted.

Interview respondents concurred with the findings from the analysis of policy documents and made the point that these policies need to be updated to reflect the evolving nature of health communication – advertising included – and its community orientation rather than a focus on profit. One of the respondents – an optometrist with more than 20 years of optical practise in Zimbabwe – gave the following remarks when asked to mention the key challenges in implementing communication, marketing or public relations activities as a practitioner/organisation:

> "Outdated legislation is a huge challenge for my practice's marketing and communication activities. The laws that are governing eyecare practitioners are 10+ years ago and they need urgent updating. It is difficult to spread awareness and educate communities since the existing laws do not allow us to market or practice communication/public relations activities. Our industry legislation needs to be updated." (Practitioner 2, 2022)

An optometrist with an optical practice in Bulawayo also added:

> "The current laws governing the eye healthcare [industry] are very outdated. They no longer make sense towards our efforts to spread awareness on eye health and educate communities on the importance of eyecare. Unfortunately, our industry regulators do not seem to be aware of the gap their laws are creating in terms of access to eyecare services in the country." (Practitioner 3, 2022)

What is inferred, therefore, is that policies governing the eye health industry in Zimbabwe are outdated and in need of review and amendment in line with the current needs of the modern health communication ecosystem, which is aimed at using communication to improve health outcomes through encouraging behaviour modification and social change (Schiavo, 2014: 45).

From the perspective of the health communication theoretical approach, the findings mentioned previously highlight communication as a fundamental element of policy change and promoting health behaviours for all stakeholders in society and/or communities (Schiavo, 2014: 37). Thus, in the context of this study, the data presented on policies governing communication in the eye health industry reveal that the existing policies do not favour the creation of new policies and the promotion of eye healthcare to individuals and society. Furthermore, the data indicate that health communication as a practice is not understood, and its implications appreciated in the eye healthcare industry.

From the point of view of integrated strategic communication management theory (Steyn & De Beer, 2012), the findings indicate a lack of awareness among regulators about why eye health should be integrated into key strategic communication plans within the overall healthcare system. This finding concurs with National Academies of Sciences, Engineering, and Medicine (2016) that globally eye health remains underrepresented in national strategic plans. Additionally, regulators need to be made aware of the need for strategic communication within the eye and vision health sector, in particular the need for strategic dissemination of key messages to the general public in order to improve population health (Gupta, Narain & Yadav, 2021).

Communication strategies utilised by service providers in Zimbabwe

To a great extent, eye health industry service providers in Zimbabwe use outreach programmes as their key communication strategy in an attempt to navigate around the communication restrictions imposed and enacted by the PCZ.

Our findings show that health campaigns, including outreach programmes and activities, are one of the most effective means that service providers use to communicate with their various stakeholders. The findings of our study reveal that optometrists/optometry practices, ophthalmologists, eye health NGOs and industry bodies all utilise outreach activities as their fundamental communication strategy to promote eye healthcare among communities in Zimbabwe. Stakeholder relationship and partnership events are also widely used communication strategies in the eye health industry as service providers classify them as outreach programmes. One of the practitioners interviewed in the study stated that:

> "Other stakeholders must be made aware of the need for eye health. Without advertisement and communication programme activities, eyecare services will not reach out to the deprived communities. So, the only way we are currently trying to bypass these restrictions is through outreach activities in partnership with stakeholders in other industries such as medical insurance and corporates." (Practitioner 5, 2022)

Therefore, one could argue that outreach programmes access and positively impact wider audiences for eye health communication as they may reach other family members and communities rather than existing eyecare patients only.

The study found that few eye healthcare service providers in Zimbabwe have active social media pages, websites or other online platforms, likely due to the restrictions imposed and enacted by PCZ under the Health Professions Act, Chapter 27:19. This is despite the fact that ICTs have been shown to serve as support structure for all 17 SDGs, including equity in health (ADEC, 2017). One of the representatives interviewed – a National Programmes Manager for the Zimbabwe Council for the Blind – said:

> "Our organisation has outsourced a communication specialist to help us manage our social media pages – our posts, content and updates."

> "Organisations in Zimbabwe should be free to share their content and communicate their strategies and also market their services online, as these platforms are now the most preferred by the majority of the population." (Practitioner 4, 2022)

This explains why relatively few eye healthcare service providers are active online. Social media communications for public health promotion are underutilised by eye health practitioners in Zimbabwe as they fear penalties could be imposed and practice certificates/licences be revoked by industry regulators.

Also noteworthy is that few service providers in the eye health industry have strategies for communicating with their stakeholders. Except for individuals who have already received eye health services and are contacted for follow-up examination, there is a lack of communication at the functional level between service providers in the eye health industry and their various stakeholders, especially members of the community. This was confirmed during the interviews carried out in this study, the following being an example:

> "We are only allowed to engage stakeholders such as medical aid societies and other corporate institutions on non-optical concerns and processes. Communicating eye healthcare messages to other people outside our practice databases is not possible given the strict laws on how we should communicate." (Practitioner 9, 2022)

For this reason, one could argue that there is a dearth of stakeholder communication in the eye health industry in Zimbabwe, which leads to the conclusion that, because current communication policies do not encourage service providers to share knowledge with the wider communication, health communication is not prioritised in the eye health industry. From a critical theory perspective, this study is able to unearth the inequities that are inherent in eye health communication, and in particular the fact that eye health communication favours those in power.

The study further highlights the importance of strategic communication in the eye health sector in order for communities to benefit from purposeful eye health messages. Key to note is that community involvement in healthcare decisions, actions and issues is also one of the principles of public health and practice stipulated in Chapter 15:17, Part III, Section 31(i) of the Public Health Act. Emphasis is placed on community participation as an integral role in decision-making and actions affecting their health; again, this shows unfriendly legal communication policies in the eye healthcare sector negatively influences public health in Zimbabwe broadly.

Targeted audiences and key messages

Ideally, health communication and eye health in particular should target entire communities in any context (Ruben, 2016). However, owing to the centralised nature of communication and restrictions on what eye service providers may and may not say, we find that, in the Zimbabwean context, eye health information has very limited reach among stakeholders. Our findings reveal that:

- there is more service provider–client communication;
- there is more peer–peer communication among eye health professionals themselves; and
- there are pockets of stakeholders who are reached through a few events such as outreach or wellness programmes.

Large communication gaps still exist in Zimbabwe for eye health awareness and there is virtually no mass targeting for eye and vision health messages. The key target audiences are people who have already accessed specialist eye care or visit the optometrist regularly to avoid or reduce the risk of severe eye problems.

In terms of key messages being communicated by eye health service providers in Zimbabwe, these are insignificant as service providers are practising little to no communication in the eye health industry. Similarly, mass communication messages on eye and vision health in Zimbabwe are partially evident only during the annual commemorations such as World Sight Day, where eye health practitioners encourage communities to take care of their eyes by following eye health standards, being aware of symptoms of eye complications and regularly visiting their optometrists.

While some service providers do use outreach activities and stakeholder partnership events to disseminate eye health information, the prevalent communication restrictions in the eye health industry deter them from promoting access to and knowledge on eye health in the country. Fuchs (2016: 11) argues that "communication is a tool or instrument that is used by those in power to retain their power and maintain it". As such, one could argue that the industry largely serves the literate and elite few who have an appreciation of the need for eye healthcare but neglect ordinary and marginalised citizens who lack information on eye and vision health and why this is important for their general wellbeing and development. Thus, the restrictions on communication practice in the eyecare industry indicate a deliberate intention to control perceptions and control narratives on access to healthcare thereby negatively affecting the entire population's appreciation, knowledge and information on eye health.

Implications for the attainment of SDGs in the Zimbabwean context

As mentioned, the study has found that the eye healthcare industry in Zimbabwe has a specific policy that prohibits the practice of strategic communication management to inform, educate and communicate to the public about eye health matters. As such, one could argue that this has a negative impact on the attainment of the SDGs because of the low level of awareness on basic eye healthcare among members of the public and society. As one of the optometrists interviewed commented:

> "Due to the restrictions on marketing and other communication practices in the eye healthcare industry, eyecare services and information are not reaching underserviced and remote communities, especially in rural areas. Hence there is need for improvement in the industry's marketing and advertising policies." (Practitioner 10, 2022)

In addition, the study found that exhibitions and trade fairs hosted and facilitated by stakeholders in the eye healthcare sector are not open to the general public, preventing education and information from reaching the most affected stakeholder in the eye health industry – the community. There are also low levels of awareness on the SDGs in the eye healthcare sector, and the majority of eye healthcare practitioners interviewed could not explain or describe how communication in the eye healthcare industry contributes to the attainment of the SDGs in Zimbabwe. In line with the Precede-Proceed model (Green & Kreutner, 1999), with low levels of awareness, it becomes difficult for individuals to embrace behaviour change regarding eye and vision health.

Conclusion

This study concludes that communication practices and strategies in the eye health industry in Zimbabwe are heavily restricted, with limited cooperation between the public and private sector. The relevant communication policies are set at the highest level of decision-making, namely the PCZ as the industry regulator, with support from the MoHCC. These policies, drafted and enforced by the industry regulator, restrict who eye practitioners should communicate with; how they should communicate; what they communicate, when they should communicate and for what purpose.

We conclude that the policies are the largest contributor to the dearth of knowledge on eye health education and awareness for communities in Zimbabwe. According to these policies, eye health service providers are not allowed to use any print or electronic communication methods to promote eye health to the general public, nor to market and advertise any eye-healthcare-related products or information. The fact that such information only targets individuals who have received eye services, leads us to conclude that the rest of the Zimbabwean population have remained unaware of the importance of eye health to their wellbeing.

Our analysis further revealed the absence of knowledge, understanding and appreciation of the SDGs in the eye health industry, leading us to conclude that the eye health policies found in Zimbabwe do not contribute to the attainment of the SDGs. Overall, we conclude that there is an absence of integrated strategic communication management with regards to eye and vision health and subsequently, a de-prioritisation of public eye health education and awareness in Zimbabwe.

References

Acheson D. (1988). Public Health in England: The Report of the Committee of Inquiry into the Future Development of the Public Health Function. 1st Edition. London: Stationery Office Books.

Burton, M. J., Faal H.B., Ramke J., Ravilla, B., Holland, P., Wang, N, West, S. K., Bourne, R. R. R., Congdon, N., Foster, A. (2019). Announcing the Lancet global health Commission on global eye health. Lancet Glob Health. 2Dec;7(12):e1612-e1613. https://doi.org/10.1016/S2214-109X(19)30450-4. Epub 2019 Oct 9. PMID: 31606327

Corbin, J. M., & Strauss, J. M. (2007). Basics of qualitative research: Techniques and procedures for developing grounded theory (3rd ed.). Thousand Oaks, CA: Sage. https://doi.org/10.4135/9781452230153

Chen J. (2021). *Reaching the Sustainable Development Goals through tackling poor vision*. International Agency for the Prevention of Blindness (IAPB). 22 June. [Retrieved 16 May 2022]. https://www.iapb.org/blog/reaching-the-sustainable-development-goals-through-tackling-poor-vision/

De Beer E, Steyn B & Rensburg R. (2013). The Pretoria school of thought: From strategy to governance and sustainability. In: K Sriramesh, A Zerfass and JN Kim (Eds). *Public Relations and Communication: Current Trends and Emerging Topics*. New York: Routledge.

Dutta-Bergman MJ. (2005). Theory and practice in health communication campaigns: A critical interrogation. *Health Communication*, 18(2): 103–122. https://doi.org/10.1207/s15327027hc1802_1

Fuchs C. (2016). Critical theory. In: KB Jensen & RT Craig. (Eds). *The International Encyclopaedia of Communication Theory and Philosophy*. John Wiley & Sons. https://doi.org/10.1002/9781118766804.wbiect002

Green LW & Kreuter MW. (1999). *Health Promotion Planning: An Educational and Environmental Approach.* 3rd Edition. Mountain View, California, USA: Mayfield Publishing.

Gupta, D., Jai, P. N., & Yadav, J. S. (2021). Strategic Communication in Health and Development: Concepts, Applications and Programming (SAGE). Journal of Health Management, 23(1), 95–108. https://doi.org/10.1177/0972063421994943

Habermas J. (1987). *The Theory of Communicative Action. Volume 2: Lifeworld and System:* A Critique of Functionalist Reason. Boston, USA: Beacon Press.

Hallahan K, Holtzhausen D, Van Ruler B, Verčič D & Sriramesh K. (2007). Defining strategic communication. *International Journal of Strategic Communication*, 1(1):3–35. https://doi.org/10.1080/15531180701285244

International Agency for the Prevention of Blindness (IAPB). (2020). Eye health: Why it matters. Downloads - The International Agency for the Prevention of Blindness (iapb.org)

Kreps GL. (1993). Relational communication in healthcare. In: BC Thornton & GL Kreps (Eds). *Perspectives on Health Communication*, Prospect Heights, USA: Waveland Press. 51–56.

Kreps GL & Thornton BC. (1992). *Health Communication: Theory and Practice.* 2nd Edition. Long Grove, USA: Waveland Press.

Lederman, L., Kreps, G., and Roberto, A,. (2017). Health Communication in Everyday Life, First Edition, Kendall Hunt Publishing.

Ministry of Health and Child Care (MoHCC). (2014). *National Eye Health Strategy (2014-2018) for Zimbabwe.* http://zdhr.uz.ac.zw/xmlui/bitstream/123456789/1384/1/Eye%20Health%20Strategy.pdf

National Academies of Sciences, Engineering, and Medicine (2016). Making Eye Health a Population Health Imperative: Vision for Tomorrow. Washington, DC: The National Academies Press.

Pandit R. (2017). Book Review: Subhash Sharma, new ideas in strategic thinking & management. *Vision,* 21(3):336–337. https://doi.org/10.1177/0972262917716801

Pharmacists Council of Zimbabwe (PCZ). (2010). Optometrists and Dispensing Opticians: Professional Conduct Regulations. Health Professions Act, Chapter 27:19.

Pharmacists Council of Zimbabwe (PCZ). (2022). Organisational Brochures, Flyers and Policy Documents. Harare, Zimbabwe: Pharmacists Council of Zimbabwe

Ruben BD. (2016). Communication theory and health communication practice: The more things change, the more they stay the same. *Health Communication,* 31:(1):1–11. https://doi.org/10.1080/10410236.2014.923086

Schiavo R. (2014). *Health Communication: From Theory to Practice.* 2nd Edition. San Francisco, USA: Jossey-Bass.

Steyn B & De Beer E. (2012). Conceptualising strategic communication management in the context of governance and stakeholder inclusiveness. *Communicare,* 31(2):29–55. https://doi.org/10.36615/jcsa.v31i2.2081

Teutsch S.M., Herman A, Teutsch C.B., (2016). How a Population Health Approach Improves Health and Reduces Disparities: The Case of Head Start. Prev Chronic Dis 2016;13:150565. https://doi.org/10.5888/pcd13.150565

Teutsch D, Masur PK & Trepte S. (2018). Privacy in mediated and non-mediated interpersonal communication: How subjective concepts and situational perceptions influence behaviors. *Social Media + Society*, 4(2). https://doi.org/10.1177/2056305118767134

Wilkins, K. G., & Mody, B. (2001). Reshaping development communication: Developing communication and communicating development. Communication Theory, 11(4), 385–396. https://doi.org/10.1111/j.1468-2885.2001.tb00249.x

World health statistics 2017: monitoring health for the SDGs, Sustainable Development Goals. Geneva: World Health Organization; 2017. Licence: CC BY-NC-SA 3.0 IGO.

World Health Organization (WHO). (2019). *World report on vision.* Geneva: World Health Organization. https://www.who.int/publications-detail-redirect/9789241516570

Zhang JH, Ramke J & Mwangi N et al. (2020). Global eye health and the Sustainable Development Goals: Protocol for a scoping review. *BMJ Open*, 10(3):e035789. https://doi.org/10.1136/bmjopen-2019-035789

Chapter 9

Citizen Engagement and Power Asymmetry in Class Divided Societies: Some Reflections on South Africa

Mandla J. Radebe

Various scholars valorise the role of citizen engagement as crucial for public sector communication in democratic societies. Not only is it argued that citizen involvement is vital but benefits such as the ability to solicit feedback and input are advanced. In emphasising the centrality of public sector organisations' interaction with citizens, Piqueiras, Canel and Luoma-aho (2020: 277) present citizen engagement as vital in "involving those who are served ... for a thriving society". Sanders and De Los Monteros (2020: 329) position the incorporation of principles of high-reliability organisations into the public sector as crucial in fostering a "communication culture for the benefit of citizens". Equally, the legitimacy of organisations has been located in their ability to respond to stakeholders' demands (Luoma-aho, Olkkonen & Canel, 2020). Again, at the heart of this disposition is the role of citizen engagement.

At face value, this valorisation may appear to be good, positive and progressive and even seductive to public sector communicators. Thus, various public sector institutions genuinely believe this to be the case – that when properly executed – citizen engagement may positively impact on the lives of ordinary citizens. This is precisely the reason it is deemed a crucial part in the delivery model of public good. However, stripped of all the bells and whistles, it is apparent that the way citizen engagement is implemented, lacks the ability to play a crucial role in the redistribution of power in society (Arnstein, 1969). To this effect, it becomes part of the tool for negotiating consent with the underclasses, who remain oppressed and marginalised in most democratic capitalist societies. To sell the idea that something is done about their plight, citizen engagement is unleashed with the primary purpose of gaining the consent of the oppressed. When consent is effective, the marginalised become the defenders of the status quo.

In this context, the objective of this chapter is to present a deeper analysis of citizen engagement – as part of the broader citizen participation discourse – in a class-divided capitalist state. The chapter advances the notion that meaningful citizen engagement must contend with the fundamental question of power redistribution. In this regard, the chapter grapples with the question of the extent of the effectiveness of current citizen engagement approaches in addressing power asymmetry in class-divided societies. To respond to this question, broad practices of citizen engagement, as part of the communication regime, are analysed. The conclusion is drawn that while current approaches in South Africa are dominated and premised on theories from the Global North, this work remains pertinent for a progressive developmental state grappling with myriad socio-economic challenges. However, it is incumbent on communicators to connect the current citizen engagement efforts to the broader objective of the developmental state and the revolutionary agenda of the governing party to transfer the wealth of the country into the hands of the people.

Indeed, while the current approaches may be useful tools in temporarily calming down tensions among the classes, these approaches may not be able to deal with deep-seated structural issues underlying the socio-economic challenges faced by the majority. Hence, the subalterns often resort to other methods beyond citizen engagement, such as public strikes and service delivery protests where they break ranks with civil society and negotiate their own communicative power – a creation of a new or parallel public sphere – to express their own dissatisfaction (Tivaringe & Kirshner, 2021). In the final analysis, public sector communicators would do well to interrogate the inherent contradictions of citizen engagement in the context of participatory democracy.

The chapter begins by unpacking South Africa's background and its position as the world's most unequal society facing a plethora of socio-economic challenges such as high levels of poverty and unemployment (Francis & Webster, 2019) in the context of stagnant economic growth (Radebe, 2020). This is followed by some theoretical approaches, particularly the need to infuse some critical analysis in relation to citizen engagement. To this end, Arnstein's (1969) Ladder of Citizen Participation model is instructive, particularly as it locates the fundamental notion of redistribution of power in citizen participation. A gap analysis in the context of some approaches from the South African perspective is discussed. Consequently, the high-level thoughts discussed under the section include the re-grounding of citizen engagement within participatory democracy and citizenship in the context of civil society. A discussion and concluding remarks on the need to re-imagine a new public sphere are presented.

Background: The World's Most Unequal Society

South Africa is ranked as one of the most unequal countries in the world with half the population living below the poverty line and a staggering unemployment rate estimated at 30% (Francis & Webster, 2019). Many indicators such as the Gini Index, a measure of the distribution of income across a population, paint the country as one of the most unequal in the world with a Gini coefficient that is close to 0.70 (Ataguba, 2021). In the past decade, the country has experienced slow economic growth coupled with mounting public debt and the deteriorating state of public finance (Radebe, 2020). The country has also experienced below-forecast tax revenue collection, the rapid rise of debt and the poor performance of state-owned enterprises (Muller, 2019). This has been exacerbated by the impact of the global outbreak of COVID-19. Hence, Francis and Webster (2019) argue that the inability to meaningfully address the high levels of inequality is due to insufficient attention to the way power reproduces inequality.

South Africa's poverty and inequality are also racialised. Poverty maintains a strong spatial dimension and is concentrated in the previously disadvantaged areas such as homelands, a reflection of the enduring legacy of apartheid (World Bank Group, 2018). These challenges notwithstanding, South Africa continues to aspire to being a developmental state to address the current levels of poverty, inequality and unemployment while diversifying the economy and reversing the process of deindustrialisation (Edigheji, 2010). Nevertheless, through its constitution, the country has an inbuilt public participation mechanism. As Nyati (2008: 102) posits, the participatory aspect of our constitutional democracy "goes further than regular elections every five years in that it guarantees involvement of each citizen in public life in between elections". Even at local government level, the community participation in, for example, the construction, implementation and evaluation of integrated development planning is guaranteed (Williams, 2006).

Therefore, it is in this context that citizen engagement takes place in South Africa. Taking into account socio-economic challenges, citizen engagement in a resource-constrained context such as South Africa is not a straightforward process, and this, coupled with the lack of citizens' capacity and knowledge of their rights to hold government accountable (Pade-Khene, 2018) makes this problem even more cumbersome. In the context of a developmental state agenda, the government's ability to involve citizens in crucial decisions through citizen engagement (Siebers, 2018) is regarded as pivotal. Thus, citizen engagement is expected to help improve social cohesion, liveability and the safety of communities (Held, 1987; Irvin & Stansbury, 2004; Horlick-Jones et al., 2007; Nabatchi & Leighninger, 2015).

Theoretical Approaches: A Critical Analysis of Citizen Engagement

Citizen engagement and participation is now central in public management, based on the assumption that it is useful for a thriving democratic society to involve recipients of public service. Most of the contemporary literature departs from Arnstein's (1969) Ladder of Citizen Participation model whose central thesis is on redistribution of power. Arnstein (1969) perceives citizen participation in relation to citizen power and hence at the centre must be redistribution of power. "It is the redistribution of power that enables the have-not citizens, presently excluded from the political and economic processes, to be deliberately included in the future" (Arnstein, 1969: 216). At the heart of this engagement and participation is the drive of social reforms by the marginalised through, inter alia, determining the sharing of information, policy direction, resource allocation and the distribution of services and patronage (Arnstein, 1969).

Figure 9 illustrates the eight 'rungs' that describe three general forms of citizen power in democratic decision-making, namely:

- Nonparticipation (no power);
- Degrees of tokenism (counterfeit power); and
- Degrees of citizen power (actual power).

As Arnstein (1969: 216) puts it "... participation without redistribution of power is an empty and frustrating process for the powerless. It allows the powerholders to claim that all sides were considered but makes it possible for only some of those sides to benefit. It maintains the status quo."

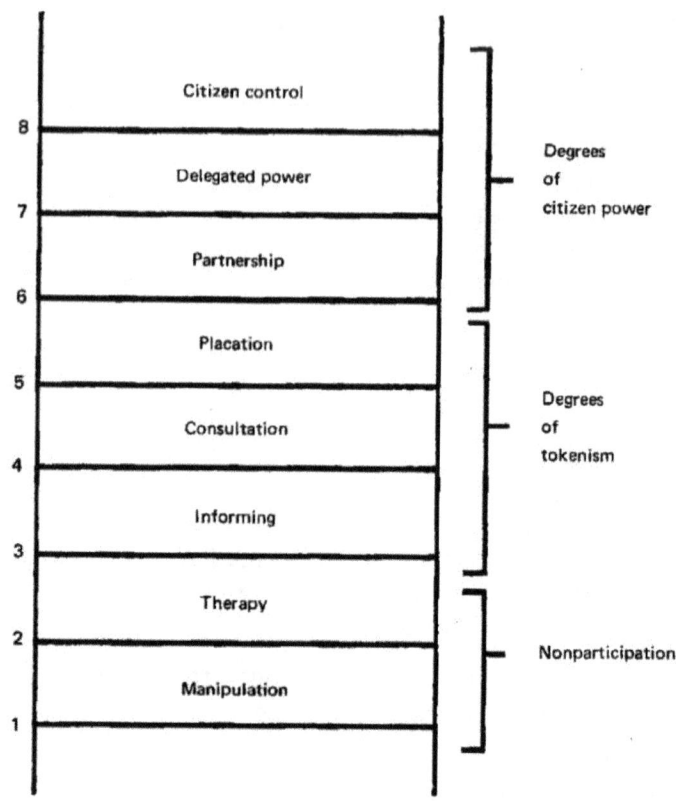

Figure 9: Eight rungs on a ladder of citizen participation (Source: This is the original 1969 illustration of Sherry Arnstein's Ladder of Citizen Participation as it appeared in the *Journal of the American Planning Association*.)

The ladder exposes the social and political cleavages that citizen engagement theories must contend with in the interaction between the subalternised and powerholders. In class-divided societies and bourgeois democracies such as South Africa's, the powerful politicians act as proxies of the ruling capitalist class whose objective is to maintain the status quo that, inter alia, entails class exploitation. Of course, the two dominant social classes, the capitalists and proletarians (Drucker, 1994), are not homogeneous. There are divergent views, often determined by proximity to the control of the means of production. Nevertheless, within the two dominant classes there is generalisation, with the subalterns regarding the capitalists as monolithic exploiters and the contrary holding that the powerful perceive the downtrodden as ill-informed masses (Arnstein, 1969).

However, citizen engagement encapsulates public institutions' efforts to develop more participatory forms of governance (Reddel & Woolcock, 2004). Thus, the underlying assumption is that public service is likely to improve when citizens are involved through engagements (Piqueiras, Canel & Luoma-aho, 2020). Engagement entails listening to citizens (Marlowe, 2005) since it is believed that this will ultimately improve the reputation of public institutions. As Piqueiras, Canel and Luoma-aho (2020: 277) posit, "new forms of citizen engagement entail undertaking dialogue and real collaboration in the form of coproduction between citizens and authorities". The most recent example of this approach in South Africa was the public hearings held across the country on the land expropriation without compensation Bill (Radebe & Chiumbu, 2022).

Of course, in the digital age, citizen engagement now takes place digitally, the digital divide and access in an unequal country like South Africa notwithstanding. This is additional to the range of platforms being employed to enable public participation, such as the traditional media (television, radio, print media and electronic media) and face-to-face interactions (Vivier, Seabe, Wentzel & Sanchez, 2015). Essentially, citizen engagement ought to be a bottom-up process that is crucial in resolving complex societal problems. This represents a departure from the traditional one-way communication culture entrenched in the public sectors (Bowden, Luoma-aho & Naumann, 2016; Canel & Luoma-aho, 2015 cited in Piqueiras, Canel & Luoma-aho, 2020). As part of participation (Steward, 2009), citizen engagement enables interaction between individuals and groups impacted by the public organisation (Bruce & Shelley, 2010). Hence, it is defined as "the intangible asset which measures the capacity of an organization to get citizens involved in public administration processes" (Canel & Luoma-aho, 2018).

Ma and Wu (2020) employ the concept of "coproducing public services with citizens" to analyse the impact of citizen engagement and found that, for government websites in China, citizens pay more attention to websites at higher administrative levels, which receive more citizen reports, in comparison with lower levels of government. Nevertheless, this study demonstrates some of the positive aspects of citizen engagement. However, the concept is not without its limitations and challenges. For example, Denhardt, Terry, Delacruz & Andonoska (2009: 1268) cite the lack of "democratic culture and civil society, profound poverty, time pressures and demands for immediate results, and the lack of an institutional infrastructure" as being among the barriers to citizen engagement in developing countries. Another issue raised is international aid programmes, which are believed to "thwart citizen engagement efforts" (Denhardt et al., 2009: 1268). This simplistic outlook on the Global South and democracy demonstrates some of the shortcomings in the analysis of citizen engagement in the context of liberal democracy spread by the west to the Global South.

Fundamentally, citizen engagement is premised on the promotion of liberal "democracies" by the Global North where citizenship is a normative term and a buzzword linked to the development rhetoric such as "participation", "accountability", "civil society", "social capital" and "good governance" (Robins, Cornwall & Von Lieres, 2008). As with all institutions and practices of liberal democracies transplanted from the Global North, it is assumed that citizen engagement will foster participatory democracy. Political apathy notwithstanding as reflected in low voter turnout, among others (see Sitto-Kaunda in this volume), South Africa's liberal constitution is embedded in Global North values such as participatory democracy as characterised by the Integrated Development Plans. This approach is purported to involve local government and the community to find the best solutions towards sustainable development. However, for citizen engagement to be meaningful and impactful, it must consider "everyday experiences in particular social, cultural and historical contexts" (Robins et al., 2008: 1070).

Some current approaches and considerations in South Africa: A gap analysis

While some citizen engagement strategies are executed with the reputation of the relevant entity in mind, many are aimed at attaining the strategic objectives of relevant entities and are thus designed to enhance the credibility of the public entity and improve the citizens' lives. Others are designed to enhance the public's knowledge of the relevant entity and access to services. Public engagement is driven and achieved through existing touchpoints such as *izimbizo* (public meetings), as well as traditional and social media platforms. While communication through these platforms is often accurate and transparent, some engagements are designed as marketing tools for brand positioning.

In some instances, citizen engagement is used as a mechanism to receive and monitor input, suggestions and complaints directly from the citizens. Indeed, in many instances, such as those pertaining to supreme audit institutions and public protectors (ombuds), these inputs are considered as leads – to borrow a marketing term – when auditing or investigations are conducted. However, for this to be realised, the relevant institution must ensure that multi-type, but relatively fixed, engagement methods exist in order to disseminate specific knowledge among citizens and ensure proper understanding and appropriate involvement.

Another crucial aspect pervasive in current practice is the crude categorisation of citizens as stakeholders for engagement as 'specialised' and 'non-specialised' (Mur-Dueñas & Lorés, 2022). Specialised citizens are considered to have some degree of knowledge on the subject at hand. Usually, they possess some form of training or experience in the understanding of the work at hand such as auditing, taxation, and so on, and of the role of good governance in general, or they may have a good grasp of the political system, principles of democracy and governance in the public sector. Engagement with citizens whose frame of reference enables them to understand and engage with the matter at hand is often differentiated from those classified as 'non-specialised citizens' to whom the technical concepts are abstract. Although specialised citizens are in the minority, they are still prioritised for engagement through professional bodies, business associations and political structures, among others.

Then there is the role of engaging civil society that is utilised as part of citizen engagement. Often couched as citizen education, this form of engagement takes place through existing communication channels such as social media and traditional media, including adverts and advertorials. Often, existing engagement channels such as public lectures are leveraged and expanded through media and social media engagements. Furthermore, opportunities such as brand exhibitions, sponsorships, corporate social investment, branded collateral and many more are used to drive this form of citizen engagement.

While some of these approaches are useful as engagement programmes, they are limited in achieving the essence of participation and redistribution of power (Arnstein, 1969). The following sections present some thoughts for consideration that may reposition citizen engagement as part of the crucial tool of re-imagining and building a better world.

Re-grounding citizen engagement within participatory democracy

In countries in the Global South such as South Africa, where the historical context of the relationship between the people and the state is characterised by "disenfranchisement, authoritarianism and clientelism", continuities of a dichotomous relations formed in the struggle years often persist (Robins et al., 2008: 1071). There are conditions for "dramatic ruptures with the past" to occur to develop a "normative version of the new citizenships" (Robins et al., 2008: 1071). This includes, inter alia, the redistribution of power, which lies in making people citizens. Of course, citizenship is a nebulous and contested term. It is no longer the domain of national citizens, and as Gaudelli (2009: 69) posits, "is being reconstituted around a constellation of other affiliations, including race/ethnicity, gender, place, ability, and class, to name a few".

Nevertheless, citizenship within this context must be reconstituted and the narrow western definition which often ignores that societies in flux, such as South Africa, have different characteristics should be jettisoned (Haste, 2004). Otherwise, this becomes eurocentrism that seeks to transplant Global North practices to the Global South. This amounts to coloniality of power that, according to Quijano (2007), is part of a global hegemonic model of power that "articulates race and labour, space and people, according to the needs of capital and to the benefit of white European peoples" (cited in Escobar, 2007: 185; Radebe, 2017). Indeed, stable western democracies are largely intact and, even in crises, individual citizens can participate through various ways. There are numerous variables at play in such societies, including skills sets, literacy, and so on, whereas it is the opposite in societies such as South Africa facing various socio-economic challenges. Hence, individual citizens often do not "have any more real power than in a stable state" and are thus "likely to feel more personally affected by the changes and thus potentially more engaged" (Haste, 2004: 416). This nuance is crucial to appreciate when dealing with citizen engagement.

Furthermore, the public sphere, where citizen engagement occurs, is equally rooted in dominant ideologies that seek to entrench established patterns of power relations. The assumption that "citizenship from below" simply translates to agency for democracy (Robins et al., 2008) is often found wanting. Essentially, citizen participation is informed by concrete material conditions linked to hitherto existing power relations beyond the abstraction of democratic institutions.

Part of the problem with current approaches is their influence by the donor-driven participatory discourse that is biased towards the ideas of the middle class. This is premised on the assumption that people participate due to altruism. The participation of the working class is driven by multiple factors, including desperation to access "services and whatever other resources they can get to improve their lives" (Robins et al., 2008: 1078). This explains the emergence of movements from below such as Operation Dudula, *Abahlali baseMjondolo* and many others with varying ideologies. Therefore, the middle-class utopia "that people struggling to survive would 'participate' simply for the love and virtue of participating" is unrealistic (Robins et al., 2008: 1078).

The subalterns' participation is survivalist. They activate their networks as patronage dependents to gain access to public services required. This may lead to the dangers of corruption but, as Robins et al. (2008: 1079) posit, it "often involves getting to know people who can do you a favour, establishing personal relationships with bureaucrats to 'smooth the way' and to make things possible". Citizen engagements strategies should not be oblivious to this reality. There are tactics employed by the marginalised to engage with power, including through social movements.

In fact, South Africa has a proud history of social movement activism, dating back to the struggle against apartheid (Sinwell, 2010). In the 1990s there was an emergence of 'new' social movements primarily focusing on social and economic justice issues (Chiumbu, 2012) as the country experienced growing inequality. This is essentially the marginalised response to their exclusion, and, through social movements, they reassert welfare politics in a neoliberal context where states pursue "market-based solutions to capitalism's problems of poverty, unemployment and welfare" (Subuddhi, 2005: 9). Nevertheless, social movements are not homogeneous, with some driven by 'emancipatory' or 'liberationist' politics focused on social justice issues (Haste, 2004: 419).

Citizenship and civil society

Citizens and civil society can be best understood in the analysis of the interplay between the state, markets and society (Radebe, 2020). To this effect, the state as an instrument of class rule, can apply forcible coercion to maintain the dominance of the ruling class, preserve existing property relations and keep all other classes in subjection (Draper, 2011). This debunks the notion of the state as "a neutral arbiter of competing interests" when in reality it is "the power and influence of corporate interests over government policy" that reigns supreme (Flew, 2007: 47). Governments are acutely aware of the need to maintain the capitalist arrangements otherwise this can unleash economic chaos that often undermines their legitimacy (Radebe, 2020). Thus, to remain in power they must "secure the profitability and prosperity of the private sector: they are dependent upon the process of capital accumulation which they have for their own sake to maintain" (Held, 2006: 170).

Citizen engagement approaches must contend with this context, intertwined with a civil society perceived differently by various traditions. On the one hand, liberals regard civil society "as a public space between state and individual citizen, comprised of voluntary associations autonomous of the state", while on the other, Marxists perceive it from a class and conflict point of view (Subuddhi, 2005: 2). In class-divided societies, also often layered with race and gender divisions, how the marginalised negotiate power can be best understood from a historical materialist perspective. This is a product of social and economic conditions driven by the developments in relation to the means of production (Marx, 2016).

Nevertheless, civil society enables the poor to reassert their rights as citizens "through forms of collective action, solidaristic networks and popular education" (Robins et al., 2008: 1071). However, civil society organisations are not inherently progressive or possessing of automatic democratising power (Robins et al., 2008). In fact, some are reactionary with anti-democratic tendencies. Civil society theories are useful in grounding citizen engagement. For example, both liberal and Marxist tradition considers the citizen as "a private individual with a set of private rights – the right to liberty, privacy and property"; class interests are crucial and hence the bourgeoisie as a class often tends to assign citizenship (Subuddhi, 2005: 3). Even public opinion is laden with class interest and thus the communication power rests with those who control the means of production and therein lies their ability to construct hegemony (Radebe, 2020).

The close relationship between the state and civil society limits avenues for the marginalised because while the state is "an institution of political coercion for the dominant classes", on the other hand, civil society is "the domain of cultural and ideological practices where consent is forged for the governance of the state" (Subuddhi, 2005: 3). It is crucial for citizen engagement theories to appreciate the connection between the state and economy, especially in capitalist economies. This is how engagement as tokenism occurs where the marginalised are placated with 'ground rules' that make it possible for them to express their views while the 'powerholders' retain the right to decide (Arnstein, 1969: 217). Of course, the underclasses have agency and hence civil society is a site of struggle where "power is always matched with a counter-force and therefore always potential for counter-hegemonic movements" (Subuddhi, 2005: 3). Nevertheless, civil society can be co-opted into the state/market matrix.

Indeed, the concept of citizenship itself is value laden as it is linked to nation states and often denotes status and class location. For example, in South Africa during apartheid, black people were denuded of their nationhood and thus citizenship was reserved for whites, and particularly white males. Therefore, citizenship and its concomitant rights "are often the products of power and struggle, based on contested conceptions of rights and justice, between the state and civil society" (Subuddhi, 2005: 6). When dealing with public engagement and participation, such historical background is useful. In this regard, civil society activism may appear to offer an opportunity to include the marginalised and excluded "whose needs and demands do not find adequate representation in the constitutional arrangements but have become a matter of ideological and political contestation" (Subuddhi, 2005: 7).

Towards a new public sphere

The psychology concept of 'motive engagement', where issues with "moral connotation engage the individual through compassion, anger, or moral outrage" (Haste, 2004: 420), may be useful in theorising citizen engagement. How particular narratives find expression in the public sphere such as "shared narrative, competing narrative, narratives that are taken for granted, narratives that locate, explain, and justify the citizen and the nation" (Haste, 2004: 420), are crucial for public participation.

At the heart of South Africa's problem is the unresolved national question stemming from the history of the country, which was divided into many 'nations' by apartheid. This included bogus nations, the Bantustans, constituted along ethnic lines, with large parts of the country constituted by whites. The African majority were regarded as non-historic nations (Hoffman & Mzala, 1990). Post-apartheid, the country lacks a uniform public sphere, which has resulted in public engagement with citizens located within specific historical groups, whether culturally or from a class perspective. In this context, citizenship is not homogeneous and thus cannot be straitjacketed through various descriptors such as race, gender and class. In this regard, citizen engagement cannot succeed without fully comprehending the essence of culture and environment from which an individual citizen emerges. This entire infrastructure facilitates how messages are processed, consumed and interpreted (Haste, 2004).

Conclusion

This chapter has presented some thoughts on approaches towards theorising and implementing citizen engagement in a

Global South context such as South Africa. Although a useful component of public participation enshrined in the country's Constitution, citizen engagement has limitations when it comes to redistribution of power (Arnstein, 1969). It is this limitation that the chapter argues makes citizen engagement part of negotiating consent to manage and placate the marginalised. On this basis, Arnstein's (1969) Ladder of Citizen Participation model has been employed to analyse citizen engagement in the context of "citizen participation," "citizen control", and "maximum feasible involvement of the poor". Fundamentally, the chapter argues that current citizen engagement approaches by the public sector, premised on advancing liberal democracies and their concomitant concepts of 'participation' and 'accountability', are inadequate in unravelling the lived experienced of the subalterns from the Global South.

Among the approaches that the chapter posits may be useful in power redistribution include re-grounding citizen engagement within participatory democracy. To this effect, the chapter has argued that current citizen engagement should eschew Western approaches that ignore or impose western practices on the Global South (Haste, 2004). Essentially, this amounts to coloniality of power where problems of the Global South are articulated and resolution is sought using western theories and lenses (Quijano, 2007). Citizenship and civil society are other elements that the chapter has argued are useful in theorising citizen engagement. Through civil society, the subalterns can reassert their rights as citizens through collaboration and solidarity (Robins et al., 2008). However, in bourgeoisie democracies it is instructive to appreciate the interplay between the state, markets and society (Radebe, 2020) and the role of class.

In order for the subalternised working class to achieve power redistribution objectives through citizen engagement, the chapter argues that a new public sphere must be considered. To this end, the current disjointed public engagements that follow cultural or class form are unsustainable. It is citizen engagement that should foster new platforms that would unite citizens across race and class lines. This public engagement outcome is unsurprising as current citizen engagement efforts are underpinned by an ideology that is not supportive of a popular uprising from below that will eventually enable the marginalised to confront the conditions that lead to their oppression and exploitation.

References

Arnstein, S. R. (1969). A ladder of citizen participation. *Journal of the American Institute of Planners*, 35(4):216–224. https://doi.org/10.1080/01944366908977225

Ataguba, J. E. (2021). The impact of financing health services on income inequality in an unequal society: The case of South Africa. *Applied Health Economics and Health Policy*, 19(5):721–733. https://doi.org/10.1007/s40258-021-00643-7

Bowden, J., Luoma-aho, V. & Naumann, K. (2016). Developing a spectrum of positive to negative citizen engagement. In: RJ Brodie, L Hollebeek & J Conduit (Eds). *Customer Engagement, Contemporary Issues and Challenges*. New York and London: Routledge. 257–277.

Bruce, P., & Shelley, R. (2010). Assessing stakeholder engagement. *Communication Journal of New Zealand*, 11(2), 30–48.

Canel, M. J. & Luoma-aho, V. (2015). Crisis en la Administración Pública, oportunidad para la intangibilidad [Crisis in public administration: An opportunity for intangible assets]. In: J. Villafañe (Ed). *La Comunicacion Empresarial y la Gestion de los Intangibles en Espana y Latinoamerica* Madrid, Spain: Gedisa. 121–132. https://doi.org/10.1002/9781119135630

Canel, M. J., & Luoma-aho, V. (2018). *Public sector communication. Closing gaps between public sector organizations and citizens*. Boston, MA: Wiley-Blackwell.

Chiumbu, S. (2012). Exploring mobile phone practices in social movements in South Africa: The Western Cape Anti-Eviction Campaign. *African Identities*, 10(2):193–206. https://doi.org/10.1080/14725843.2012.657863

Denhardt, J., Terry, L., Delacruz, E. R. & Andonoska, L. (2009). Barriers to citizen engagement in developing countries. *International Journal of Public Administration*, 32(14), 1268–1288. https://doi.org/10.1080/01900690903344726

Draper, H. (2011). *Karl Marx's Theory of Revolution III* (Vol. 2). Aakar Books for South Asia.

Drucker, P. F. (1994). *Post-Capitalist Society*. New York: Harper Bus.

Edigheji O. (2010). *Constructing a Democratic Developmental State in South Africa: Potentials and Challenges*. Cape Town: HSRC Press. https://doi.org/10.1515/9780796926531

Escobar, A. (2007). Worlds and knowledges otherwise: The Latin American modernity/coloniality research program. *Cultural studies*, 21(2-3):179–210. https://doi.org/10.1080/09502380601162506

Flew, T. (2007). *Understanding global media*. Palgrave Macmillan. https://doi.org/10.1007/978-1-137-28579-9

Gaudelli, W. (2009). Heuristics of global citizenship discourses towards curriculum enhancement. *Journal of Curriculum Theorizing*, 25(1):68–85.

Hallahan, K., Holtzhausen, D., Van Ruler, B., Verčič, D. & Sriramesh, K. (2007). Defining strategic communication. *International Journal of Strategic Communication*, 1(1):3–35. https://doi.org/10.1080/15531180701285244

Haste, H. (2004). Constructing the citizen. *Political Psychology*, 25(3):413–439. https://doi.org/10.1111/j.1467-9221.2004.00378.x

Held, D. (1987). *Models of Democracy*. Cambridge UK: Polity Press

Held, D. (2006). *Models of Democracy*. Stanford: Stanford University Press.

Hoffman, J. & Mzala, N. (1990). 'Non-historic nations' and the national question: A South African perspective. *Science & Society*, 54(4):408–426.

Horlick-Jones, T., Walls, J., Rowe, G., Pidgeon, N., Poortinga, W., Murdock, G., & O'Riordan, T. (2007). *The GM debate: Risk, politics and public engagement*. Routledge. https://doi.org/10.4324/9780203945933

Irvin, R. A., & Stansbury, J. (2004). Citizen participation in decision making: is it worth the effort?. *Public administration review*, 64(1), 55-65. https://doi.org/10.1111/j.1540-6210.2004.00346.x

Luoma-aho, V., Olkkonen, L. & Canel, M. J. (2020). Public sector communication and citizen expectations and satisfaction. In: Luoma-aho V & Canel MJ. (Eds). *The Handbook of Public Sector Communication*. John Wiley & Sons. 303–314. https://doi.org/10.1002/9781119263203.ch20

Ma, L. & Wu, X. (2020). Citizen engagement and co-production of e-government services in China. *Journal of Chinese Governance*, 5(1):68–89. https://doi.org/10.1080/23812346.2019.1705052

Marlowe, J. (2005). Fiscal slack and counter-cyclical expenditure stabilization: A first look at the local level. *Public Budgeting & Finance*, 25(3), 48-72. https://doi.org/10.1111/j.1540-5850.2005.00367.x

Marx, K. (2016). Capital. In: W Longhofer & D Winchester (Eds). *Social Theory Re-Wired: New Connections to Classical and Contemporary Perspectives*. New York, USA: Routledge. 145–151.

Muller, S. M. 2019. *South Africa's economy is in a perilous state and is running out of time to get fixed*. Quartz Africa. 7 August. https://qz.com/africa/1683190/south-africas-economy-rising-debt-no-jobs-and-political-crisis/.

Mur-Dueñas, P. & Lorés, R. (2022). When science communication becomes parascience: Blurred boundaries, diffuse roles. *Publications*, 10(2):14. https://doi.org/10.3390/publications10020014

Nabatchi, T., & Leighninger, M. (2015). *Public participation for 21st century democracy*. John Wiley & Sons. https://doi.org/10.1002/9781119154815

Nyati, L. (2008). Public participation: What has the Constitutional Court given the public? *Law, Democracy & Development*, 12(2):102–110. https://doi.org/10.4314/ldd.v12i2.52896

Quijano, A. (2007). Coloniality and modernity/rationality. *Cultural Studies*, 21(2-3):168–178. https://doi.org/10.1080/09502380601164353

Pade-Khene, C. (2018). Embedding knowledge transfer in digital citizen engagement in South Africa: Developing digital literacy. *Reading & Writing Journal of the Reading Association of South Africa*, 9(1):1–9. https://doi.org/10.4102/rw.v9i1.193

Piqueiras, P., Canel, M. J., & Luoma-aho, V. (2020). Citizen engagement and public sector communication. *The handbook of public sector communication*, 277-287. https://doi.org/10.1002/9781119263203.ch18

Radebe, M. J. (2017). Corporate Media and the Nationalisation of the Economy in South Africa: A critical Marxist political economy approach. PhD thesis. Johannesburg: University of the Witwatersrand.

Radebe, M. J. (2020). Constructing Hegemony: The South African Commercial Media and the (Mis)Representation of Nationalisation. Pietermaritzburg: University of KwaZulu-Natal Press.

Radebe, M. J., & Chiumbu, S. H. (2022). Frames and marginalisation of counter-hegemonic voices: Media representation of the land debate in South Africa. *African Journalism Studies*, 43(1), 89-106. https://doi.org/10.1080/23743670.2022.2033289

Reddel, T. & Woolcock, G. (2004). From consultation to participatory governance? A critical review of citizen engagement strategies in Queensland. *Australian Journal of Public Administration*, 63(3):75–87. https://doi.org/10.1111/j.1467-8500.2004.00392.x

Robins S, Cornwall A & Von Lieres, B. (2008). Rethinking 'citizenship' in the post colony. *Third World Quarterly*, 29(6):1069–1086. https://doi.org/10.1080/01436590802201048

Sanders, K. B. & De Los Monteros MDLVE. (2020). Citizen communication in the public sector: Learning from high-reliability organizations. In: Luoma-aho V & Canel MJ. (Eds). *The Handbook of Public Sector Communication*. John Wiley & Sons. 329–343. https://doi.org/10.1002/9781119263203.ch22

Siebers, V. (2018). Citizen engagement in South Africa: The case of Prince Albert. *International Journal of Public Leadership*, 14(4):232–244. https://doi.org/10.1108/IJPL-05-2018-0025

Sinwell L. (2010). Defensive social movement battles: Need to engage with politics. *South African Labour Bulletin*, 34(1):37–39.

Steward, J. (2009). *Dilemmas of engagement: The role of consultation in governance*. Canberra, AU: ANU E-press. https://doi.org/10.22459/DE.06.2009

Subuddhi, K (2005, February 8 – 10). State, Civil Society and Citizenship: Liberal and Marxist Perspectives [Conference presentation]. III International Conference on Citizenship and Governance, organized by PRIYA, Benaras Hindu University, India. https://www.researchgate.net/profile/Karunamay-Subuddhi/publication/236656998_Benaraspaper2ofinal1/data/02e7e518b94f1be98f000000/Benaraspaper2ofinal1.rtf

Tivaringe, T., & Kirshner, B. (2021). Learning to claim power in a contentious public sphere: A study of youth movement formation in South Africa. *Journal of the Learning Sciences, 30*(1), 125-150. https://doi.org/10.1080/10508406.2020.1844713

Vivier, E., Seabe, D., Wentzel, M. & Sanchez, D. (2015). From information to engagement: Exploring communication platforms for the government-citizen interface in South Africa: Informatics for development. *The African Journal of Information and Communication*, 15:81–92.

Williams, J. J. (2006). Community participation: Lessons from post-apartheid South Africa. *Policy Studies, 27*(3):197–217. https://doi.org/10.1080/01442870600885982

World Bank Group. (2018). *Overcoming poverty and inequality in South Africa: An assessment of drivers, constraints and opportunities.* World Bank. https://openknowledge.worldbank.org/entities/publication/7ae40441-e472-58d3-9b3c-b87b41ea3d4e

Chapter 10

Exploring Government Transparency as a Path to Open Government

Anna Oksiutycz

The calls for, and declarations of, commitment to transparency by government have come from many quarters, including politicians, lawmakers, business managers, customers, activists and civil society. In South Africa, both government and business organisations are under the increased scrutiny of the public, media and civil society, and as such, there is a growing emphasis on government and public sector organisations becoming more transparent and consequently accountable to the citizens.

Transparency and accountability are critical issues in South Africa, considering the prevalence of corruption, mismanagement, fraud, misappropriation of funds and other malaises that have been identified at all levels of government. At the local level, it has been reported that many municipalities experience abuses of power and public resources are diverted to serve private interest (BusinessTech, 2022, Corruption Watch 2021), severely impacting local government's ability to deliver essential services to communities.

Government transparency has become a prerogative of modern democracy, yet according to the Organisation for Economic Co-operation and Development (OECD, 2020), less than 10% of governments consider transparency and stakeholder participation as the focus of their government communication strategy. The concept of transparency has gained prominence in the past two decades, not least because it reflects the ideals of a fair and just society. Transparency is closely linked to governance and accountability (Wehmeier &

Raaz, 2012; Alcaide-Muñoz, Bolívar & Villamayor-Arellano, 2022). However, transparency as a concept is frequently oversimplified and reduced to information provision without questioning the process, decision-making and expectations about transparency. This chapter analyses the complex nature of transparency in the context of government and public service, highlighting its contradictions and paradoxes, particularly how they emerge in the digital age.

In this chapter I argue that information is not neutral and that providing information is a process loaded with subjectivity, reflecting deliberate choices and the established institutional order and culture. Although information is a precondition of transparency, it is not a guarantee of transparency. Therefore, principles of communication should be applied by governments to foster transparency and its outcomes: accountability, engagement and efficiency. Furthermore, transparency needs to be institutionalised within the government by instilling the ideas of open government among government departments and designing and implementing policies that facilitate transparency.

The chapter begins with an overview of the concept of government transparency, followed by a discussion on initiatives promoting open government, e-government and access to information. The final section of the chapter presents the case of the South African government's progress towards achieving an open and transparent government.

Perspectives on Government Transparency

Scholars who research contemporary transparency discourse (Wehmeier & Raaz, 2012; Schnackenberg & Tomlinson, 2016) have consistently underscored the multiplicity of views on transparency. Far from being a simple concept, the literature highlights various approaches to government transparency.

Transparency is presented in contrast to closure, opacity and secrecy (Rawlins, 2009; Birchall, 2011). Government transparency is described in similar terms; for example, Johnson (2021) refers to government transparency as openness in decision-making, policy outcomes and access to, and provision of, information. Hood (2007: 701) defines government transparency in terms of rules guiding information disclosure, stating that "transparency denotes government according to fixed and published rules on the basis of information and procedures that are accessible to the public". Porumbescu, Meijer and Grimmelikhuijsen (2022) state that government transparency is the availability of information which enables external actors to monitor the internal workings or performance of that government. However, given the complexity of government transparency and the multiplicity of approaches to studying it, there is some consensus in the literature that an agreed upon definition of government transparency is lacking (Bauhr & Grimes, 2012).

Government transparency can be analysed at different levels. The institutional level pays attention to rules and priorities in terms of their general orientation towards openness and information priorities (Roberts, 2020). Organisational level focuses on transparency practices in different government organisations (Porumbescu et al., 2022). These two levels are interrelated because the government is a social institution that organises the lives of citizens according to socially established rules, and at the same time, it is a network of public sector organisations that enact these rules. As such, it is pertinent to consider government transparency as a form of organisational transparency.

Another consideration of government transparency is based on broadly understood government activities: transparency of decision-making processes, transparency of policy content and transparency of policy outcomes or effects (Grimmelikhuijsen & Welch, 2012). In addition, government transparency comprises fiscal, administrative and political transparency (Cucciniello, Porumbescu & Grimmelikhuijsen, 2017). Fiscal transparency deals with budgets and how the money is spent; administrative transparency refers to structures, procedures and functions of different departments; and political transparency is information about elective process and officials.

Government transparency is closely linked to the democratic process, legitimacy and trust in government. Meijer, Hart and Worthy (2018) refer to these aspects as a political dimension of government transparency. The complementing dimension is what they refer to as the administrative dimension, which has to do with good governance, curbing corruption and improved decision-making. Thus, government transparency is seen as a desirable state of affairs; it is a goal to be achieved by government organisations. From this perspective, the most fitting definition is provided by the King IV code of governance, which defines transparency as an "unambiguous and truthful exercise of accountability such that decision-making process and business activities, outputs and outcomes – both positive and negative – are easily able to be discerned and compared with ethical standards" (IoDSA, 2016: 24).

The alternative approach considers transparency a dynamic, evolving, complex and sometimes contradictory social process (Oksiutycz, 2021). The former view is based on the assumption that degrees of transparency can be objectively determined or that there is a clear-cut distinction between the presence or absence of transparency. The process view highlights the socially constructed nature of transparency, which emanates from continuing societal and organisational discourses and values. From the process perspective, Meijer (2013: 429) defines government transparency as a relational process "constructed through complex interactions between a variety of political and social actors, within sets of formal and informal rules, and with the availability of constantly evolving technologies".

Transparency as intrinsic value

Transparency is primarily seen as a positive phenomenon. It is associated with government actions that reflect the universal ideals of democracy, principles of human rights and the beliefs of rationality and justice embedded in the "right to know" and human rights (Klaaren, 2013; Christensen & Cheney, 2015). Transparency is also linked to ethics and moral values that guide the conduct of government departments. Transparency as a normative intrinsic value is usually referred to as a "principle" (IoDSA, 2016; Marais, Quayle & Burns, 2017) corresponding with the "right to know" perspective. On the other hand, transparency as an extrinsic value is an avenue to strengthen democratic processes and build relationships, trust and the social capital of a society (Oksiutycz, 2021).

Transparency as purposeful information disclosure

Although definitions of transparency are numerous and varied, most of them revolve around the provision of information. Rawlins (2009: 75) defines transparency as "the deliberate attempt to make available all legally reasonable information – whether positive or negative in nature – in a manner that is accurate, timely, balanced and unequivocal, to enhance the reasoning ability of publics and hold government organisations accountable for their actions, policies and practices". Forssbaeck and Oxelheim (2015: 6) state that transparency is "the production, the processing, the use and the flow of, as well as the access to the control over, the information". Bushman, Piotroski & Smith (2004) consider transparency as "an output of a collective process of gathering, validating and disseminating information, to those outside of an organisation".

The interpretation of transparency as information disclosure exposes taken-for-granted assumptions about the nature of information. This view assumes that information is objective, precise and explicit and leads to indisputable truth (Christensen & Cheney, 2015; Lee & Comello, 2019). Transparency as a purposeful information sharing view perceives message construction and transmission mainly from the perspective of the sender's intent to attain a particular effect on the audience based on the aims of the sender (Rawlings, 2009; Schnackenberg & Tomlinson, 2016. Furthermore, when transparency is linked to information disclosure, organisations are presented as senders of impartially selected information, whereas the complexity behind the construction and reception of messages is ignored, particularly the asymmetrical and purposeful nature of information disclosure and concealment. Instead, it is assumed that organisations are senders of neutral and unbiased information, ignoring the fact that disclosure of the information is a deliberate and political process. Many government documents are created with a specific aim in mind, such as upholding reputation or political gains, so they are far from being objective information.

Numerous authors paid attention to the nature of information, highlighting its qualities related to temporality, relevance, reliability and accessibility as conditions of transparency (Forssbaeck & Oxelheim, 2015; Almuqrin et al., 2022). Each condition has a set of more specific descriptors, as shown in Table 4.

Table 4: Characteristics of information aiding transparency

Characteristic	Descriptors
Temporality	Timeliness, instantaneous information, real-time, instant
Relevance	Beneficial to stakeholders, usable, understandable
Reliability	Quality, quantity, accuracy, truthfulness, clarity, consistency
Accessibility	Cost, availability, access, control, boundaryless nature

In the context of government communication, information is supposed to be provided for the benefit of the intended receivers – the citizens; however, this is not always the case. With easy access to all kinds of information, new forms of opacity can occur as a result of information overload, and various forms of misinformation and disinformation (Christensen & Cornelissen, 2015; Ruijer, 2017). Expanding volumes of available information and increased regulation of transparency and governance is not always a path to improved transparency. Government agencies tend to "push out" as much data as possible. The implicit assumption is that "discerning citizen-consumers" have the skills and abilities to find, select and understand the available data (Moore, 2018: 11). In addition, the information provided by the government is often incomplete, irrelevant, difficult to grasp and sometimes expensive to access (Etzioni, 2010).

Aware of the public demands for transparency, government departments can engage in nominal transparency, a form of "transparency-washing", where transparency tokens are generated to legitimise certain decisions or to manage the organisational image or merely to create impressions of compliance with legal requirements or social norms (Bernstein, 2012; Christensen & Cornelissen, 2015; Hansen, 2015). Transparency is only helpful if the stakeholders for whom transparency is intended, have an interest in specific content, knowledge and the ability and resources to process, interpret and understand the information provided (Heald, 2012: 34). The ability of the government to provide information in formats that are comprehensible to publics with varying levels of education, who often have limited access to technological resources, makes delivering transparency particularly challenging in South Africa and other developing countries.

Transparency as communication

When looking at transparency solely through the lens of information disclosure, transparency becomes a condition, a state achieved by the organisation rather than a two-way relationship between the public sector and citizens, built on engagement and communication. In contrast to the transparency as purposeful information dissemination perspective where organisations are presented as rational senders of impartial information, a communication perspective on transparency assumes that transparency is a meaningful co-creation process whereby stakeholders' needs and resources are considered. Consequently, transparency implementation requires that the government takes cognisance of stakeholders' transparency needs and engages in strategic dialogue with the stakeholders (Willis, 2015). This requires governments to be interactive and responsive. Responsiveness is a domain of engagement, which is a way for government organisations to acknowledge the values of the stakeholders they are meant to serve.

Yet, as argued by Macnamara (2016), in the organisational settings, one-way transmissional notions persist. In particular, government departments have limited willingness and skills to listen to their stakeholders (Willis, 2015). In order to achieve constructive transparency, government must allocate requisite resources to the stakeholder research and engagement in order to better understand stakeholders' transparency requirements.

In public service and government, communication transparency is considered a catalyst for social change, entailing stakeholder engagement and collaboration of different societal actors based on inclusivity, dialogue and trust (Oksiutycz, 2021). Transparency and accountability reduce political tensions and distrust, which is particularly important for a government that suffers from a trust deficit, with only 42% of South African citizens saying they trust central government and less than 35% having trust in local government (DPME, 2021: 4).

The outcomes of government transparency

Although challenged by some academics (Christensen & Cheney, 2015; Flyverbom, Leonardi, Stohl & Stohl, 2016) a common view on transparency is that it allows those outside the government to observe and assess government actions and plans and inner workings, thus leading to better accountability to the stakeholders (Bearfield & Bowman, 2017; Radcliffe, Spence & Stein, 2017), ultimately making governments more efficient (Volta, 2019).

Ruvalcaba-Gómez and Renteria (2020) suggest that transparency and its outcomes, such as citizen participation, can maintain the balance of power by keeping the power of political elites in check. When stakeholders are aware of what a government department intends to do, they are in a better position to engage in the social discourse that defines their expectations about legitimate government behaviours. In particular, civil society organisations are able to act as "information intermediaries" and put pressure on regulators to enforce accountability (Ingrams, 2017). Transparency thus serves as a symbolic and observational control mechanism that can be exercised through various monitoring technologies, regulations and laws. Two types of control observational and regularising (or disciplinary) can be implemented (Foucault, 1977; Flyverbom, Christensen and Hansen 2015). Regularising control is coercive in its nature. Observation control creates the potential for interventions where necessary. When information about the government is available to the public, the public exercises observational control simply because it can access information about its actions or intentions. Among forms of observational control are various institutionalised reporting requirements, mandatory disclosures, audits and other legally defined mechanisms for the provision of specific information are examples of observational control. By promoting integrity in government, transparency as a form of surveillance fulfils its role as a social control mechanism.

Harrison and Sayogo (2014) argue that transparency is a precondition for accountability. Openness is thought to prevent corruption and abuse of power as it mandates the conduct of public affairs in the open, exposing it to public scrutiny (Redish & Dawson, 2012; OECD, 2020). In the past decade, South Africa has made little headway in fighting corruption, being ranked 72nd out of 180 countries, with a score of 43 on the corruption index – the same position as in 2012 (Sibanda, 2023).

Numerous authors argue that transparency leads to better utilisation of government resources (Leroy, Saez-Martin, Caba-Perez & De Avila, 2022), more accountable spending of public funds (Ruijer, 2017), sound decision-making (Bluemmel, 2021) and increased efficiency of the public sector (Alcaide-Muñoz et al., 2022; Castro & Lopes, 2022). Considering that the number of dysfunctional municipalities increased in 2022 from 64 to 66, 151 municipalities in the country are under the threat of collapse, while 43 have already collapsed and require central government rescue (BusinessTech, 2022), an increased fiscal transparency at various levels of government is a necessity.

Ultimately, transparency empowers citizens and should ideally lead to incorporating a diversity of ideas in government decision-making, whereby stakeholders can comment, object and contribute to the societal outcomes based on the information they have. Citizen empowerment and participation are linked with public policy transparency. Communication about proposed policies becomes a part of a democratic and two-way process whereby the government has the opportunity to be exposed to citizens' views and needs concerning a particular policy issue. Communication about policy can present the government's rationale for the policy and elicit citizens' support (or resistance) to the intended policy (Gelders & Ilhen, 2010).

From The Right to Information to Open Government

If government transparency is to be implemented by the government, it needs to be supported by a legal framework and practical steps. An example of the former is the freedom of information law. The latter is reflected in the ideas of open government, open data and e-government.

The right to access information

Close relationships between transparency and the right to access information, also referred to as 'freedom of information' (FoI), is a crucial component of government transparency. "The right to access information is an effective lever for inclusive growth. It increases citizens' trust in their public institutions, as well as their participation in the elaboration of public policies", states the OECD (2019). Freedom of information policy, with its aim to guarantee the "right to know" and thus create informed citizens, is, in many countries, including South Africa, guaranteed by law. However, it should be noted that public information disclosure has limitations due to restrictions related to public interest protection matters such as privacy or national security (Moon, 2020).

It should be pointed out that access to information laws preceded the widespread use of information and communication technology. Hence, the key aspect of information laws was demand-driven access to information. The interested party had to request information, and the government agencies were obliged to provide it. The key objective of FoI was to create informed information receivers. In contrast, the concepts of open government and open data are based on the premise of proactive information disclosure by the government.

Open government

In the early 2000s, many governments began to promote open government ideas by taking advantage of technological innovations (Moon, 2020). Open government is a governance model within public sector management associated with transparency, accountability, open data, access to information, interoperability, new technologies, democracy and citizen participation (Ruvalcaba-Gómez & Renteria, 2020). The concept of open government is closely related to transparency, freedom, freedom of information, human rights and development (Kurmanov & Knox, 2022).

Open government has been applied to different government and public service levels, from central government through local government structures and various public agencies. The OECD (2009) states that open government entails: "the transparency of government actions, the accessibility of government services and information and the responsiveness of government to new ideas, demands and needs".

High levels of transparency as a mechanism for public oversight are at the centre of open government, with accountability to citizens and improvements to people's quality of life being the main objective. Accountability is defined as the state of being responsible for one's actions (Christensen & Cheney, 2015: 71) and it involves fostering integrity in the public sector and strengthening the governance measures within the government. Open government is a governance regime based on "a culture of governance that promotes the principles of transparency, integrity, accountability and stakeholder participation in support of democracy and inclusive growth" (OECD, 2017: 42). Although transparency is the critical element of open government, it is not the end goal but rather the means to an end. According to the OECD (2017 :42) open government is "a foundation of inclusive institutions that offer broad citizen participation, plurality and system checks and balance which, in turn, provide better access to services".

The concept of open government is based on the idea of creating civic space where stakeholder involvement happens and where the public sector and civil society can collaborate. Providing information about government activities is the foundation towards involving the citizens in decision-making and public policy formulation. The ultimate outcome is identifying appropriate solutions with the help of civil society and a broad spectrum of stakeholders (Kurmanov & Knox, 2022). On the one hand, open government enshrines the rights of citizens to be informed, and on the other hand, it is meant to enforce civic responsibility as communities become part of the space created due to open government (Volta, 2019).

The key elements of such a space are civic freedoms (e.g. access to information, protection of whistle-blowers and activists), free media (e.g. independent media, free internet, data protection), and an environment that enables strong civil society through capacity building, the availability of funding and a low administrative burden. The fourth element is citizen involvement through fostering inclusion, institutionalised engagement mechanisms and support for citizen-led initiatives (OECD, 2019).

Civic freedoms refer to ensuring access to government information, both legally mandated and voluntarily and proactively provided by the government. Bearfield and Bowman (2017) note the importance of the local press and the presence of government watchdogs as the factors influencing the degree to which government is open. The media – traditional and online – have been considered an important governance mechanism. Through their coverage, media engage in legitimising or de-legitimising practices framing and selecting arguments and rhetorical devices that may influence the publics' perceptions of the legitimate behaviour of government departments. The citizen involvement dimension focuses on co-production (co-designed co-delivery) and networked collaborative governance (Moon, 2020) through knowledge and idea sharing. Transparency, as a facet of communication between government and citizens, fulfils its constitutional role of strengthening democratic institutions through citizens' participation. In addition to enabling stakeholder participation in government decisions, open government is also intended to create platforms for collaboration between civil society and the government.

Open government has mainly been prioritised in the central administration of countries (Volta, 2019), with a much lower adoption rate by local governments and municipalities, particularly in the developing world. However, in the global north countries, open government is increasingly being adopted across different levels of government (Bearfield & Bowman, 2017). To advance the idea of open government, the Open Government Partnership (OGP, n.d.) was established in 2011. The partnership comprises 77 participating governments, 106 local authorities, civil society advocates and reformers who are united under a common objective, "to make governments more transparent, accountable and participatory" (OGP, n.d.). Notwithstanding initiatives such as the OGP, less than 2% of commitments contained in OGP National Action Plans aim to improve public communication (OECD, 2019). Sandoval-Almazána, Criado and Ruvalcaba-Gómez (2021) note that, generally, there are two aspects to open government. The first one has to do with fostering democratic values and transparency, and the other with applying technology and innovation to deliver more efficient public service through e-government and open data.

Open data

Open government transparency is one of the pillars of open data, which is data that is either produced or managed by the government, and which is made publicly available. The open government and open data concepts are based on the premise of proactive information disclosure by the government. Open data also means that the data is provided licence-free, so citizens can use it without restrictions. Furthermore, data should be provided in open access formats without the need to acquire any special software to retrieve it. Digitalising public information allows governments to make data accessible online to multiple citizens simultaneously and instantaneously through multiple channels. Furthermore, Wamukoya (2012) draws attention to the need to provide government records in context, without which the value and usability of such data to users diminishes.

While governments have made some effort to provide data using computer and online applications, as noted by Wamukoya (2012), little attention has been paid to government record-keeping processes, data integrity, trustworthiness and data safety – issues that are particularly acute in sub-Saharan Africa. Record keeping is also an essential element in inhibiting corruption and mismanagement. Along with accounting and auditing, robust record management systems can provide documentary evidence to support financial accountability and responsible management of government budgets. The lack of a paper trail is one of the main problems in tracing mismanaged and misappropriated public funds, preventing successful investigations by the authorities and thus indirectly enabling corrupt practices.

E-government

E-government – also called digital government or government 2.0 – is a concept closely associated with open government as it relates to delivering services via digital platforms, open data and information provision. It is based on the coherent use of technology by the government. The use of technology facilitates integrated policies and public services and promotes s effective, resilient and transparent institutions (UN, 2022a). Developing e-government allows for the promotion of sustainable development, particularly in developing and transition economies (Castro & Lopes, 2022).

The World Bank (2015) describes e-government as "the use by government agencies of information technologies (e.g. wide area networks, the internet and mobile computing) that have the ability to transform relations with citizens, businesses and other arms of government". The OECD (2003: 11) defines e-government as "the use of information and communications technologies (ICTs), and particularly the internet, to achieve better government". Examples of e-government applications are the use of technology to provide government services such as issuing documents, customer relationship management systems and, increasingly, electronic voting. Among the benefits of e-government are improved delivery of government services, lower costs, timesaving, improved administrative capacity and democratic governance, improved efficiency of government and revenue growth (Castro & Lopes, 2022).

By providing more equitable access, e-government facilitates basic service delivery in areas such as health, employment, education and social welfare (Castro & Lopes, 2022). It allows citizens to access government services without dealing with long-distance travel and inconvenient service hours. E-government has become a measure of development, and as a developing country, South Africa still has a long way to go in terms of fully-fledged e-government.

Government transparency and the use of communication technology

As ICTs expand their grip on sharing information, communication, service delivery, and other aspects of life, governments increasingly incorporate ICTs into various aspects of their activity, including communication with stakeholders. Transparency is implemented by using different communication media, communication channels, platforms and genres to communicate with stakeholders. Internet communication and social media increase the freedom for citizens and the government to communicate with each other. The internet also enhances accessibility and reduces the cost of communication. Therefore, there is less justification for governments not to be transparent (Mason, 2008).

Today, it is almost unthinkable for any government not to have an online presence. Most public service organisations have elaborate portals and websites and utilise social media platforms (Hofmann, Beverungen, Räckers & Becker, 2013) but does using these platforms automatically lead to an open and transparent government? There seems to be a disconnect between technology implementation and transparency for reasons that include challenges in terms of accessibility, relevance and clarity. A study by Hoffman et al. (2013) indicates that the online communication behaviour of local governments is based on disseminating information in a traditional way without adapting their communication habits to the particular characteristics of the online medium. The successful use of digital media for communication by many governments during the COVID-19 pandemic is a refreshing example of the unexhausted possibilities for governments to apply them beyond crisis communication.

One of the shortcomings holding back effective government communication and transparency is the lack of professional development of government communicators. Government officials may also be reluctant to fully engage online for lack of expertise or time and also because of the perceived reputational risks stemming from the lack of control of online communication as opposed to the carefully planned transparency of the pre-digital age. Furthermore, some research indicates that digital communication technologies are used to enhance the reputation of the government rather than engage with stakeholders (Alcaide-Muñoz et al., 2022). Another primary environmental constraint on government communication is "the lack of importance often placed on communication by management" (Liu & Horsley, 2007), as if the achievement of policy and political goals can be dissociated from stakeholder communication.

The use of social media opens vast opportunities for public sector organisations to connect with the public and derive the benefits from such engagements, such as sharing ideas, coming up with solutions and soliciting public support for government policies (Lim, Rasul & Ahmad, 2022). Engagement requires that the government creates spaces for dialogue about public life and invites the public to participate in shaping it (Oksiutycz, 2021; Cezar, 2018). Yet, as noted by Macnamara (2018), even in advanced democracies, public consultations face limitations such as the narrow framing of questions, short-term notice of public meetings, use of official and technical language, failing to acknowledge submissions from the public, not taking into account the needs of different publics and not providing feedback on the result of consultations. Despite the possibilities of immediate exchange of information and opinions provided by digital platforms, citizen engagement is challenging for government departments owing to a lack of resources and skills on the one hand and the digital divide on the other, affecting those left behind by the digital revolution. Shao and Saxena (2019) note barriers to transparency, such as the complexity of data formats, the inability to identify the appropriate data, no incentive for users to participate and the high cost to users (e.g. data or devices).

Challenges to open government

Despite heralding the value of transparency, the OECD (2019) estimates that less than 10% of governments list promoting transparency or encouraging stakeholder participation as one of their key objectives. The research identified different issues that affect the implementation of open government policies, depending on the political and economic makeup of the particular society. Factors such as government resources, administrative professionalism and organisational networks were found to be factors in government transparency (Bearfield & Bowman, 2017). Other aspects include culture, political pluralism and robust political competition (Bearfield & Bowman, 2017). To date, the implementation of the open government concept in South Africa has been slow. The research on why it is so is scarce is limited; however, studies by Ingrams, Piotrowski and Berliner (2020) in other parts of the world suggest that political manipulation, goal ambiguity, inherent value conflicts, inter-sectoral complexity and coordination problems, policy conflict between departments, structural barriers, technological and economic dependency, political conflicts and political faddism and short-term interest prevent the adoption of e-government.

Kurmanov and Knox's (2022) research in the countries of Central Asia revealed the resistance among state officials to implement open government policies, as they perceived it as "extra work". Some government officials believe that disclosure of information will lead to ill-informed or unnecessary public debate about government policy (Bluemmel, 2021). Government officials are often more concerned with creating a particular image of their departments than with broader objectives and transparency benefits (Marland, 2017).

Progress towards Open Government: The Case of South Africa

Since 1994, South Africa has made a tangible effort to improve various aspects of open government and transparency. Notable developments were the establishment of the Government Information and Communication System in 1998, the adoption of the Promotion of Access to Information

Act (PAIA) in 2000 and the introduction of the Government Communication Policy in 2018. In addition, relatively advanced telecommunication infrastructure, a free press and a strong legal system create favourable conditions for promoting government openness. However, there is a lot of room for improvement. According to the UN e-government ranking, South Africa is in the top 30% of countries. It is ranked 65th out of 193 countries in the e-government development index and 61st in the e-participation index (UN, 2022). This relatively high position does not always correspond with the everyday experiences of ordinary citizens and government employees. For example, Mawela, Ochara and Twinomurinzi (2017) highlight various difficulties and outright failures of the South African government to introduce e-government at the local level due to a lack of ICT skills, poor leadership and structural issues such as organisational siloes. The State Information Technology Agency (SITA) performance, by its own admission, is far from effective. SITA has 170 services hidden in "a very obscure website", and with merely 300 000 registered e-Gov portal users and only 1.3 million total users (2.4% of the population) of government digital services. South Africa trails behind the world and even neighbouring countries (Mzekandaba, 2024).

South Africa was one of the first countries in sub-Saharan Africa to promulgate an access-to-information law, the Promotion of Access to Information Act (PAIA), in 2000. PAIA's main objective is "to give effect to the constitutional right of access to any information held by the State and any information that is held by another person and that is required for the exercise or protection of any rights" (Republic of South Africa, 2000). Despite the progressive nature of the PAIA, its implementation in practice is challenging as there are many instances (see Moosajee & Makan, 2020) of civil society organisations only being able to obtain information from the government after successful court challenges. Furthermore, access to information requires functional records and data management systems, which are a challenge in many sub-Saharan countries (Wamukoya, 2012). Marais et al. (2017) all point out that processes and procedures for recording, storing, accessing and retrieving information are crucial to fulfilling the legal obligations of PAIA, yet in reality, these elements are often absent in South Africa (Marais et al., 2017).

South Africa is a founding member of OGP, but its progress since 2011 towards open government is, at best, lacklustre. South Africa did not submit an action plan for 2018–2020. The new plan (2020–2022), the fourth such plan, is an attempt to revive the OGP process in the country (DPSA, 2020). The plan has three main commitments: commitment to open data, transformative fiscal transparency and beneficial ownership transparency. Sadly, in the assessment of the OGP, only the first of these commitments is "verifiable" and has modest potential for a positive result. The other two obligations were considered vague, without explicit activities and milestones (OGP, 2020). However, in an effort to avoid being grey-listed, the country enacted legislation in December 2022 to require disclosure of beneficial ownership.

By its own admission, the fiscal transparency of the South African government leaves a lot to be desired. According to the DPSA (2020: 8), "The budget transparency that South Africa currently has and which is globally recognised, is unfortunately not sufficient to achieve oversight of public expenditure, including public procurement. While high-level budget data is available, much of the government's granular level spending data and its procurement and contracting data is simply not available. This contributes to a lack of real-time monitoring both by government and civil society, resulting in inadequate oversight of spending". There are some moderate initiatives for introducing e-Government services in South Africa. The province of Gauteng has a department of e-Government, which defines its role as creating a network infrastructure connecting government facilities, including schools, hospitals, offices and economic zones (Provincial Government of SA, n.d.). Currently, the department has a page on the Provincial Government of South Africa site, with very limited functionality and information.

The GCIS Government Communication Policy, introduced in 2018, is an attempt to create a cohesive approach to government communication. The policy deals with matters such as the role of government communication, media engagement, online communication platforms, crisis communication, marketing, internal communication and research. It does not explicitly refer to open government and hardly refers to transparency. In fact, transparency is mentioned twice in the policy. On one occasion, transparency is referred to as a democratic principle: "Government communication is driven by democratic principles of openness and participation and is guided by the basic principles of transparency, accountability, consultation" (GCIS, 2018: 7). The second mention is in the context of information disclosure, being "To promote transparency in Government operations and decisions, requests for the sharing of various types of information must be timeously dealt with" (GCIS, 2018: 36). However, the policy document does not use the word 'transparency' to label the information and instead 'provision of information' to the public is more frequently used. For example, the role of government communication is to "provide the public with timely, accurate and clear information about government policies, programmes, plans, services and initiatives in a non-partisan way, thus making it accountable to the public it serves" (GCIS, 2018: 8) and "make information widely accessible to all South Africans with diverse needs". Another document, the government guide for website communication (GCIS, 2012), states that the aim of the government entities' websites is to "provide current, factual and official information to the public".

The Government Communication policy also references another vital aspect of open government – public participation in policymaking. The key methods listed in the policy are *imbizos*, Thusong service centres, which aim to enable two-way communication between citizens and government, and council/ward committees (GCIS, 2018). The government commits to allocating 1% to 5% of the institutional budget to the communication function, based on the strategic communication plan and the size of the institution (GCIS, 2019). However, due to limited financial transparency, it is not clear how much is spent on communication activities. While the normative goals of transparency are clear, the practical application in the South African public service is another matter because research indicates that, in the view of citizens, government communication is ineffective due to the superficial nature of public consultation and communication methods and practices that do not resonate with the publics (Rasila & Musitha, 2017; Shabangu & Oksiutycz, 2018).

Conclusion

This chapter analysed the nature of transparency in the context of its application to achieving open government, which is said to improve government efficiency, promote democracy and contribute to sustainability and development. The study indicates that creating an open and transparent government requires a deep understanding of the complexity of the transparency concept, which has multiple antecedents and outcomes: ethical, organisational and social. In the context of government, transparency was considered a result of three broad processes: information provision, communication and stakeholder engagement. Transparency cannot be achieved just by making available government-generated information but needs to incorporate stakeholder needs and expectations about openness. The content of government communication should include accountability for past actions and debates on future policies. Furthermore, financial and budget transparency is lacking, yet it is crucial in South Africa, where accusations of fruitless and wasteful expenditure, maladministration, mismanagement, nepotism, and dereliction of duty are the order of the day.

To create conducive conditions for stakeholder engagement, a strategic and systematic approach to improving public sector transparency must be applied by developing, implementing and refining policies and procedures that facilitate the culture and practice of transparency. To achieve open government, transparency must become a dominant institutional logic worldview, be embedded in organisational culture and become a key principle of government communication. Governments need to build internal capacity for open government and put transparency at the top of the hierarchy of government goals. It can be argued that transparency is only one antecedent of effective controls that should be used in conjunction with other enforcement and surveillance mechanisms, such as laws and government regulations. Conscious efforts should be made to change the organisational logic and culture to promote transparency as an internalised norm within the government. Open government cannot be achieved without an enabling environment, relevant resources and skills development for communication practitioners and public servants at all levels, including politicians. Furthermore, possibilities opened up by ICT technology in terms of information provision, communication, stakeholder engagement and service delivery should be fully utilised.

Transparency is not a simple construct. It needs further development in the context of public service and government communication in terms of a deeper understanding of its dimensions and to foster the institutionalised forms of transparency – a foundation of open government leading to new and robust forms of governance necessary for South Africa's development.

References

Alcaide-Muñoz L, Bolívar MPR & Villamayor-Arellano CL. (2022). Factors in the adoption of open government initiatives in Spanish local governments. *Government Information Quarterly* 39(4):101743. https://doi.org/10.1016/j.giq.2022.101743

Almuqrin A, Mutambik I, Alomran A, Gauthier J & Abusharhah M. (2022). Factors influencing public trust in Open Government data. *Sustainability*, 14(15): 9765. https://doi.org/10.3390/su14159765

Bauhr M & Grimes M. (2012). *What is government transparency: New measures and relevance for quality of government?* The Quality of Government Institute (QoG) Working Paper Series 2012:16. Department of Political Science, University of Gothenburg.

Bearfield DA & Bowman AOM. (2017). Can you find it on the web: An assessment of municipal e-Government transparency. *The American Review of Public Administration,* 47(2):172–188. https://doi.org/10.1177/0275074015627694

Bernstein ES. (2012). The transparency paradox: A role for privacy in organizational learning and operational control. *Administrative Science Quarterly,* 57(2):181–216. https://doi.org/10.1177/0001839212453028

Birchall C. (2011). Introduction to 'secrecy and transparency': The politics of opacity and openness. *Theory, Culture & Society,* 28(7-8):7–25. https://doi.org/10.1177/0263276411427744

Bluemmel S. (2021). Government transparency in decision making. *Law in Context,* 37(2):119–124. https://doi.org/10.26826/law-in-context.v37i2.162

Bushman RM, Piotroski JD & Smith AJ. (2004). What determines corporate transparency? *Journal of Accounting Research,* 42(2):207–252. https://doi.org/10.1111/j.1475-679X.2004.00136.x

BusinessTech (2022). *More municipalities in South Africa declared dysfunctional.* 10 November. https://businesstech.co.za/news/government/642281/more-municipalities-in-south-africa-declared-dysfunctional/

Castro C & Lopes C. (2022). Digital government and sustainable development. *Journal of Knowledge Economy,* 13:880–903. https://doi.org/10.1007/s13132-021-00749-2

Cezar LC. (2018). Reflections on communication in public policies: Proposal for an evaluation model of government communication. *Brazilian Journal of Public Administration.* 52(1):52–70.

Christensen LT & Cheney G. (2015). Peering into transparency: Challenging ideals, proxies and organizational practices. *Communication Theory*, 25(1):70–90. https://doi.org/10.1111/comt.12052

Christensen LT & Cornelissen J. (2015). Organizational transparency as myth and metaphor. *European Journal of Social Theory*, 18(2):132–149. https://doi.org/10.1177/1368431014555256

Corruption Watch (2021). *CW report reveals municipal managers commit most corruption in local govt.* 18 August. https://www.corruptionwatch.org.za/cw-report-reveals-that-most-local-government-corruption-occurs-in-municipal-managers-office/

Cucciniello M, Porumbescu G & Grimmelikhuijsen S. (2017). 25 years of transparency research: Evidence and future directions. *Public Administration Review*, 77(1):32–44. https://doi.org/10.1111/puar.12685

Department of Policy Monitoring and Evaluation (DPME) (2021). Policy brief trust in government. Accessed from: https://www.dpme.gov.za/publications/research/Documents/2021_DPME_Policy%20Brief_Trust%20in%20Government.pdf

Department of Public Service and Administration (DPSA) (2020). *Reviving the OGP Process in South Africa OGP 4th National Action Plan 2020-2022.* Accessed from: https://www.opengovpartnership.org/documents/south-africa-action-plan-2020-2022/

Etzioni A. (2010). Is transparency the best disinfectant? *Journal of Political Philosophy*, 18(4):389–404. https://doi.org/10.1111/j.1467-9760.2010.00366.x

Foucault, M. (1977). *Discipline and Punish: The Birth of the Prison.* London: Allen Lane.

Flyverbom M, Christensen LT & Hansen K. (2015). The transparency-power nexus: Observation and regularising control. *Management Communication Quarterly*, 29(3):385–410. https://doi.org/10.1177/0893318915593116

Flyverbom M, Leonardi PM, Stohl C & Stohl M. (2016). The management of visibilities in the digital age. *International Journal of Communication*, 10:98–109.

Forssbaeck J & Oxelheim L. (2015). The multifaceted concept of transparency. In: J Forssbaeck & L Oxelheim (Eds). *The Oxford Handbook of Economic and Institutional Transparency*. Oxford, UK: Oxford University Press. 3–32. https://doi.org/10.1093/oxfordhb/9780199917693.001.0001

Gelders D & Ilhen O. (2010). Government communication about potential policies: Public relations, propaganda or both? *Public Relations Review*, 36(1):59–62. https://doi.org/10.1016/j.pubrev.2009.08.012

Grimmelikhuijsen SG & Welch EW. (2012). Developing and testing a theoretical framework for computer-mediated transparency of local governments. *Public Administration Review*, Hansen HK. (2015). Numerical operations, transparency illusions and datafication of governance. *European Journal of Social Theory*, 18(2):203–220.

Harrison TM & Sayogo DS. (2014). Transparency, participation and accountability practices in open government: A comparative study. *Government Information Quarterly*, 31(4):513–525. https://doi.org/10.1016/j.giq.2014.08.002

Heald D. (2012). Why is transparency about public expenditure so elusive? *International Review of Administrative Science*, 78(1):30–49. https://doi.org/10.1177/0020852311429931

Hood, C. (2001). Transparency. In PB Clarke & J Foweraker (Eds), *Encyclopaedia of Democratic Thought*, (pp. 700–705). London: Routledge.

Hofmann S, Beverungen D, Räckers M & Becker J. (2013). What makes local governments' online communications successful? Insights from a multi-method analysis of Facebook. *Government Information Quarterly*, 30(4):387–396. https://doi.org/10.1016/j.giq.2013.05.013

Ingrams A. (2017). The transparency performance puzzle: A fuzzy set qualitative comparative analysis of policy failure in open government initiatives. *Information Polity* 22(1):25–39. https://doi.org/10.3233/IP-160014

Ingrams A, Piotrowski S & Berliner D. (2020). Learning from our mistakes: Public management reform and the hope of open government. *Perspectives on Public Management and Governance*, 3(4):257–272. https://doi.org/10.1093/ppmgov/gvaa001

Institute of Directors South Africa (IoDSA). (2016). King IV Report on Corporate Governance for South Africa. Accessed from: https://www.iodsa.co.za/page/king-iv-report [Retrieved 14 April 2024]

Johnson GE. (2021). The law: Government transparency and public access. *Presidential Studies Quarterly*, 51(3):705–724. https://doi.org/10.1111/psq.12731

Klaaren J. (2013). The human right to information and transparency. In: A Bianchi & A Peters (Eds). *Transparency in International Law*. Cambridge, UK: Cambridge University Press. 223–238. https://doi.org/10.1017/CBO9781139108843.013

Kurmanov B & Knox C. (2022). Open government and citizen empowerment in authoritarian states. *Journal of Eurasian Studies*, 13(2):156–171. https://doi.org/10.1177/18793665221104118

Lee TH & Comello MLG. (2019). Transparency and industry stigmatization in strategic CSR communication. *Management Communication Quarterly*, 33(1):68–85. https://doi.org/10.1177/0893318918807566

Leroy RSD, Saez-Martin A, Caba-Perez MC & De Avila LAC. (2022). Scientific progress of fiscal transparency research at national governments level. *Spanish Accounting Review*, 25(2):316–328. https://doi.org/10.6018/rcsar.412231

Lim WM, Rasul T & Ahmad A. (2022). A unified theory of open government and social mediatization. *Business Information Review*, 39(3):98–106. https://doi.org/10.1177/02663821221104393

Liu BF & Horsley JS. (2007). The government communication decision wheel: Toward a public relations model for the public sector. *Journal of Public Relations Research*, 19(4):377–393. https://doi.org/10.1080/10627260701402473

Macnamara J. (2016). Organizational listening: Addressing a major gap in public relations theory and practice. *Journal of Public Relations Research*, 28(3-4):146–169. https://doi.org/10.3726/978-1-4539-1739-8

Macnamara J. (2018). Toward a theory and practice of organizational listening. *International Journal of Listening*, 32(1):1–23. https://doi.org/10.1080/10904018.2017.1375076

Marais DL, Quayle M & Burns JK. (2017). The role of access to information in enabling transparency and public participation in governance: A case study of access to policy consultation records in South Africa. *African Journal of Public Affairs*, 9 (6):36–49.

Marland A. (2017). Strategic management of media relations: Communications centralization and spin in the Government of Canada. *Canadian Public Policy*, 43(1):36–50. https://doi.org/10.3138/cpp.2016-037

Mason, M. 2008. Transparency for whom? Information disclosure and power on global environmental governance. *Global Environmental Politics*, 8(2):8–13. https://doi.org/10.1162/glep.2008.8.2.8

Mawela T, Ochara & Twinomurinzi H. (2017). e-Government implementation: A reflection on South African municipalities. *South African Computer Journal*, 29(1):147–171. https://doi.org/10.18489/sacj.v29i1.444

Meijer A. (2013). Understanding the complex dynamics of transparency. *Public Administration Review*, 73(3):429–439. https://doi.org/10.1111/puar.12032

Meijer A, Hart P & Worthy B. (2018). Assessing government transparency: An interpretive framework. *Administration & Society*, 50(4):501–526. https://doi.org/10.1177/0095399715598341

Moon MJ. (2020). Shifting from old open government to new open government: Four critical dimensions and case illustrations. *Public Performance & Management Review*. 43(3):535–559. https://doi.org/10.1080/15309576.2019.1691024

Moore S. (2018). Towards a sociology of institutional transparency: Openness, deception and the problem of public trust. *Sociology*, 52(2):416–430. https://doi.org/10.1177/0038038516686530

Moosajee A & Makan V. (2020). *SCA takes firm approach to PAIA request refusals by public bodies.* ENSafrica. 9 June. https://www.ensafrica.com/news/detail/2860/sca-takes-firm-approach-to-paia-request

Mzekandaba S. (2024). *SITA to ramp up access to digitised govt services.* ITWeb. 16 February. https://www.itweb.co.za/article/sita-to-ramp-up-access-to-digitised-govt-services/j5alr7QAN157pYQk

Open Government Partnership (OGP) (n.d.). *OGP strategy.* https://www.opengovpartnership.org/mission-and-strategy/

Open Government Partnership (OGP) (2020). *South Africa action plan review 2020–2022.* https://www.opengovpartnership.org/documents/south-africa-action-plan-review-2020-2022/

Organisation for Economic Co-operation and Development (OECD) (2003). *The e-Government Imperative.* Paris: OECD. Accessed from: https://www-oecd--ilibrary-org.eu1.proxy.openathens.net/governance/the-e-government-imperative_9789264101197-en

Organisation for Economic Co-operation and Development (OECD) (2019). *Institutions guaranteeing access to information: OECD and MENA Region.* https://www.oecdilibrary.org/sites/d1916f07en/index.html?itemId=/content/component/d1916f07-en

Organisation for Economic Co-operation and Development (OECD) (2020). *Innovative citizen participation and new democratic institutions: Catching the deliberative wave.* https://www.oecd.org/gov/innovative-citizen-participation-and-new-democratic-institutions-339306da-en.htm

Oksiutycz A. (2021). Social capital, stakeholder engagement and the public sphere. In: S Verwey, R Benecke & T Phumo (Eds). *Strategic Communication: South African Perspectives.* Cape Town, RSA: Oxford University Press. 88–111.

Porumbescu, G, Meijer A & Grimmelikhuijsen S. (2022). *Government Transparency: State of the Art and New Perspectives.* Cambridge, UK: Cambridge University Press. https://doi.org/10.1017/9781108678568

Provincial Government of South Africa. (n.d.). *Gauteng department: e-Government.* https://provincialgovernment.co.za/units/view/32/gauteng/e-government

Radcliffe VS, Spence C & Stein M. (2017). The importance of accountability: The relationship between greater transparency and corporate reform. *Contemporary Accounting Research,* 34(1): 622–657. https://doi.org/10.1111/1911-3846.12277

Rasila BN & Musitha ME. (2017). Assessing challenges to ineffective communication in government institutions: A case study of Vuwani area, Limpopo, South Africa. *Africa's Public Service Delivery & Performance Review* 5(1):a177. https://doi.org/10.4102/apsdpr.v5i1.177

Rawlins B. (2009). Give the emperor a mirror: Toward developing a stakeholder measurement of organizational transparency. *Journal of Public Relations Research*, 21(1):71–99. https://doi.org/10.1080/10627260802153421

Redish, M.H & Dawson, E.N. (2012). Worse Than the Disease: The Anti-Corruption Principle, Free Expression, and the Democratic Process, *William & Mary Bill Rights Journal*, 20 (4) 1053-1084. Accessed from: https://scholarship.law.wm.edu/wmborj/vol20/iss4/3

Republic of South Africa. Government (2000). Promotion of Access to Information Act 2 of 2000. Accessed from: https://www.gov.za/documents/promotion-access-information-act

Republic of South Africa. Government Communication and Information System (GCIS). (2012). Policy guidelines for South African government websites. Accessed from: https://www.gcis.gov.za/sites/default/files/docs/resourcecentre/guidelines/Government_%20website_guidelines_version1_final121015_layout.pdfRepublic of South Africa. Government Communication and Information System (GCIS). (2018). Government Communication Policy. [Retrieved 15 October 2019] https://www.gcis.gov.za/sites/default/files/government%communication%20policy%online%20cabinetapproved.pdf

Republic of South Africa. Government Communication and Information System (GCIS). GCIS (2019). Government Communication and Information Systems (GCIS). (2019). *Communication policy*. PowerPoint presentation.

Roberts A. (2020). Bridging levels of public administration: How macro shapes meso and micro. *Administration & Society*, 52(4):631–656. https://doi.org/10.1177/0095399719877160

Ruijer HJM. (2017). Proactive transparency in the United States and the Netherlands: The role of Government Communication Officials. *American Review of Public Administration*, 47(3):354–375. https://doi.org/10.1177/0275074016628176

Ruvalcaba-Gómez EA & Renteria C. (2020). Contrasting perceptions about transparency, citizen participation, and open government between civil society organization and government. *Information Polity*, 25(3):323–337. https://doi.org/10.3233/ip-190185

Sandoval-Almazána RJ, Criado I & Rubalcaba-Gómez EA. (2021). Different perceptions, different open government strategies: The case of local Mexican public managers. *Information Polity*, 26(1):87–102. https://doi.org/10.3233/IP-180100

Schnackenberg AK & Tomlinson EC. (2016). Organizational transparency: A new perspective on managing trust in organization-stakeholder relationships. *Journal of Management*, 42(7):1784–1810. https://doi.org/10.1177/0149206314525

Shabangu PE & Oksiutycz A. (2018). Stakeholders' perceptions of the local government stakeholder engagement practices in the Bekkersdal Township. *Journal of Public Administration*, 53(2):199–214.

Shao S & Saxena S. (2019). Barriers to Open Government Data (OGD) initiative in Tanzania: Stakeholders' perspectives. *Growth and Change*, 50(1): 470–485. https://doi.org/10.1111/grow.12282

Sibanda OS (2023). *South Africa stagnates on the global Corruption Perception Index, but there are glimmers of hope on the horizon. Daily Maverick.* 31 January. https://www.dailymaverick.co.za/opinionista/2023-01-31-south-africa-stagnates-on-the-global-corruption-perception-index-but-there-are-glimmers-of-hope-on-the-horizon/

The World Bank (2015). *E-Government.* https://www.worldbank.org/en/topic/digitaldevelopment/brief/e-government

United Nations (UN) ((2022a). UN E-Government Survey 2022. Accessed form: https://desapublications.un.org/sites/default/files/publications/2022-09/Web%20version%20E-Government%202022.pdfUnited Nations (UN) (2022). *UN e-Government knowledge base.* https://publicadministration.un.org/egovkb/en-us/Data/Country-Information/id/159-South-Africa

Volta CA. (2019). Local open government model for rural municipalities: Opportunities and barriers from the experience of Calle Larga. *Journal of Democracy*, 11(2):32–59. https://doi.org/10.29379/jedem.v11i2.569

Wamukoya JM. (2012). The role of record keeping and open government data initiatives in fostering a critical development of open government policies and public services in sub-Saharan Africa. *Mousaion*, 30(2):117–127.

Wehmeier S & Raaz O. (2012). Transparency matters: The concept of organizational transparency in the academic discourse. *Public Relations Inquiry*, 1(3):337–366. https://doi.org/10.1177/2046147X12448580

Willis P. (2015) Preach wine and serve vinegar: Public relations, relationships and doublethink. *Public Relations Review*, 41(5):681–688. https://doi.org/10.1016/j.pubrev.2014.02.004

Conclusion

Contextualising the Complexities of Public Sector Communication

Karabo Sitto-Kaunda

This volume presents the overarching complexities of the interconnectedness of communication in the public sector. The importance of government communication has attracted significant academic attention; however, this book attempts to paint a broader picture of the economic and administrative structures owned, controlled and operated by the government in the context of technological disruption. We also outline public sector communication with the recognition of the three branches of government, namely the executive, the legislature and the judiciary.

The complexity of this public sector communication system involves various institutions that are charged with public service delivery and the equitable management of public resources, funded by the public purse. The acceleration of infrastructure development that facilitates and supports public sector communication is critical in a 4IR age, where the public have greater access. Through internet-enabled platforms and media, to engage with various sections of the public sector and their representatives. The COVID-19 pandemic and subsequent global lockdowns increased the reliance on digital communication technologies to drive reach for government, and yet, even post-COVID-19, evaluation of public sector communication efforts demonstrates the growth of the digital divide among the public.

South Africa has worked hard to address the ills of the past embedded in the pre-democratic public sector communication machinery and has developed commendable policies. However, upon closer inspection, the structure of the public sector and the appointment of the principals in office through party-political structures perpetuate the principal-agent problem for professional communicators in the public sector. Chapter 1, by Themba Maseko, effectively outlines the key challenges of professional communicators, whose responsibility should lie with the South African public's interests, in maintaining a balance between the public and their principals' interests. The ethical conduct of public sector communicators and their professional integrity is challenged when government officials seek to re-capture the public sector machinery for their own political aims, in contrast with the policies put in place.

Transparency, accountability and the right to access information are constitutionally enshrined, requiring all public sector entities in South Africa's democratic society to adhere to these principles. However, as Margaret Dingalo points out in Chapter 5, the nature of government systems is bureaucratic, with high levels of concentrated control over all aspects, including the communication system. Furthermore, new 4IR-driven technologies are forcing the democratisation of information, demanding interactive communication from public sector institutions and public transparency from their communication employees. Bureaucracy is being challenged, along with public sector employees, in the level of information control possible, with new technologies enabling the formal and informal sharing of key information, which may be unreliable or from anonymous or unknown sources working against public institutions. This requires rethinking and re-evaluation of public sector communication practices in managing public information integrity and authority through official channels of the public sector.

Transparency and accountability are the key issues that influence the effectiveness of public sector communication. Anna Oksiutycz, in Chapter 10, draws attention to the fact that in South Africa, corruption, mismanagement, fraud, misappropriation of funds and other wrongdoings plague all levels of government. In order for the South African government to meet the prerogative of a modern democracy, transparency needs to be institutionalised within the public sector, through ideas of open government among government departments, as well as through designing and implementing policies that facilitate transparency, fostered through communication. The contribution posits the communication approach to transparency, where transparency is approached as a meaningful co-creation process that takes into account stakeholders' expectations, needs and resources. Thus, the social context is critical to transparency, with the public sector required to understand citizen expectations as key stakeholders. Transparency in public sector communication can form the foundation for open government, leading to new and robust forms of governance that are needed for South Africa's development.

Stakeholder engagement in the public sector is more critical than ever, requiring a strategic approach to communication and relationship management. Public sector employees engage in collective bargaining with respect to labour matters, which involve unions, local government, employees, media and other stakeholders. The environment of collective bargaining is governed by several policies, which influence the flow of information from, and between, the various stakeholders. In Chapter 3 Pay Shabangu outlines the sometimes-dire consequences of misunderstandings during the bargaining process, such as killings and protest action. The deep mistrust among stakeholders, based on the way communication is handled in this public labour process, demands that a new approach be considered that is more cooperative, transparent and co-created. The proposition of a strategic communication approach to collective bargaining would allow stakeholders to participate meaningfully, to harness the advantages of communication technologies for engagement, and to facilitate authentic dialogue in reaching agreement among stakeholders. The strategic communication paradigm proposes that the shift from consent to conflict drives more authentic engagements and often can result in better outcomes for stakeholders.

Digital technologies have provided a different means for the public sector to demonstrate its efforts in serving communities. Social media has grown in popularity for public sector entities, political figures and even elected officials. Lakela Kaunda and Ricky Mukonza, in Chapter 2, focus on the use of Facebook by municipalities to showcase their public service delivery efforts through online communication. Social media promotes public participation in matters influencing their communities, and the main aim of municipalities is to reach as many members of the public as possible. However, public sector communicators and their principals need to consider how their approach can be changed, as their current practices do not adequately harness the interactive power of social media. Municipalities were observed to be using Facebook as a bulletin board, with limited feedback or responses to comments by members of the public, driving frustration. The public perceived some interactions as dismissive, reducing the social media communication efforts of municipalities. However, the key driver of the quality of communication from the public sector is inextricably linked to the perceived quality of public service delivery – a key insight for public sector leaders in looking to improve the quality of their stakeholder engagements on social media.

In Chapter 9, Mandla Radebe addresses the influence of power and class on citizen engagement outcomes for public sector communication. While citizen engagement is lauded as a positive exercise by the public sector, even considered a critical element of public service delivery, the manner of its implementation through communication falls short of being able to redistribute power in society. The consequences of the limited citizen engagement approaches reveal deep-seated social challenges that lead to public strikes and service delivery protests in an effort for those citizens feeling powerless to negotiate their own communicative power. South Africa is one of the most unequal societies in the world, which influences the quality and effectiveness of citizen engagement communication, especially in the absence of a redistribution of power because it can leave powerless citizens feeling frustrated. The chapter focuses on the importance of bottom-up communication to ensure meaningful citizen engagement and participation, through redistribution of power, not simply as a placation tool to be used by the public sector communicators, but rather a means for building social cohesion.

Public wellness includes the critical aspect of health. One of the key challenges of any government is ensuring a healthy citizenry, driven through public health communication and policy setting. Public health communication by government, as Elizabeth Lubinga highlights in Chapter 7, is critical for informing, persuading and maintaining healthy behaviour among citizens. In South Africa, a significant portion of the national budget is committed to the health portfolio – a demonstration of the importance of public health and its communication in influencing healthy behaviour among the public. There are, however, challenges with respect to health information access, which the public sector, through various stakeholder partnerships, needs to combat, particularly along the urban/rural divide. In South Africa, the challenges of access to health information very often leads to the exclusion of certain segments of the South African population, inadvertently creating health disparities. The issue of health literacy is also key to understanding public health messages and behaving accordingly in response to these messages, irrespective of the medium used to disseminate them. The COVID-19 pandemic, HIV/AIDS crisis and other health crises are discussed in the context of the effectiveness, reach and understanding of the health communication messages developed by the government for dissemination by the public sector. Public health communication may only be effective through the collaborative partnership of community-level stakeholders, alternative health providers such as traditional healers and local leaders to drive healthy citizen behaviour.

Key to effective public health communication is the engagement between public policymakers and healthcare practitioners. Vincent Tshuma and Sibongile Mpofu, in Chapter 8, outline the eye healthcare communicative landscape in

Zimbabwe, highlighting the policy restraints that widen the information gap among the public. The restrictive policies of regulatory bodies on the private sector in Zimbabwe's healthcare communication activities may contribute to the low levels of participation by citizens in seeking eye healthcare services due to a gap in public knowledge. The proposed approach to tackling the current challenges includes a re-evaluation of the existing policies, in line with the availability of multiple channels of communication, especially the growth of digital communication technologies to promote eye health messaging. Paramount to successfully raising awareness through communication among Zimbabwe's public is the redefinition of the strategic stakeholder partnership between eye health practitioners and public policymakers to facilitate a more flexible communicative environment.

Maphelo Malgas and Andiswa Mrasi consider the public/private partnership reliance for effective public sector communication from a small business lens in Chapter 6. The COVID-19 pandemic and lockdown period had a devastating effect, particularly on small businesses, which were recognised by the government as needing support. The South African government's legislation, and other small business-supporting agencies such as the SEDA, SEFA, IDC and the CSBP, are critical for successful public sector engagement with small business. However, the number of institutions and departments responsible for stakeholder communication among small businesses leads to fragmentation, with frustrations building from a lack of clarity in the communication with respect to the varying roles of the public institutions.

The COVID-19 crisis caught the small business-supporting agencies underprepared, with limited means to engage and communicate the various interventions designed to support small businesses to weather the pandemic storm. The existing institutional communication challenges were made far more apparent during COVID-19, because of the limited success in meaningfully supporting small businesses through public sector interventions because of a lack of access

Conclusion

to clear information. The proposal from this volume is for the implementation of a collective intelligence communication framework involving government and public sector entities openly collaborating through engaging small business owners to co-create and co-design for a specific output. The important role of digital and social media channels being used in this framework is considered central to the success of the collaboration through the power of these tools.

Karabo Sitto-Kaunda, in evaluating the increased use of digital and social communication for public engagement, considers the South African IEC and its communication of voting matters in Chapter 4. South African voter turnout has experienced significant decreases since the first publicly held elections in 1994, potentially linked to the diminishing efforts of public voter education through mass communication channels and limited digital access by the public, especially along the rural/urban divide. The 2021 local government elections, which took place during the COVID-19 lockdown period, highlighted the challenges of voter communication, linked to health behaviour imperatives and voter turnout. The IEC itself faces a principal-agent problem, between serving the interests of voters and political parties. The public communication activities of the IEC have reduced visibility, are less frequent and have led to a younger voting population with limited understanding of the power of their participation to influence democratic outcomes. The IEC as a Chapter 9 institution, tasked with safeguarding the participation of citizens voting, needs to reevaluate the effectiveness of its communication strategy in increasing voter turnout through a more consistent, participatory and converged approach.

Public Sector Communication Framework

The volume engages public sector communication at various levels of government, including the legislation and agencies in place to deliver on the public promise. Throughout the chapters, this volume highlights that stakeholder centricity is inextricably linked to public sector performance and communication effectiveness. At the heart of public sector communication's effectiveness is quality public service delivery. The reflexive perspective of stakeholders, if taken by the public sector, would enhance critical processes such as labour bargaining, voter participation and digital and social media engagement and foster increased transparency to the South African public. The government needs to consider the increased empowerment of the public to engage with its public agencies through 4IR-driven communication technologies such as social media and reconsider its communication strategies to take advantage of avenues to improve stakeholder relations.

In its strategic approach, government needs to consider the numerous factors – both internal and external – that influence public communication. The investment in public communication infrastructure – particularly expanding internet access – is critical in increasing public participation among citizens, as is raising public literacy, which involves linguistic access and digital literacy. Diversifying the channels to access public sector messages through bridging inequality of access will increase communication reach. The reach of public sector messages may be increased by:

- diversifying the channels by bridging inequality of access;
- using a converged media approach;
- delivering options for the recognition of differences in communication channel access; and
- strategically addressing the digital divide.

Public sector communication practitioners need to possess professionalism, excellent communication and linguistic skills and be adept at bargaining with stakeholders. The media's role in influencing public perceptions of public sector messages is significant, particularly because of media agenda-setting. The media raises questions of the interests of citizens, and public sector communicators' media relations effort should be linked to the government institutions they serve, and not just their principals. The matter of transparency, balanced against bureaucratic systems, requires a communicative approach by

Conclusion

the public sector that aims to balance stakeholder interests. Agency among public sector communication professionals is key to ensuring clarity of whose interests are represented, as well as autonomy with respect to communication activities across all communication. The GCIS's coordination of government communication at national level has contributed towards some gains in successful public sector communication; however, with no holistic national public sector communication strategy in place, there continues to be limited alignment at different government levels.

Basic service delivery influences the attitudes and reception of all public sector communication, and a perceived lack of service delivery renders important public sector communication ineffective. The current political climate in South Africa, because of the way government is constituted, is often divisive, along party political lines – in some instances perpetuating segregation along historical lines. The political climate makes public sector communication non-cohesive and reduces public trust in critical government institutions.

Some of the outcomes of effective public communication, if a stakeholder-centric approach is pursued, would be informed citizens, increased public trust, meaningful public engagement, an engaged and active citizenry and successful public/private partnerships. Informed citizens improve the performance of the public sector, with better relationships between citizens and institutions and a clear understanding of roles across different public sector spheres. When government-controlled entities are considered to be transparent and acting in an ethical manner, the public are far more inclined to engage, and their scepticism is reduced, and they are thus more receptive to government communication efforts across the public sector. Citizens will then be able to engage with public sector messages on multiple levels, beyond basic service delivery, and provide feedback in a relevant manner to the public sector on public input required. Engaged and active citizens improve the health of a democracy, leading to improved stakeholder engagements and strong public/private partnerships and relationships, uplifting the health of a democracy.

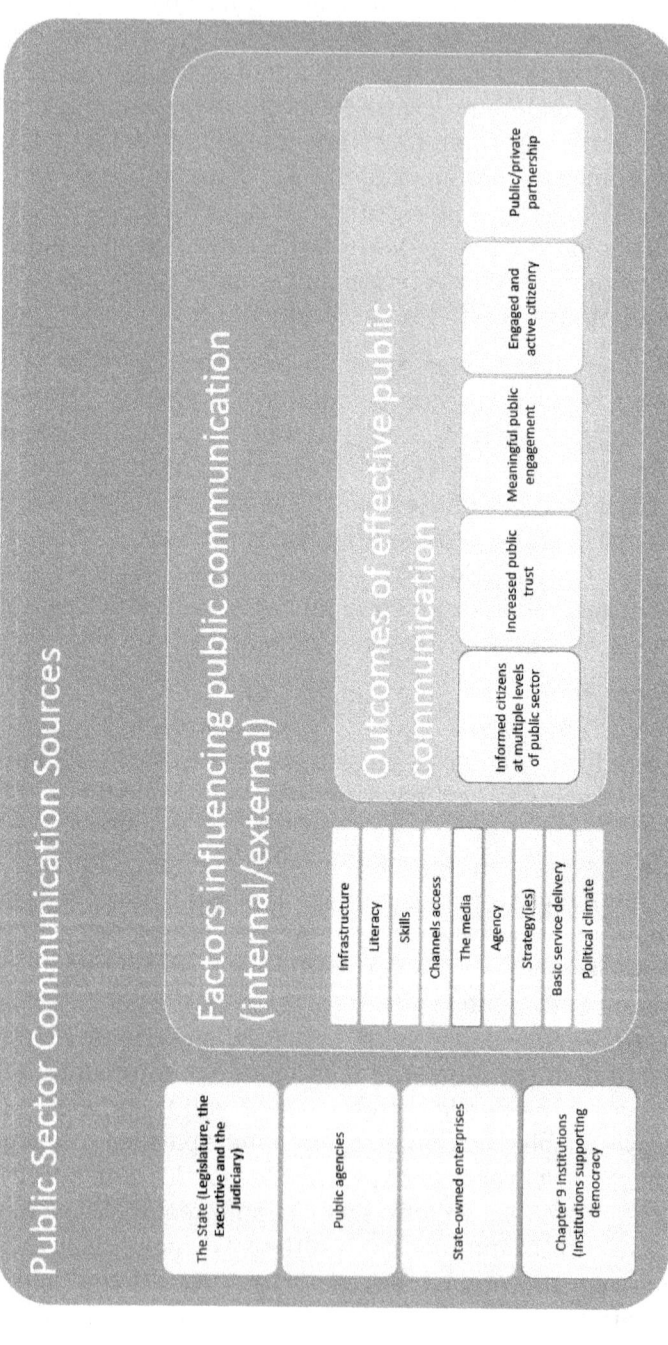

Figure 10: Public sector communication framework

Contributors

Margaret Dingalo boasts a 30-year career as a marketing and communications expert, excelling in reputation management, brand strategy and stakeholder communications. Notably, she led global communications as Executive Manager: Corporate Affairs at Transnet Limited South Africa's National Ports Authority. Serving as Convener and Chairperson of the 2010 FIFA World Cup Marketing and Communications Forum, she played a pivotal role in shaping South Africa's communication strategies for the event. Holding a Master's degree in communication science from the University of South Africa, she is currently pursuing a PhD in the same field.

Lakela Kaunda is a seasoned communication and journalism expert and public service executive with many years of experience in government and the media, having worked as a journalist and newspaper editor and having headed communication in government departments including the Presidency. Dr Kaunda has a keen interest in the advancement of government communications, in particular the use of technology to communicate with citizens. She is a Deputy Director-General in the National School of Government where she champions the training of government communicators and political office staff. She is a former Chief Operations Officer in the Presidency where she also headed the Private Office of the President.

Elizabeth Lubinga holds the position of Associate Professor in the Strategic Communication Department at the University of Johannesburg. Her scholarly pursuits centre around health communication, encompassing facets like knowledge and awareness, the intersection of digital and health communication, digital health inequalities, and the realm of Communication for Development.

Maphelo Malgas is a lecturer at Sol Plaatje University in Kimberley, South Africa, responsible for diverse modules in the School of Economic and Management Sciences. Previously, he lectured at Cape Peninsula University of Technology in Cape Town. His research focuses on small business retailing (formal and informal), entrepreneurship, and small business financing. He has over 20 years of experience, including management roles in investment and retail for 7 years and his work has been featured at local and international conferences, and has been published in local and international journals. Beyond academia, Dr Malgas is an entrepreneur with interests in hospitality, food retailing, and skills development.

Themba Maseko, (Adjunct) Professor and Director of Executive Education at Wits School of Governance, holds degrees including a BA and an LLB from the University of the Witwatersrand and an MBA from De Montfort University. His extensive career encompasses roles such as Chief Executive Officer of the Government Communication and Information Service, Government Spokesperson, and Director-General in the Department of Public Service and Administration. He has also held positions in the private sector, including Managing Director of Damelin Education Group and Communications Director at Business Leadership South Africa. Maseko serves on the Boards of Corruption Watch and the Council for the Advancement of the South African Constitution. He is also a trustee of the Nelson Mandela Foundation and the author of the book *For My Country*.

Sibongile Mpofu is a Research Associate in the Department of Strategic Communication at the University of Johannesburg. Her areas of specialisation are: Journalism; Strategic Communications and Gender. Her research interests include: gender and the political economy of digital media spaces; feminist political thought; contemporary critical theory; journalism education and strategic communication. She is also a Fulbright Fellow.

Andiswa Mrasi, an academic and researcher at Cape Peninsula University of Technology, is the Manager: Strategic Initiatives and Projects in the Faculty of Business and Management Sciences. With 15+ years in academia and industry, she specialises in strategic management, stakeholder engagement, retail and brand management, corporate affairs, and Small Medium Micro Enterprises research. Holding a Master's degree in Retail Business Management, she is pursuing a PhD in Marketing (Branding). Outside her roles, Mrasi actively serves on the Board of Trustees of the Carel Du Toit Trust and the CPUT Convocation Executive Committee.

Ricky Mukonza is an Associate Professor in the Department of Public Management and the Academic Manager in the Faculty of Humanities, Polokwane at Tshwane University of Technology. To date, he has published over 60 journal articles, 3 book chapters and numerous conference proceedings. He has successfully supervised several Master's and Doctoral students to completion. His areas of interest in research are Public Administration and Governance, Migration, Digital Governance, International Administration, Local Government, Intergovernmental Relations and Public Policy Analysis. Prof Mukonza has received a number of institutional awards for his efforts in research.

Anna Oksiutycz, an Associate Professor in the Department of Strategic Communication at the University of Johannesburg, specialises in strategic communication, business management, marketing communication and research. With a record of supervising numerous postgraduate students, she teaches research and strategic communication modules. As the Editor-in-Chief of *Communicare: Journal for Communication Studies in Africa*, Anna promotes African scholars' contributions to global communication theory. Her involvement spans collaborative projects with organisations like the UN International Organisation for Migration and South African Depression and Anxiety Group.

Mandla J. Radebe is an Associate Professor in the University of Johannesburg's Department of Strategic Communication and serves as the Director for the Centre of Data and Digital Communication. He is the author of numerous academic journals focusing on the political economy of communication. Notably, he penned, *Constructing Hegemony: The SA Commercial Media and the (Mis)Representation of Nationalisation* (UKZN

Press) and *The Lost Prince of the ANC: The Life and Times of Jabulani Nobleman 'Mzala' Nxumalo* (Jacana Media).

Pay Shabangu is a Research Associate in the Strategic Communication Department at the University of Johannesburg. He also holds the position of Deputy Director: Website, Intranet, Social Media, and Publications Content at the Gauteng Department of Cooperative Governance and Traditional Affairs. He holds a PhD in Strategic Communication from the University of Johannesburg, with his research centred on strategic communication within local government collective bargaining. His scholarly work includes publication in the *Journal of Public Administration*.

Karabo Sitto-Kaunda holds the position of Associate Professor in the Department of Business Management at the University of Pretoria. Karabo instructs at both undergraduate and postgraduate levels, and she has experience supervising postgraduate students. Her research interests encompass digital and online communication, convergence in health communication, identity, social representations, and pedagogical approaches to teaching and learning.

Vincent Tshuma is a communication practitioner in the eye healthcare sector and a Master of Science in Strategic Communication student at the Department of Journalism and Media Studies, National University of Science and Technology, Zimbabwe.

www.ingramcontent.com/pod-product-compliance
Lightning Source LLC
Chambersburg PA
CBHW070836160426
43192CB00012B/2206